2 - 3 - 96

Shepherd of an Immigrant
People

The Story of
ERLAND CARLSSON

Pastor Erland Carlsson

Shepherd of an Immigrant People

The Story of

ERLAND CARLSSON

by
Emory Lindquist

1978
Augustana Historical Society
Rock Island, Illinois

Augustana Historical Society
Publication no. 26

Ernest M. Espelie, Editor

Printed in the United States
Wagners Printers, Inc.
Davenport, Iowa

To
Conrad Bergendoff

Preface

Biography always embraces the life and thought of an individual. Occasionally the significance encompasses the wider arena of a generation or an era. The latter is especially true of Erland Carlsson. His career, with its deep piety and unflagging dedication, was truly characteristic of the man. But in his representative capacity as a pastor, church leader, promoter of education, missions, charitable institutions, and the printed word, he became symbol and fact of the best of the immigrant tradition in American life during the nineteenth century. Moreover, he was an important influence in the Americanization of Swedish immigrants with whom he came in contact.

A casual observer could not have sensed the potential of young Erland who grew up in the depths of the dark but beautiful forests of Älghult Parish in Kronobergs *län*, Småland, Sweden, during the second quarter of the past century. But the determination of this unusual boy to gain an education and to be a Lutheran pastor transcended almost insurmountable obstacles. When his ambition was finally recognized, later encouraged, and then developed, the future was transformed for him.

Erl. Carlsson's academic record at Lund University was distinguished by fine scholarship which was officially recognized by the faculty. His faith in and genuine commitment to the Word of God was enriched with a dynamic quality during these years. Although his convictions on certain church and social issues resulted in conflict with the church leadership, his potential was widely recognized. In the spring of 1853 the call to serve Swedes in America as a pastor at Chicago came through his friend, Dr. Peter Fjellstedt, well-known evangelical leader and missionary. He faced the unknown future in a strange land with confidence and hope.

Pastor Carlsson served Immanuel Lutheran Church, Chicago, for more than two decades during the years 1853-1875. Moreover, his talent and energy also produced gratifying results in a wider area. He became one of the founders of the Evangelical Lutheran Augustana

Synod, Augustana College and Theological Seminary, Augustana Hospital, Chicago, and the Lutheran Publication Society. As a home missionary he organized six congregations in three states. His own congregation grew from some thirty-six members in 1853 to 2,200 in 1875 and became a force for good among the immigrants and others. In later years he served with distinction as pastor of the historic Andover, Illinois, Lutheran Church.

Transcending the contribution of Erl. Carlsson as president of the Augustana Synod, long-time chairman of the Board of Directors of Augustana College and Theological Seminary, first chairman of the board of Augustana Hospital, chairman of home and foreign mission boards, the principal force in providing the *Catechism,* hymn book, and service manual for the immigrant church, was the personality of the man and his dedication as a pastor. Literally thousands of Swedish immigrants knew and esteemed Erl. Carlsson for his faithful pastoral care, his unfailing concern for their welfare, and his sacrificial help in a variety of situations. In the midst of a busy career of service, Pastor Carlsson shared in the rich resources of happy family life and rewarding fellowship with friends. Although the pathway of his life brought important official responsibilities, he never lost the touch of being a friendly person and a sympathetic pastor. The source of his strength has been described by a contemporary: "Erl. Carlsson's life's and heart's fellowship with God set a stamp upon his whole personality."

The chronicle of Erl. Carlsson's life records the agonies caused by hardship and conflict in various forms. Personal illness and active participation in the massive distress during the cholera epidemics of the 1850s, and severe criticism by those who were hostile to the Christian gospel in which he so firmly believed, were aspects of that record. Concern about his inability to live up to his own expectations caused times of great anxiety, even to the end of his life. But through it all he was sustained by the Risen Christ whose faithful servant he remained.

A century and a quarter of time has passed since Erl. Carlsson first came to America, but his contribution to the church and to individuals still lives on.

Acknowledgments

The student of Swedish immigration in the American scene is the legatee of extensive research and writing, past and present, in the United States and in Sweden. This is especially true in writing a biography of Erl. Carlsson.

The most striking indebtedness is to Eric Norelius, friend and associate of Erl. Carlsson for four decades. Outstanding in materials from Norelius' prolific pen are the two volumes of his definitive work, *De Svenska Lutherska församlingarnas och Svenskarnes historia i Amerika* (1890, 1916). In addition to providing exemplary background material, volume one makes available, sometimes by direct quotation and again by paraphrase, the most complete source for the autobiography which was written in 1889-90, at the request of Norelius, describing Carlsson's early life. In a less direct but important area is the work of the late O. Fritiof Ander, especially his volume *The Cultural Heritage of the Swedish Immigrant: Selected References* (1956).

The accumulated research and writing of G. Everett Arden, Conrad Bergendoff, Ulf Beijbom, Emeroy Johnson, Evald B. Lawson, Helge Nelson, I. R. Nothstein, Ernest W. Olson, Oscar N. Olson, Sam Rönnegård, George M. Stephenson, and Gunnar Westin, among others, provided excellent materials. The twenty-five volumes of the Augustana Historical Society contain invaluable materials, especially those volumes which include translations of congregational, conference, and synodical sources. An important source is the series of volumes in the annual, *Älghults-Krönika.*

Several individuals in Sweden and in the United States have given much assistance and support. Included among the former are Ola Christensson, archivist, Göteborg University; Ulf Beijbom, director of the *Emigrantinstitutet,* Växjö, and Lars-Johan Johansson, his associate; Sten Almqvist and Karl Olin, also of Växjö; Sven Blomén, Älghult; *Rektor* Erik Larsson, Älmhult; and Catharina Svensson, Finspång, who traces her ancestry to Lovisa, Erl. Carlsson's sister. In this country Joel Lundeen, Chicago, associate archivist of

ix

the Lutheran Church in America, has provided valuable manuscript material and bibliographical items. Others who have been helpful are Dixie Lanning, Bethany College librarian; Thoburn Taggart, Jr., inter-loan librarian, Wichita State University; Marjorie M. Miller, special collections librarian, Augustana College; Daniel T. Moore, photographer in the media resources center, Wichita State University; Mrs. Clarence Mumford, Highland Beach, Florida; Paul Mumford, La Grange, Illinois; and L. E. Carlsson, Olympia, Washington. The last three persons are descendants of Erl. Carlsson.

Gratitude is expressed in memory of Dr. O. V. Anderson, well-known Augustana pastor and church leader, who collected valuable sources in his research about Erl. Carlsson during the process of writing his biography. It was unfortunately not completed because of the author's untimely death. Dr. Anderson's material, which Mrs. Anderson kindly made available, has been used extensively. His translation of Carlsson's immigrant guide is found in the appendix.

Hearty appreciation is extended to Perry Mason, director of publications, Augustana College, who has so diligently and expertly supervised the typesetting and keylining for this volume. Thanks go also to Teresa Burkhart Ulbrich and Linda Koch for typing the manuscript.

Once again I express my obligation and thanks to Ernest Espelie, editor of the Augustana Historical Society publications, who during all stages of the project, and as editor of the volume, has been unfailing in his excellent professional support. I appreciate also the knowledgeable help of Mary Belle Espelie on many occasions.

I am especially grateful for the support and encouragement which I have received from Wichita State University.

Finally, I thank members of my family, my brother Ermal, who assisted me at various stages, and especially Irma, who is always my helpful co-worker and critic.

The author acknowledges with gratitude the privilege of studying and recording the life and thought of Erl. Carlsson. It has been an interesting, and at times, an exciting, and always, a rewarding experience. The only regret is that the printed page does not convey the presence and achievement of Erl. Carlsson as fully as it is known and felt.

Contents

1

The Early Years
in Sweden

On August 24, 1822, a son was born to Carl and Stina Carlsdotter Jonsson of Suletorp, Älghult parish, Kronobergs *län*, Småland. He was given the name Erland. Two sisters were born later, Anna Lovisa in 1824 and Vendla in 1828. The Jonssons were simple, honest, and pious people who owned and tilled a small farm.[1]

Erland's remembrances from the age of three or four included regular attendance at the worship services of Älghult church where he was especially attracted by a wooden crucifix on the north wall dating from the year 1500. The puzzled child asked many questions about the crucifix. Erland was baptized on September 1, 1822, quite likely at the hewn-stone baptismal fount of 1650. The exact date of the founding of the congregation in the medieval era is not known. When he went to worship in the early nineteenth century church, he saw the mighty stone wall of the old church, *gamla sakristan* (the old sacristy), as it was called, which dated from the late thirteenth or early fourteenth century.[2]

In the limited educational conditions of the 1820s at Älghult, Erland's parents did the best they could to encourage the development of their son. At the age of six he received instruction in reading from a Christian woman at Hättemåla. This elderly and pious lady had limited knowledge, as exemplified by the fact that she apparently did not know the difference between vowels and consonants. She was a dedicated, friendly person who devoted her

1

best efforts to the young people. Erland was encouraged by her kindness and responded favorably. Her religious insight seemingly impressed the boy. In a few weeks of instruction he learned the basic principles of reading and continued the effort with the help of his parents. He studied his lessons seated by his mother as she was sewing, spinning, and weaving. On Saturday evenings he read aloud to his parents, thus demonstrating what he had learned during the week.[3]

Erland's father died when he was ten years old. His mother has been described as "a religious, resolute, alert, and capable woman." Firm discipline prevailed in the family. Breakfast was not served until the children were properly washed, combed, and dressed. Food was eaten only after certain scriptural passages were recited by the children while standing. Before going to bed, each child would drop to his knees near the mother as they read Bible verses and hymns. Thereafter, Martin Luther's evening prayers were read, after which members of the family recited the Apostle's Creed, the Lord's Prayer, and the benediction. Erland recounted that hymns were often sung as the family assembled around the crackling winter fire at the end of the day's work. The family attended church services on Sunday mornings, and in the afternoons devotions were held in the home. A short sermon was read and the well-known hymn book, *Mose och Lamsens Visor* and *Zions sånger* provided many selections. When Erland's mother married Erland Danielson, the life in the home continued in the same pattern. Three children were born in that marriage—Gustaf Peter, 1835, Johanna Charlotta, 1837, and Emma Sophia, 1842.[4]

The restricted opportunity for formal schooling in the area known as "darkest Småland," is apparent. At the age of thirteen Erland attended for only two weeks the sessions of the schoolmaster known as Kryck-Anders. The principal objective was learning to write. The teacher interspersed writing exercises with catechetical sessions twice weekly. These sessions, brief as they were, made deep impressions on the serious-minded boy.[5]

A crucial event in the life of Erland occurred at Pentecost, 1838, at his confirmation and first communion in Älghults church. He recounted that he was in a miserable condition. The weeks of preparation for the great events associated with confirmation had not achieved the hoped-for goal. He did not feel worthy to meet his Lord and Saviour in the communion or to renew the baptismal vow. His heart was heavy as he joined the other children who seemed deeply moved in spirit and sobbed loudly as they assembled around the altar. However, as he has written, "When he bent his knees at the altar ring and bowed his head, the Lord heard his prayer and satisfied his need. When he got up, the heavy burden on his heart was lifted." But his joyous feeling was short-lived. When the confirmation class gathered at his parental home that afternoon, Erland soon left them feeling that the flippancy that prevailed was not in keeping with the solemnity of the day. He went to his room and read the *Bible*.[6]

Erland devoted much time to Bible reading and prayer during this period. He read by candlelight the Holy Scriptures and studied Luther's *Catechism* intensely, learning the long Bible passages in the Swedish explanation by memory. He also read other devotional books.[7]

Although encountering many obstacles, the youth felt that the Holy Spirit was present as the conviction grew that he should become a pastor. Erland Danielson, his step-father, opposed the boy's desire. The pastors of the congregation discouraged him, contending that his age (sixteen at this time), his limited formal education, and his timid manner did not suggest a good basis for success in the ministry. The situation is best described in Erland's words:

> I felt a great need to consult with an experienced and wise person about my spiritual condition and especially about my intense inner longing to become a pastor; but bashful and timid as I was I had a hard time to talk to anyone. I, therefore, decided to write a letter to the pastor's assistant, Bengt Eklundh, from whom I had confirmation instruction. In that letter I recounted in simple and straightforward language my spiritual experience and at my conversion, the intense inner desire to become a pastor.[8]

Erland brought the letter with him to church one Sunday morning. When Eklundh came out of the church, the youth took off his hat, and handed the letter to the clergyman, who accepted it without comment. Later that summer, when Erland had an errand at Eklundh's home, he was cordially greeted and invited to enter the pastor's study. The conversation began with a discussion of Erland's desire to become a pastor. Eklundh advised against it, stating that it would be difficult and quite likely an impossibility. The discussion soon centered about repentance and the nature of the Christian life, a rather interesting topic for the sixteen-year-old boy with such limited formal education. Eklundh emphasized the need for a deep acknowledgment of sin and full understanding of salvation by the grace of Christ. Erland then told Eklundh, as he recalled later: "I have felt sin deeply and I have almost despaired, and then the Lord has allowed His Grace to flood my poor heart. But at the same time I have felt especially weak and poverty-stricken in prayer and must often sigh. I do not know for what and how I should pray."[9]

The Älghult pastor's assistant was well impressed with young Erland by this time. He recommended a volume by A. H. Franke, *Anvisning att bedja på ett rätt och Gudi behaglig sätt* (Guide to Praying in a Repentant and God Pleasing Manner), as eminently suited for Erland's need. At the boy's request he wrote down the name of the author and full title of the volume. [10]

When Erland a few days later climbed on the wagon-load of lumber which he was assigned to deliver to Kalmar, about forty miles distant, the note about Franke's book was a prized possession. After unloading the lumber at Kalmar and providing for the horses, he hurried to a book store. He soon learned that the book was available at a price of 24 *skilling riksgälds.* Erland had no money but he was not lacking in other resources. He decided to seek out *Patron* Kramer, the man for whom the lumber had been delivered. Good fortune favored the youth because as he walked, he met Kramer. Erland has described the meeting: "I took off my hat, bowed deeply and said: 'I was on my way to see *Herr Patron.*' He replied cordially: 'What do you want, my boy?' I said: 'I have hauled lumber for five years to the *Patron* and I have never asked for a gratuity. Today I am asking for one.' 'What do you drink?' he replied." Then Erland told him that he did not drink, and immediately showed him the piece of paper with the title of the book on it. When the *Patron* heard that Erland needed money to purchase the volume, he gave it to him without further question. Erland bowed, thanked him, and according to his description, "Rushed like a rocket to the bookshop and purchased the volume."[11]

Erland read the Franke volume on the way home from Kalmar

and many times subsequently. He now had a good source on how to use Bible verses and hymns in deepening his devotional life. This was a landmark experience for the sixteen-year-old youth.

The year 1838 provided the setting for another important event in young Erland's life. In Advent of that year he sought out Pastor Peter Lorenz Sellergren, a well-known evangelical preacher at Hälleberga in Småland, in order to discuss with him his spiritual experiences and desire to become a pastor. This kind man suggested that the objections of those who said that Erland was too old and had not attained enough education were invalid. On the other hand, he told Erland that his conversion experience and deep feeling about saving souls did not necessarily mean that he should become a pastor. His advice to the boy was that he should go home, "Be quiet and earnestly pray to God, that if it were not His will for you to become a pastor, He would remove the burning and ceaseless desire; on the contrary, if it is His will that the desire may continue, then the Lord will open doors for you to begin your studies. That you are too old, poor and simple does not mean anything, because God will provide the opportunity, resources, and means for what He wishes to happen."[12]

Erland followed Pastor Sellergren's advice as he worked on his step-father's farm and reflected on the future. In the autumn he acquired a complete Bible, with concordance and topical subjects. He selected certain subjects, sought out the appropriate Bible verses, thus enriching his knowledge of the Holy Scriptures.

On Shrove Monday (shortly before Lent) 1839, another decisive development occurred. A lady who knew Erland well and was fully aware of his intense desire to become a pastor approached *Komminister* (assistant to the chief pastor) J. P. Hultbring with a pertinent question: "Why are you pastors so opposed to this boy continuing his studies?" The response was heartening. Hultbring stated that he had recently accepted a young man for tutorial instruction and if Erland came to the church next Friday, he would discuss the possibility of accepting him also. The parents' permission was received. Hultbring agreed to accept Erland for a three-month trial period. Arrangements were made for Carl Johan Fowelin, later a pastor in the Växjö diocese, and Erland to live in the home of an elderly couple in the congregation. Erland's mother was enthusiastic about the plans. His step-father consented reluctantly, telling the boy that he would squander his small inheritance, and moreover become unsuitable for farm work, while also failing to achieve his objective. Erland responded that if it were God's will, he would be success-ful. [13]

On March 26, 1839, Erland began his studies. This period was critical for Erland's future. The principal emphasis was on Latin, with Sjögren's *Latin Grammar* as the basic text. Although the work was very difficult, the youth's burning desire to learn and his unflagging zeal, won the victory. At the end of the three-month period, *Komminister* Hultbring declared that if Erland continued in good health and maintained the same zeal and industry, he most likely would achieve his goal. [14]

Studies continued for two years under Hultbring's direction. The subjects included Latin, Greek, history, geography, and mathe-matics. Fowelin, his companion, and Erland worked in helping to support themselves by carrying water from a distant well, chopping wood, and preparing their own meals. They studied in a room at the *prästgården* (home of the pastor). Fowelin left for Kalmar in the spring of 1841, but Erland studied with Hultbring until the spring of the following year. At that time he became a tutor for *Patron* Slettengren's son, Janne, and moved to Lenhovda. He studied German and French with the pastor's assistant. [15]

Erland lived in the inn which Slettengren owned. This was an uncertain period for the young student. Lenhovda was a dark, cold and rather isolated area. He sought to deepen his spiritual life by reading carefully Arndt's *Sanna Kristendom* (True Christianity) and Nohrberg's, *Postilla* (Sermons), volumes which were to be greatly cherished by Swedish immigrants. The sermons of Petrus Anderson encouraged him. God's grace was not always abundantly present in Erland's feeling about life, but he prayed and struggled to find faith and meaning. [16]

The studies at Lenhovda ended in December 1842. After spending the Christmas season at his parental home, he lived alone in two rooms in an empty house near Älghult church. It was his good fortune to receive instruction from Fredrik Thelander, a recent Uppsala University graduate, and the pastor's assistant. The youth studied Greek, Hebrew, and higher mathematics under Thelander's direction and Latin on his own. He also studied several of the *pensa* (prescribed studies) required for *student examen* (an examination required for entrance in a university). In September 1843, Erland went to Lund where he attended lectures and received private instruction for subjects in the *student examen*. He was enrolled as no. 1999 in *Smålands Nation* (students from Småland) in 1843. He passed this examination at the end of the spring term, 1844.[17]

Erl. Carlsson had now completed the first phase of his goal of becoming an ordained clergyman in the Church of Sweden. Before beginning his theological studies in the autumn, he decided to spend the summer in his native Småland in order to rest after strenuous study and to earn some greatly needed funds through preaching assignments. His first stop was at Växjö where he received from Bishop Esaias Tegnér, the famous poet and theologian, his first *venia concionande*, the permission to preach. He had never appeared as a lay preacher in any situation prior to this time. His first sermon was preached at Älghult, his home congregation, on the fourth Sunday after Trinity, on the subject, "The True Light in a Man's Heart." He preached later that summer at Ekeberga, Hovmantorp, Fagerhult, Hälleberga, and again at Älghult before returning to Lund.[18]

It was a thrilling experience for Erl. Carlsson to begin his theological studies at the University in Lund in September 1844. But it soon became a trying time when he was afflicted seriously with gastric nerve fever. He was often ill and alone. He began to improve at the end of the first term and was able to begin the new term with enthusiasm. He purchased books as extensively as his finances permitted, including detailed exegetical volumes, Gesinius' *Hebrew Grammar*, Winer's *Grammar for New Testment Greek*, Guericke's *Church History*, books on symbolics, dogmatics, and the New Testament. He worked so hard that at times it seemed as if his health would be impaired. Pastor Sellergren had told him: "It would be well if all our pastors were learned men."[19]

Erl. Carlsson passed with honors at Lund University the theoretical examination in theology in April 1848, and the practical examination in December of the same year. In the first examination he received the citation *cum eximia laude Adprobatur* (passed with special distinction) in Old Testament Exegetics; *cum laude Adprobatur* (with distinction) in New Testament Exegetics, Symbolics, and

Church History; and *Adprobatur* (passed) in Dogmatics and Moral Theology. In the practical theology examination the results were as follows: in Catechetics, Homiletics, and Casuistics, *cum laude Adprobatur* (with distinction), in Church Law and Liturgics, *non sine laude Adprobatur* (not without distinction). Per Welander and Erl. Carlsson received stipends from the faculty in recognition of having the highest academic marks in the class.[20]

The theological student from Älghult had attained academic distinction in the midst of illness and financial problems. In addition to his studies he tutored young students in Latin, Greek, and Hebrew ten to twelve hours per week for which he was paid modest fees. He also served as a pulpit supply during his later years at Lund. He assisted *Kyrkoherde* (chief pastor) Wieselquist at Gylle at Christmas and New Years in 1847 and Pastor Tegnér the next summer at Källstorp. In the summer of 1848, he served as pastor in the resort town of Ramlösa. His friends at Lund had been few in number, but they were serious Christians. In addition to his formal studies, he spent much time reading the Bible and the writings of Luther, Schartau, Arndt, Nohrborg, and Rosenius. On the way home to Småland, after completing his studies at Lund, he preached on the first Sunday in Advent at Osby, where his friend and later a pastor in America, O. C. T. Andrén, was pastor's assistant. [21]

Since there was no scarcity of pastors in the Växjö diocese, no special cause prompted Erland to seek ordination immediately. He preached at the *Julotta* (Christmas matins) service and on other occasions at Älghult. Pastor's assistant Fr. Thelander and he conducted Bible studies in various places in the congregation with gratifying results. People came to hear him from a wide area. Spiritual revival occurred especially among young people. After several months the response continued to be strong, an encouraging development for the young theological graduate. [22]

Towards Shrove-tide in 1849, Erl. Carlsson went to Växjö, the diocesean headquarters, to prepare for the pastor's examination before the *Konsistorium* (cathedral chapter) as a prerequisite for ordination. Through the influence of his friend, E. G. Tillström, he received an assignment to preach in Växjö cathedral and thus met some new people. He went to Hovmantorp at Easter to be with his university friend, J. P. Dahlstedt, who was a tutor and assistant *komminister* at Furuby. Erland preached in both churches. When he was ready to leave for Växjö, a messenger came from *Bergsrådet* (mine executive), Johan Lorentz Aschan asking him to conduct services at the *Brukskyrkan* (mill church) at Lessebo the next Sunday. He accepted the invitation.[23]

On the day following the Sunday service, Erl. Carlsson was asked by *Bergsrådet* Aschan if he would accept a call as pastor at Lessebo and tutor of the sons of Countess Carie Cederström, his daughter. After careful consideration for several days, Carlsson responded in the affirmative. The call provided that he should preach on alternate Sundays at Lessebo, but live in the household of Countess Cederström in Växjö in the winter and at *Åry bruk* in the summer. His compensation was to be 300 *riksdaler* as pastor and 200 *riksdaler* as tutor, and free maintenance. On April 25, Erland had a conference with Bishop Heurlin who authenticated the call and proposed that he be ordained at Växjö.[24]

The goal of ten years of striving was reached on June 19, 1849, the first Sunday after Trinity, when Erl. Carlsson was ordained with four other young men into the holy ministry at Växjö by Bishop Christopher Heurlin. The official document setting forth the results of his pastoral examination was signed by Bishop Heurlin and included the following: "Erland Carlsson . . . has proven his knowledge with distinction and thus, as far as human evaluation is able to ascertain, is found qualified to assume the serious calling as a Christian pastor." On May 17, Ascension Day, he preached his ordination sermon in Växjö Cathedral. His first sermon as an ordained pastor was preached on the second Sunday after Trinity at Älghult. On the following Sunday he preached for the first time at Lessebo. His topic was "How Jesus Seeks and Saves Lost Sinners."[25]

The attitude of Erl. Carlsson as a recently ordained pastor at Lessebo is clearly understood from the contents of a letter to Peter Wieselgren shortly after his arrival there: "May God show his grace and mercy so that I may carry out my mission as the pastor of the congregation and teacher of children faithfully and conscientiously, with wisdom and energy, with gentleness and earnestness, before my own conscience and that of others. . . . And may I rejoice in the richness of His grace and power both towards me and those whom he has entrusted to me."[26]

Pastor Erl. Carlsson entered enthusiastically into his work at Lessebo. Many of the congregation, which numbered 250 in 1850, were employed in Aschan's iron and paper mills. The new pastor was authorized, to his great joy, to conduct Bible study on Sunday afternoons. On the first Saturday of his pastorate at Lessebo, he held a church school which was attended by all children of the parish and by many adults. The wife of *Bergsrådet* Aschan joined with her daughter, the Countess, in sharing deep religious experiences. The young pastor was supported by Aschan until shortly after the death of the latter's wife. Then his attitude changed. He ceased attending the church services and complained about reports that so many people from other congregations came to the Lessebo church that the resident members were crowded out. Erland had used a room for conferences with individuals in the company building, and Aschan complained that the building was deteriorating and the carpet worn out by the many *läsare* (readers, pietists) who came to see the pastor in such large numbers. [27]

The private sessions were then moved to the church with the result that even more prople sought to consult with Pastor Carlsson. Aschan criticized him for this development, using such terms as "hypocrisy" and "ingratiation." Carlsson, however, demonstrated the seriousness of the counselling relationship so that Aschan finally said: "Let us not think any more about this matter, but let us go and smoke a pipe." They smoked the "peace-pipe" and the pastor continued to preach, conduct Bible studies, and counsel with the people privately. [28]

Pastor Carlsson's responsibility as a tutor of Countess Cederström's children—ages 18, 9, and 6—was exacting but rewarding. In addition to regular academic studies, he provided Bible studies and devotional exercises. In the winter months at Växjö, increasing numbers of people attended the prayer and Bible study sessions in the home of the Countess. The pastor had secured the permission of *Domprost* (Dean of Cathedral) Ahlstrand for these religious meetings outside the church. Soon there were several of these informal but regular devotional meetings in Växjö and in country homes. Bishop Heurlin was critical and raised the issue in the *Konsistorium*. But *Domprost* Ahlstrand informed the Bishop that Erl. Carlsson had been authorized to hold such meetings. [29]

This criticism by Bishop Heurlin was the beginning of a situation that in time developed into hostility toward Erl. Carlsson. The young pastor soon received a *missiv,* or order, that he had been assigned to a remote corner of the diocese. After consultation with a friend who was a member of the diocesean consistory, he was advised to bring the *missiv* to the Bishop, lay it on the table, and declare: "My call as a *brukspastor* [at Lessebo] is a firm call, the consistory has no right to execute this *missiv*, and I neither can nor will leave my post." Carlsson followed this advice. The Bishop yielded and the problem was temporarily solved. [30]

The continued hostility of Bishop Heurlin was soon apparent. On May 12, 1852, he received another *missiv.* Erland turned again to his friend and advisor who said to him:

> Although I and some others both spoke and voted against this action as illegal and unjust, some joined the bishop's side, since the appointee would become the bishop's own assistant in the prebendary of Hemmesjö and Tegnaby [in the Växjö area]. Although I was against the decree, I cannot do otherwise than urge you to accept it since I heard the conversation between the ecclesiastical minister and the bishop, and I know, if you do not obey and conduct the worship service at Hemmesjö next Sunday, the bishop will declare there was *mässfall* [default of a worship service] and Carlsson will be suspended because of that, and if Carlsson appeals to His Majesty, one knows in advance what the decision will be. [31]

The conversation referred to by Erl. Carlsson's friend between the newly appointed ecclesiastical minister, Professor Henrik Reuterdahl of Lund, high church theologian, and the bishop, occurred at Växjö when the latter held a reception for Reuterdahl who was enroute to Stockholm to take up his new assignment. When most of the guests had left and only a few members of the consistory remained, the designated ecclesiastical minister made inquiry about conditions in the diocese. Bishop Heurlin then described the resistance of Erl. Carlsson to the first *missiv* and his refusal to follow the instructions of the consistory. The future ecclesiastical minister is reported to have said: "Should the bishop feel it necessary to take action that will remove him from his present position and should he [Erl. Carlsson] refuse or appeal to His Royal Majesty, I will see to it that the decision is made in harmony with your wishes." [32]

Although Erl. Carlsson was generally well-liked and dearly loved by many, there were some who opposed him. There seemed to be no further conflict with *Bergsrådet* Aschan. However, in a letter to his son he wrote: "On the basis of a *missiv,* that man of spirit, Pastor Carlsson, has left Lessebo, and that is a good thing." In October 1849, Erl. Carlsson had written to Peter Wieselgren: "My area of work is certainly limited here . . . Should God by His Spirit, make me capable of a wider area of service through experience and study, He will provide it for me." Carlsson was destined for a "wider area of service," but the circumstances that provided it were rather unusual. [33]

Pastor Carlsson conducted the morning service at Hemmesjö the Sunday following receipt of the *missiv.* He called on Bishop Heurlin the next day. The conversation was pleasant until the bishop said to the young pastor: "There is one thing that I wish the pastor to understand fully from the outset; I do not want to learn about any conventicles in my congregation." Erl. Carlsson then asked what the bishop meant by "conventicles," and received the response that "you surely know what a conventicle is." The pastor responded that he knew what a conventicle was but he was not sure that the two of them had the same understanding. The bishop then gave his definition: "I understand by conventicles such meetings of men and women, younger and older, assembled for special worship services." [34]

On hearing the bishop's definition, Erland replied that he was afraid that he had already violated the bishop's wish. On the previous day there had been a wedding at Hemmesjö at the home of a deacon, who asked the pastor to conduct a Bible study as an appropriate dedication of a beautiful Bible that the deacon had purchased as a gift for the bride and groom. Carlsson gladly consented. The guests sang hymns, the pastor prayed, presented the Bible to the newly-weds, and conducted a Bible study which was followed by another prayer and singing. When Erland told the bishop that he planned to continue such "conventicles," he was asked: "What authorizes the pastor to do so?" Erland replied: "My call as pastor and the Apostle Paul when he said: 'Preach the word in and out of season.' " [35]

In the conversation which followed, the bishop told the pastor that if he continued to be bold and hold conventicles, he would send the *länsmanen* (police officer). The courageous pastor replied: "The bishop may do that but it will not frighten me. But since the bishop is so opposed to Bible studies in the homes of church members, how would he feel if they were presented in the church?" The bishop gave the only possible answer under the circumstances: "I really do not have anything against Bible studies in the church." Carlsson hastened to tell him that such Bible studies would begin next Sunday. [36]

When Erl. Carlsson finished the sermon at Tegnaby the next Sunday, he announced that after a fifteen minute intermission, the church bell would call the members for Bible study. Almost the entire congregation participated. After the meeting, a deacon invited the pastor to join his family for the noon meal. Others came later. They conversed, sang hymns, read the Bible, prayed, thus holding a conventicle. Bishop Heurlin apparently made no further protest. [37]

Another problem soon developed between Bishop Heurlin and Erl. Carlsson. In the middle of August of that year the latter accepted the invitation to present temperance talks in Konga *härad* of the Växjö diocese. This activity was greeted with indignation by Heurlin who didn't like what he called "this temperance business." Since Carlsson's work was in congregations directly under the bishop's jurisdiction, the latter wished to transfer the pastor. A vacancy had occurred among the cathedral clergy because of illness. The dean urged that someone be appointed immediately. The bishop said he knew of no one except "the fanatical zealot," Pastor Carlsson who could be assigned. The dean said he would gladly accept him. Erland then began service with the cathedral clergy in October 1852, according to *Wexjö Stifts-Tidningar.* [38]

Carlsson entered into his assignment determined to do the best possible. He was an effective preacher and it is reported that the attendance was larger than usual when he was scheduled to preach. He was assigned to hold *husförhör,* sessions in which he went in the homes of members to discuss devotional life, personal relations, temperance, etc. At a large gathering of socially prominent persons, he was amazed to see that a table with alcoholic drinks was set up in connection with the luncheon, and that in an intermission, card playing occurred. When the meeting resumed, Carlsson spoke sternly about the evils of alcohol, drawing a reprimand for his strong language from some of the pastors in attendance. Although he did not criticize the card players, he left abruptly when the games started, thus showing his displeasure. Erl. Carlsson responded in keeping with the evangelical and pious *läsare* tradition in which he believed. [39]

Pastor Carlsson's temporary appointment at Växjö ended when the pastor for whom he was substituting regained his health. In Januray 1853, he was assigned as *Komminister* to the parish of Härlöv and Öjaby in the Växjö area, prebendaries of his friend, *Lektor* A. Melander. He was happy at the prospect of service in these congregations. But, unknown to him, other developments were taking place. After six weeks at Härlöv and Öjaby, he received a call to serve in far-away America. [40]

FOOTNOTES

[1]"Elghults födelse och dopbok, 1800-31," p. 507; "Elghults husförhörslängd, 1825-30," p. 38. Catharina Svensson, Linkoping, Sweden, a descendent of Erl. Carlsson's sister, Anna Lovisa, has traced the family antecedents to the early 1700s. Eben Carlsson, Erland Carlsson's oldest son, and his wife named their oldest son Erland. The present Erland Carlsson IV is the great, great-grandson of the immigrant pastor.

[2]Eric Norelius, *De Svenska Lutherska församlingarnas och Svenskarnes historia i Amerika* (Rock Island: Lutheran Augustana Book Concern, 1890), I, 393. Hereafter cited *De Svenska Lutherska . . . historia i Amerika.* Sven Blomén, *Älghult. Vår hemsocken* (Nybro: Johansson och Svenson Boktryckeri AB, 1955), pp. 124-30; "Elghults födelse och dopbok, 1800-31," p. 507. Norelius, cited above, based his account of the early life of Erl. Carlsson directly on the autobiography which the latter prepared for him in 1890. See the letters from Carlsson to Norelius August 6, 1889, February 25, 1890, and April 2, 1890, as described *infra*, Chapter XIII, p. 192. Norelius used this material by direct quotation or paraphrase. Carlsson's "Sjelfbio-grafi" is presently available only for the years 1853-54 and in a form copied by Norelius from the original with some editing. Norelius' *De Svenska Lutherska . . . historia i Amerika* is basically Erl. Carlsson's autobiographical material related to his early life. The use of "Erl. Carlsson" rather than "Erland Carlsson" corresponds with the manner in which he always signed his name.

[3]Norelius, *De Svenska Lutherska . . . historia i Amerika,* I, 393-94.

[4]"Elghults husförhörslängd, 1831-39," p. 328; Norelius, *De Svenska Lutherska . . . historia i Amerika,* I, 394.

[5]Norelius, *De Svenska Lutherska . . . historia i Amerika,* I, 395.

[6]Norelius, *De Svenska Lutherska . . . historia i Amerika,* I, 396; Esther Dahlén, Bondpojken från Suletorp som blev president för Augustanasynoden i Amerika," *Älghults-Krönika,* IV (1947), 55.

[7]Norelius, *De Svenska Lutherska . . . historia i Amerika,* I, 396.

[8]*Ibid.,* I, 397.

[9]*Ibid.*

[10]*Ibid.,* I, 398.

[11]*Ibid.*

[12]Norelius, *De Svenska Lutherska . . . historia i Amerika,* I, 399; Dahlén, "Bondpojken från Suletorp . . . ," p. 55. See *Älghults-Krönika* IV (1947) for a discussion of various aspects of Lorenz Sellergren's life, pp. 103-14.

[13]Norelius, *De Svenska Lutherska . . . historia i Amerika,* I, 400.

[14]Norelius, *De Svenska Lutherska . . . historia i Amerika,* I, 400-402; *Svenskt biografiskt lexikon,* Bertil Boethius (editor), VII, 570.

[15]Norelius, *De Svenska Lutherska . . . historia i Amerika,* I, 401.

[16]*Ibid.*

[17]Norelius, *De Svenska Lutherska . . . historia i Amerika,* I, 401; *Svenskt biografiskt lexikon,* VII, 570; Carl Sjöstrom, *Smålands nation i Lund, 1668-1921. Biografiska och genealogiska anteckningar* (Lund: 1922), p. 345.

[18]Norelius, *De Svenska Lutherska . . . historia i Amerika,* I, 403; L. G. Abrahamson, "Doktor Erland Carlsson," *Minneskrift. Illustreradt album utgivet af Svenska Ev. Lutherska Immanuelsförsamlingen i Chicago* (Rock Island: Lutheran Augustana Book Concern, 1903,), p. 35. Hereafter referred to as *Minneskrift-Immanuelsförsamlingen.*

[19]Norelius, *De Svenska Lutherska . . . historia i Amerika,* I, 403; *Svenskt biografiskt lexikon,* VII, 570.

[20]"Utdrag af protocollet hallet uti theologiska faculteten i Lund d. 8 April 1848, d. 6 Dec. 1848."

[21]Norelius, *De Svenska Lutherska . . . historia i Amerika,* I, 403-404.

[22]*Ibid.,* I, 405.

[23]Norelius, *De Svenska Lutherska . . . historia i Amerika,* I, 406-407; Gustaf Clemensson, *Lessebo 1658-1850* (1954), pp. 323-24.

[24]Norelius, *De Svenska Lutherska . . . historia i Amerika*, I, 407.

[25]Erland Carlsson's ordination certificate was signed June 10, 1849, by Bishop Heurlin of Växjö diocese.

[26]Erl. Carlsson to Peter Wieselgren, Chicago, October 26, 1849.

[27]Norelius, *De Svenska Lutherska . . . historia i Amerika*, I, 409; Clemensson, *Lessebo 1658-1850*, pp. 317, 323-34; Dahlén,"Bondpojken från Suletorp," pp. 56-58. In 1838 Peter Wieselgren, upon Aschan's invitation and with his support, had organized a temperance society at Lessebo with more than 100 members. The mill owner distributed Psalm Books and New Testaments to people in the area.

[28]Norelius, *De Svenska Lutherska . . . historia i Amerika*, I, 409-10.

[29]Erl. Carlsson to Peter Wieselgren, Chicago, October 26, 1849; Norelius, *De Svenska Lutherska . . . historia i Amerika*, I, 410-11.

[30]Norelius, *De Svenska Lutherska . . . historia i Amerika*, I, 411.

[31]*Ibid.*, I, 411-12.

[32]*Ibid.*, I, 411.

[33]Clemensson, *Lessebo 1658-1850*, p. 324; Erl. Carlsson to Peter Wieselgren, Lessebo, October 26, 1849.

[34]Norelius, *De Svenska Lutherska . . . historia i Amerika*, I, 412.

[35]*Ibid.*

[36]*Ibid.*

[37]*Ibid.*, I, 413.

[38]Norelius, *De Svenska Lutherska . . . historia i Amerika*, I, 413; *Wexjö Stifts-Tidningar*, October, 1852, p. 74.

[39]Norelius, *De Svenska Lutherska . . . historia i Amerika*, I, 413-14.

[40]Norelius, *De Svenska Lutherska . . . historia i Amerika*, I, 416; *Wexjö Stifts-Tidningar*, December 1852, p. 90.

2

Emigration to America

The transformation of the life of Erl. Carlsson from service in two congregations in the quiet countryside of Småland to that of a pioneer pastor in the far-away city of Chicago was caused by a variety of factors. A basic element in that story had its origin in the emigration to America of Pastor and Mrs. Lars Paul Esbjörn, Hille, Gästrikland, with 146 persons, on June 29, 1849. Esbjörn was supported by a travel grant from the Swedish Missionary Society. The minister of ecclesiastical affairs at Stockholm had authorized his departure with the privilege of continuing membership in the ministerium and of returning to the service of the Church of Sweden when he wished to do so. Esbjörn's emigration was a personal venture and not an official act under the auspices of the Church of Sweden. He was the first Swedish Lutheran pastor in America in the nineteenth century immigration and the first ordained clergyman in the future Augustana Lutheran Synod.[1]

After a few days in New York, Esbjörn and his party decided to travel to Illinois arriving in the Andover area on the twenty-fourth of October. On March 18, 1850, Esbjörn, a graduate of Uppsala University, organized a church with ten charter members. The Swedish Lutheran Church in America had been formally launched.

Esbjörn kept in close contact with friends and sympathetic supporters in Sweden, especially with Pastors Peter Fjellstedt and Peter Wieselgren, urging them to recruit pastors for service in

17

America. In August 1852, Pastor and Mrs. Tuve Nilsson Hasselquist from Åkarp, Skåne, left Sweden with 100 immigrants to become co-laborers with Esbjörn in Illinois. Hasselquist, a graduate of Lund University, almost immediately upon arrival began his pastorate at Galesburg in the same month that Esbjörn organized the congregation. The early arrival of this outstanding pastor and leader was another decisive factor in shaping the course of the Swedish Lutheran Church in America.[2]

The emigration of Pastors Esbjörn and Hasselquist in the mid-century years had antecedents that reflected developments in the state Church of Sweden. A key person in these background factors was Carl Olof Rosenius, who had been closely identified with George Scott, the English Methodist pastor whose church, Bethlehem Chapel, Stockholm, had become the focal point for a far-reaching revival movement. Rosenius, editor of *Pietisten,* a religious journal which emphasized personal piety, emotional and subjective factors in Christian experience, and the role of moral imperatives in sanctification, had a large forum and many followers. He had been a theological student at Uppsala, but never sought ordination in the Church of Sweden. He resisted any movement related to the separatists. The pioneer Swedish American pastors owed much to Rosenius and his ideas as expressed in numerous writings.[3]

Moreover, three pastors within the Church of Sweden were especially noteworthy for their personal influence upon the immigrant pastors: Peter Fjellstedt, who established a school for training Christian leaders at Lund, located successively in Stockholm and Uppsala; Peter Wieselgren, long-time dean of Göteborg Cathedral and national leader of the temperance movement; and P. A. Ahlberg, founder and director of Ahlberg's School in Småland. The pioneer pastors were intimately associated with these leaders while still in Sweden and across the years in America. Restive over conditions within the Church of Sweden and in conflict with the church hierarchy, the support, especially of Fjellstedt and Wieselgren, was a decisive factor as they faced the challenge of service to God and man in far-away America.

This was a time of exploration and pioneering among Swedes far from their homeland, who were earnestly seeking to establish themselves in a new world. A heavy burden of responsibility was carried by Esbjörn and Hasselquist. Although emigration from Sweden was still relatively modest, there were many places where immigrants had settled and still other areas which would be key points in the future. Chicago was one of these places. Twenty-nine Swedes, supported by Pastor Paul Andersen of the Norwegian Lutheran Church, sent a letter to Hasselquist at Galesburg, asking the pastor "if he would have the great kindness to make the great effort to come to us in Chicago immediately after New Years to preach again God's Word to us ... [and] that he might with God's help organize a Swedish congregation, and thirdly, that he might write to Sweden for a pastor with a view of having him come to Chicago as early as possible next spring." On January 16, 1853, Hasselquist organized the Swedish Evangelical Lutheran Church in Chicago.[4]

The meeting in January provided that the call to serve the Chicago Swedes would go to Pastor Peter Fjellstedt at Lund for transmission to Pastor J. P. Dahlstedt at Hovmantorp. Since there was no certainty that he could or would accept the call, no name was inserted in the form. It was agreed that if Dahlstedt did not accept, Fjellstedt should seek a candidate and insert the name. This was a wise decision because Dahlstedt could not accept the call because of illness.[5]

A difficult situation faced Fjellstedt in his serious desire to respond to the appeal for a pastor from the Chicago Swedes. It has been reported that after reflecting on the matter for several days, he dropped on his knees one morning at his home in Lund and prayed that God would guide him in selecting someone to accept the call. At that moment he heard a knock on the door, and when he opened it, a student greeted him with these words: "I do not have time to come in but I wish to leave a letter from Pastor Erl. Carlsson." Fjellstedt was confident that this was an answer to prayer. He wrote immediately to Carlsson, urging him to accept the Chicago call. He was so certain of the result that he inserted Erl. Carlsson's name in the blank space of the document which had been sent from Chicago.[6]

Erl. Carlsson had no knowledge of the possible contents of the letter from his friend and counselor, Peter Fjellstedt, as he opened it that February day in 1853. There is no evidence to indicate that Erland had considered emigration to America. He reflected on it seriously and prayerfully. Looming large in his contemplation was his strong endorsement by Peter Fjellstedt, a man highly esteemed by the young pastor. He had lived in the Fjellstedt home during a period of his Lund residence. Although Erland had good friends in Sweden and relationships with his family were excellent, he had no deep roots in any one place and no personal family obligations. Moreover, he has written that he had recently read in a newspaper a long account from Chicago of the need for a pastor to serve the immigrants there and others who passed through the city enroute to other places. As he prayed one morning, two Bible verses came to him: "The earth is the Lord's and the fullness thereof, the world and they who dwell therein" (PS 24:1), and "He who loved father and mother more than me is not worthy of me" (Matt 10:37). This experience seemed to give an answer to his prayer for guidance.[7]

The young pastor went immediately to Växjö to consult with his physician who told him that it was quite likely that his health would be improved in a new climate. He then wrote to Fjellstedt stating that in Jesus' name, he had decided to accept the call as soon as he received permission from the King to emigrate.[8]

On March 11, Fjellstedt wrote to Erland declaring: "It pleases me that my dear brother has decided to accept this important call." The former then informed his friend about the procedure for gaining permission to emigrate, namely, that he should write to *Högwällborne Herr Friherr* (his lordship, Baron) Joh. A. Posse, of the *Kungliga Riksarkivet* (amanuensis at the Royal Archives) Stockholm. Posse wrote a very encouraging letter to Carlsson later that month, informing the applicant that his request had been transmitted to the Växjö authorities. Posse urged Carlsson to contact *Fil. dr.* Melander in Växjö in order to speed up the procedure, also assuring him that he would personally talk with Ecclesiastical Minister Reuterdahl in his behalf. On April 22, Carlsson was informed that permission to emigrate had been granted in the form of a leave-of-absence for six years with the understanding that he could return to the service of the Church of Sweden before the expiration of that period.[9]

Erl. Carlsson immediately began preparations for emigration. He preached his farewell sermon at Härlöv on May 5, and on the following Sunday at Öjaby. He then went to Älghult to make final preparations and to say good-bye to relatives and friends. He preached at Älghult, his home congregation, on May 29. The ticket for passage from Kalmar to New York had been purchased earlier at Växjö from an agent of a Hamburg shipping line. A few families and some single persons from the Växjö and Älghult areas had discussed emigration with him. When he came to Kalmar on June 2, he was amazed to see a throng of emigrants, 146, planning to travel to America on the same ship. He was accompanied to Kalmar by Erland Danielson, his step-father. On Friday morning, June 3, Pastor Carlsson preached to a large crowd of emigrants and others in Kalmar Cathedral, including Bishop Genberg. [10]

Although Erl. Carlsson was surprised to see so many emigrants ready to leave with him for America on June 3, background factors afford at least a partial explanation. It was known in April that he had been granted permission to emigrate to America. Meanwhile C. Fr. Eckström, an emigrant agent in Växjö, was actively promoting the June 3, date for departure. In the pages of *Nya Wexjö-Bladet,* he announced the plans. On April 18, he described the plans and on April 29, 150 people met at Växjö to receive information. On May 10, he announced final details for the departure of the *Gauthiod* from Kalmar on June 3. Seventeen emigrants from Älghult, the first from the congregation, were included in the Carlsson party. The pastor was well-known in several areas of Kronobergs *län* and he had gained followers through his sermons and Bible studies. His popularity and Eckström's promotional activities provide reasons for the large number of emigrants from Kronobergs *län* that June day. [11]

On June 3, 1853, Erl. Carlsson boarded the paddle-steamer *Gauthiod* for Lübeck. After saying good-bye to his step-father, he turned to the large crowd at dock-side, and cried out with a loud voice: "Good-bye in Jesus' name. We will meet at the throne of grace and within the gate of heaven. Jesus' promise: 'I am with you always, even unto the end of the world,' applies to us in our homes and in our journey to America as well as in Sweden, until he has brought us unto himself, when we shall be with the Lord always." Many handkerchiefs were waved, many tears were shed, and many prayers were raised to God as the ship began the voyage. [12]

The first newspaper account of the departure of the Carlsson party was printed in *Barometern,* published in Kalmar on June 4, 1853. In two paragraphs is a news account and an editorial opinion:

Yesterday afternoon not less than 146 emigrants all from Kronobergs *län*, left on the paddle-steamer *Gauthiod*, P. O. Nylen, captain. They will travel via Hamburg and Liverpool to America. Their destination is New York, from whence they plan to continue their journey to Chicago on Lake Michigan, where about 200 Swedes have already settled and to which the accompanying *Adjunct* Erland Carlsson from Härlöv in Kronobergs *län*, has been called as pastor.

Among the emigrants are several land owners, who sold their farms for cash; the rest consist of *torpare* [crofters] in addition to a large number of women and small children. The group—it is reported—bring with them more than 100,000 *riksdaler*, which certainly will enable them to make a good start in the new world; however, the countenances of the emigrants created a depressing feeling. They fully understand that many adversities face them before they reach their destination and perhaps on first arriving in a foreign land they will regret that they left the fatherland, especially since prosperity and fairly good conditions are not lacking. [13]

The route of the Carlsson party was from Kalmar, on the east coast of Sweden, to Lübeck, then to Hamburg, old and famous Hanseatic towns on the Baltic Sea, and then to England. They arrived at Lübeck on the morning of June 5, where they boarded the train for Hamburg. This was a new experience for the pastor and his fellow travelers. Johan Andersson from Hälleberga, described their wonderment about the large locomotive and many railroad cars. It was with excitement that they looked upon the passing countryside as the train moved swiftly and safely on wheels that followed the long ribbon of steel tracks. The trip from Lübeck to Hamburg required only three and one-half hours. The travelers were impressed at the speed with which the train carried them over the ground and even sometimes underground. At Hamburg the Swedes were especially attracted by the gas street lights which burned throughout the night. The emigrant party was not able to leave Hamburg until June 10. Three days later they were at Hull, and by evening of that day, they arrived at the great port city of Liverpool. [14]

The experiences of the emigrants at Liverpool were not pleasant. They were required to stay there fifteen days before sailing for America. The shipping company tried to avoid the full contractual agreement relative to providing supplies for the crossing but Pastor Carlsson entered into the controversy and persuaded the agents to deal fairly with the travelers. A witness to the event praised the pastor for his skill and firmness; the emigrants hastened to raise a collection of sixty *riksdalers* as a token of appreciation for Carlsson's effective assistance. [15]

In the midst of the many preparations for departure on the long voyage to America, Erl. Carlsson reflected on the experiences of his party in the context of later Swedish emigrants who would follow them. On June 21, he wrote a letter from Liverpool addressed to "My Countrymen," which was printed in *Borås Tidning, Nya Wexjö-Bladet,* and elsewhere. Included was the following message:

> Without wishing to encourage or discourage emigrants from the fatherland, I feel it a duty to those who have already decided to emigrate to present the following announcement.
>
> Since there are few berths available Göteborg to America with the result that most of the Swedes who emigrate must go via Hamburg, it is of the greatest importance not to enter into a contract with just any company of the many who have been formed to serve emigrants. It often happens that Swedes find themselves among those who do not know the language or are not familiar with their legal rights, and are therefore badly treated by some of the companies.

Carlsson recommended the Columbia Company affiliated with the Morris Company at Hamburg. He was certain that this company would live up to the terms of its contract. He also promised that more complete information would be provided later. His quite detailed emigrant guide was available the next year. [16]

The afternoon of Midsummer Day, on June 25, the emigrants boarded the *St. Patrick* at Liverpool. It was not until 4 p.m. on the 28th that the tide and other conditions were right so that the ship could sail into the open sea. The ship's manifest signed by Master Matthew Kinney, shows that there were 554 passengers on board as the voyage to New York began. Included were people from Sweden, Norway, Germany, Great Britain, Ireland, Russia, and France. The largest contingents were from Sweden and Ireland. The names of 170 Swedes are listed. The range in age was from infants of a few months to a man aged fifty-seven. Fifty persons out of 170 were in the age range of ten and below. Only twelve persons were over forty years old. Seventeen were under the age of twelve months. There were ninety-eight males and sixty-three females for whom this information is available. The vast majority were farmers or farm workers and a sizeable number of single household women workers. Among other professions and vocations were the following: a minister, a school-master, a carpenter, a watchmaker, two blacksmiths, and two tailors. Pastor Carlsson, 30, was listed no. 125. [17]

The Atlantic crossing lasted from June 28 to August 13. A severe storm struck the *St. Patrick* shortly after leaving Liverpool, bringing much seasickness with the attendant distress. Since trunks were not fastened, there was general dislocation as the ship was struck with high waves. Fortunately the weather soon improved, and except for a stiff contrary wind, which slowed down the progress of the *St. Patrick,* there was no great danger to the passengers. But the angel of death was often present. Sixteen Swedish emigrants, about ten percent, died enroute, principally from dysentery. Nine of seventeen infants, one year or less in age, died during the passage. On July 11, Johan Anderson, a farmer, lost his wife, Ingrid, and their infant daughter. On August 1, Johann Herlin, a shoemaker, suffered the same tragedy, when his wife, Johanna, and their infant daughter passed away. Pastor Carlsson was occupied consoling the bereaved and encouraging the doubters.[18]

A worship service was conducted by Pastor Carlsson each Sunday morning. Prayer and Bible study was a regular experience each morning and evening. There were several fine singers on board and they sang their simple and beautiful hymns daily, accompanied often by Erl. Carlsson with his violin. The pastor was also involved in counselling and advising his fellow travelers who were leaving home for an uncertain venture in an unknown land. When time permitted, he studied the Bible and English grammar and vocabulary.[19]

The Swedes watched quietly and attentively as the *St. Patrick* docked at New York on August 13. Then followed a busy time in making arrangements at Castle Garden, the official station of the United States Immigration Service, and in clearing customs, checking travel documents, studying schedules, and buying tickets for the journey to Chicago. Erl. Carlsson and some members of his party attended the religious service on Sunday at the famous *Bethel Ship* in New York harbor, conducted by Olof Gustaf Hedström, the well-known Swedish Methodist minister. On Tuesday, August 16, the

Carlsson party traveled via the Hudson River Railroad to Buffalo. On Friday, they boarded a large and fine steamship, crossing Lake Erie to Detroit, disembarking there at noon the next day. On Sunday they went to Chicago via the Michigan Central Railroad, arriving there Sunday afternoon. Pastor Carlsson was met at the railroad station by members of the Swedish Lutheran congregation. Housing had been arranged for him at the home of Iver Lawsen, a Norwegian. [20]

The newly-arrived pastor immediately turned his attention to aiding members of his immigrant party. A group of seventy had chosen Chisago Lake, Minnesota, as their destination. He arranged transportation for them via canal boat to La Salle, and from there by horse-drawn vehicles to Rock Island, and then by boat to Minnesota. He negotiated a contract with the canal boat company and arranged for other tickets. Shortly thereafter, forty persons left for St. Charles, approximately forty miles from Chicago. Carlsson exchanged "sad and painful farewells" with these friends from Småland with whom he had crossed the Atlantic. [21]

Erl. Carlsson's greatest immediate problem was related to the rest of the party in Chicago who were poor and many who were ill. He found lodging, food, and medical aid for them. Moreover, another Swedish immigrant party soon arrived with 200 members, most of whom needed assistance. In a letter to a friend he wrote: "I have been here now a month and during this short period of time I have seen greater human distress here than I have ever seen in the homeland . . . I feel at the same time joy at being stationed here. This has been a difficult time. First of all I have to struggle with the language and, in addition, everything is new and strange. May the Lord give me health and strength to carry on his work here." [22]

The seventy members of the Erl. Carlsson immigrant party who went to Chisago Lake, Minnesota, in the late summer of 1853, furnished people who shared in the setting for the famous immigrant novels of Vilhelm Moberg. In the church membership book of the Chisago Lake Swedish Lutheran congregation are the names of members who arrived there in 1853 from Långasjö, Älghult, Dädesjö, Lenhovda, Hovmantorp, Linneryd, Algutsboda, and Ljuder, Kronobergs *län,* Erl. Carlsson's home area. [23]

FOOTNOTES

[1]G. Everett Arden, *Augustana Heritage. A History of the Augustana Lutheran Church* (Rock Island: Augustana Press, 1963), pp. 27-38. Hereafter cited as *Augustana Heritage.*

[2]*Ibid.*, p. 39.

[3]*Ibid.*, pp. 4-11.

[4]I. O. Nothstein (ed.), "Selected Documents Dealing with the Organization of the First Congregations and the First Conferences of the Augustana Synod and their Growth Until 1860," Part 2, *Augustana Historical Society Publications*, XI, (Rock Island: Augustana Historical Society, 1946), 5-8.

[5]Norelius, *De Svenska Lutherska . . . historia i Amerika*, I, 416.

[6]Erl. Carlsson, "Sjelfbiografi," p. 35; Norelius, *De Svenska Lutherska . . . historia i Amerika*, I, 417. There are approximately sixty-five lines to each of the numbered pages of the "Sjelfbiografi."

[7]Erl. Carlsson, "Sjelfbiografi," p. 35; Norelius, *De Svenska Lutherska . . . historia i Amerika*, I, 417.

[8]Erl Carlsson, "Sjelfbiografi," p. 35.

[9]P. Fjellstedt to Erl. Carlsson, Lund, March 11, 1853, and J. Aug. Posse to Erl. Carlsson, March 29, 1853, Gunnar Westin, *Emigranterna och kyrkan. Brev från och till Svenskar i Amerika 1849-1892* (Stockholm: Svenska kyrkans diakonistyrelses bokförlag,) 1932, pp. 64-65; Sten Almqvist "Erland Carlsson 1822-1872," *Älghults-Krönika*, 1972, pp. 34-35.

[10]Erl. Carlsson, "Sjelfbiografi," p. 36; Norelius, *De Svenska Lutherska . . . historia i Amerika*, I, 418; *Svenskt biografiskt lexikon,* VII, 571.

[11]*Nya Wexjö-Bladet*, April 18, April 29, May 10, May 20, 1853; "Statistical Table," *"Älghults-Krönika*, 1947, p. 88.

[12]Erl. Carlsson, "Sjelfbiografi," p. 36; Norelius, *De Svenska Lutherska . . . historia i Amerika*, I, 418-19.

[13]*Barometern* (Kalmar) June 4, 1853.

[14]Erl. Carlsson, "Sjelfbiografi," p. 37; Arvid Bjerking, "En Hällebergas Amerikaresa 1853," *Älghults-Krönika*, 1959, pp. 69-71; *Nya Wexjö-Bladet*, July 1, 1853.

[15]Bjerking, "En Hällebergas Amerikaresa 1853," p. 70; Norelius, *De Svenska Lutherska . . . historia i Amerika*, I, 419.

[16]*Borås Tidning,* July 14, 1853; *Nya Wexjö-Bladet,* July 15, 1853.

[17]Erl. Carlsson, "Sjelfbiografi," p. 37; "St. Patrick's Ship's Manifest, New York, August 15, 1853;" Sven Blomén, "Ut-och inflyttningar från och till Älghult 1845-1945," *Älghults-Krönika,* 1947, p. 88; Bjerking, "En Hällebergas Amerikaresa, 1853," p. 71.

[18]Bjerking, "En Hällebergas Amerikaresa, 1853, pp. 71-72; "St. Patrick's Ship's Manifest."

[19]Erl. Carlsson, "Sjelfbiografi," p. 37; Norelius, *De Svenska Lutherska . . . historia i Amerika,* I, 419, Bjerking, "En Hällebergas Amerikaresa, 1853," p. 72.

[20]Erl. Carlsson, "Sjelfbiografi," p. 37; Erl. Carlsson, letter to an unidentified friend, September 23, 1853; Bjerking, "En Hällebergas Amerikaresa, 1853," p. 72.

[21]Erl. Carlsson, letter to an unidentified friend, September 23, 1853; Norelius, *De Svenska Lutherska . . . historia i Amerika,* I, 433.

[22]Erl. Carlsson, letter to an unidentified friend, September 23, 1853.

[23]Hilding Pleijel, "The Church from which Came the Founders of the Augustana Synod," *Augustana Quarterly,* XXVII (July, 1948), 206-207; Norelius, *De Svenska Lutherska . . . historia i Amerika,* I, 555-56.

Erl. Carlsson's Parental Home
in Suletorp

Älghult Church

3

Building a Congregation

Erl. Carlsson's arrival in Chicago in August 1853 to become pastor of the recently organized Swedish Lutheran Church marks a vital date in a series of developments associated with Swedish American religious and cultural life. A few Swedes are known to have lived in Chicago as early as the mid-1840s, but no regularly organized church of the homeland was available until 1853.

Gustaf Smith, a virtually unknown layman, claiming to be a clergyman, organized in 1847 what was supposedly a Lutheran congregation among a small number of Swedes. There is no evidence to indicate that Smith had any official relations with any Lutheran synod. Construction was begun on a church building on the south side of Superior Street, between Wells and La Salle streets, an address that was destined to be long remembered among Swedish Americans. In order to gather funds for completing the church structure, Smith, accompanied by a deacon, solicited funds among German Lutherans in St. Louis. An excellent response produced $600 for the building.[1]

Meanwhile doubts about Smith had arisen among members of the congregation. On the date designated for a meeting to discuss Smith's situation he disappeared, allegedly, with a sizeable part of the money received in St. Louis. Soon thereafter a storm struck the unfinished church, moving it from its foundation and causing other damage. The prospects for the new Swedish Lutheran congregation were discouraging.

Meanwhile, some Norwegians who had not joined in Smith's plans, became associated with Paul Andersen who was a student at Beloit College, a Presbyterian institution. Andersen conducted informal services and Bible studies in Chicago. Several Norwegians urged him to join with them and organize a Lutheran congregation. In a wise and generous decision, Presbyterian officials urged Andersen to serve his countrymen in this religious tradition rather than associate himself with the Presbyterian Church. In January 1848 the first Norwegian Lutheran church was organized. Andersen was ordained as a pastor by the Evangelical Lutheran Franckean Synod. The unfinished church on Superior Street was taken over and made ready for services.[2]

Some Swedes turned to Gustaf Unonius for spiritual leadership. Unonius was a Swedish-born Episcopal priest, the first graduate of Nashotah Theological Seminary, Wisconsin. Captain Philip von Schneidau, who had known Unonius in Wisconsin, urged him to organize a congregation in Chicago. The original intent to form a Swedish Episcopal congregation, St. Erik's, was abandoned in 1849 due to the interest of some Norwegians who had belonged to the short-lived congregation founded by Smith. The decision was then made to organize St. Ansgarius Church, composed of Swedes and Norwegians.[3]

The constitution of the original congregation read in section one as follows:

> We, the undersigned, Swedes residing in the city of Chicago . . . do hereby unite, being adherents of the Evangelical Lutheran Church as it is established and maintained under Episcopal jurisdiction in our homeland, into a church to be named St. Erik's in cooperation and fellowship with the Protestant Episcopal Church of the United States of America, and the diocese of Illinois, the constitution and church ordinance of which we hereby acknowledge and to which we submit, engaging ourselves to conform to its liturgy and church order whenever the services shall be conducted in the English language.

In the final document of St. Ansgarius Episcopal Church, the words "Swedes and Norwegians" were substituted for "Swedes," according to Unonius.[4]

Intense controversy developed later in the relations of the

Swedish Lutherans and Unonius, although Erl. Carlsson was not as
heavily involved as Esbjörn and Hasselquist. Unonius returned to
Sweden in 1858. In his *Memoirs* Unonius wrote about the arrival of
Erl. Carlsson and other Swedish pastors: "But they were ministers of
the Swedish church and the Swedish immigrants naturally found it
more correct to place themselves under their care than to enter
fellowship with a church that had another name than Lutheran. My
labors as a missionary to these immigrants seemed in certain aspects
to be superfluous." St. Ansgarius Church continued for many years
but it was not a substantial influence in the religious life of the
Swedes in Chicago.[5]

The church situation among the Swedes in Chicago was largely
unchanged until new developments occurred in 1852. We learn from
the writings of Erl. Carlsson the story of immigrants from Västergötland who in that year left Chicago for Wisconsin. After the boat
brought them to Sheboygan, they were stranded on the dock for two
days, and then returned by the same boat to Chicago. Several of
them rented rooms with Norwegian families who were members of
Paul Andersen's Norwegian Lutheran church. Some of these Swedes
were stricken with cholera and their Norwegian hosts asked Pastor
Andersen to minister to them. He responded immediately, going at
night to see them. These Swedes attended Andersen's church which
was already quite large and made many demands on the time of the
pastor. Andersen, who felt that he could not adequately serve the
Swedes, and being concerned about the success of Unonius in
attracting some of them to his St. Ansgarius congregation, sought to
have a Swedish Lutheran church organized in Chicago.[6]

In September 1852, Pastor Hasselquist, when enroute from
Sweden to his congregation in Galesburg, stayed a few days with
Pastor Andersen in Chicago. The latter urged him to return soon and
organize a Swedish Lutheran congregation. In a letter, dated January
17, 1853, Hasselquist described the events leading up to the final
organization of the Chicago church. After attending the convention
of the Mississippi Conference in Moline, he went to Chicago. He
preached on Sunday morning to the Norwegians and in the afternoon
to the Swedes. On the latter occasion Hasselquist requested
intercessory prayers for the plan to organize a Swedish Lutheran
congregation: "Whereupon Brother Andersen at my request . . . of-

fered a fervent prayer on behalf of his audience which caused tears to flow from the eyes of the majority. Thereupon we entered within the altar rail and made two propositions to the Swedes in respect to the organization of a congregation: The conditions by which members may be received hereafter, and the Lutheran character of the congregation. Then the signing of the names took place, whereupon the whole procedure was concluded with prayer, the benediction and the singing of verse 6 of hymn 412 in the Swedish *Psalmbok.*" [7]

The records show that approximately 100 persons signed their names on the list that created the new congregation. Eighty members were adults who had prior membership in the Church of Sweden. On this occasion, as already described, Hasselquist was requested to write to Pastor Peter Fjellstedt in Sweden requesting him to arrange for a pastor to serve the congregation. As indicated earlier, Fjellstedt approached Erl. Carlsson.[8]

In the interval between the organization of the congregation and the arrival of Erl. Carlsson in August 1853, the members met on Sunday afternoons in the Norwegian Lutheran church where hymns, Bible reading, prayer and a sermon, read by a member, constituted the order of service. In the spring of 1853, Pastor Esbjörn of Andover preached and conducted a communion service. But there had been great changes among the members. Although eighty communicants and twenty children were on the list of members at the time of organization in January 1853, only eight families and twenty single persons for a total of thirty-six still belonged to the congregation. The others had moved or had joined other churches.[9]

On Sunday, August 28, 1853, the fourteenth Sunday after Trinity, Pastor Carlsson preached his first sermon in Chicago. The service was held in the afternoon at the Norwegian Lutheran church. It was a time of great solemnity as the newly-arrived pastor and the Chicago Swedes sang the old hymns and shared the service with deep feeling as the audience stood in keen anticipation. *Helig, Helig, Helig är Herren Sebaot! Hela jorden är full af hans härlighet.* (Holy, Holy, Holy is the Lord of hosts! The whole earth is full of His glory.) These words were to be heard by this congregation from the lips of Pastor Carlsson for the next twenty-two years. [10]

Erl. Carlsson lived only a short time at the home of Iver Lawson. He then moved to the Nicolai Tobiasons, a Norwegian family on Des Plaines Street. He has described the situation: "There was not a single family among the members of the congregation who could give hospitality to their pastor. They lived either in poor 'shanties' or in a small and crowded room. He must, therefore, at first rent a room with a Norwegian family and pay ten dollars a month for room, meals, and washing." In September, when student Eric Norelius came to Chicago, he lived with Carlsson in the Tobiason home. Early in November they both moved to the home of a Danish sea captain by the name of Nielsen, north of the Kinzie Street bridge. Norelius writes that in the spring of 1854 the pastor had a new location with an American family on Dearborn Street. There was a constant stream of visitors seeking his counsel with the result that the landlady asked them: "Are you trying to kill the pastor?" [11]

Pastor Carlsson conducted the first communion service on October 9. He had delayed this service so that he could learn to know the members better and make adequate preparations for this important occasion. Several new members were added that day. It was also decided to seek congregational membership in the Evangelical Lutheran Synod of Northern Illinois. The congregations of Paul Andersen, L. P. Esbjörn, and T. N. Hasselquist were already members. Erland and a lay delegate attended the meeting at Galesburg, the first of many meetings of this type across the decades for this loyal churchman. [12]

Christmas in this far-away land was observed by the Swedish immigrants at the traditional five-a.m. *Julotta* (Christmas matins) service. Eric Norelius, a young student who was in attendance, has provided this account: "Pastor Carlsson presented an inspirational sermon on the Christmas-day text, Isaiah 9. The church was filled with people and an indescribable joy appeared on all the countenances. The poor immigrants who fought every day for survival, now seemed to have forgotten their sorrow and needs as they sat in God's house and listened to the glad Christmas message and sang from the depth of their hearts our incomparable Christmas hymns." A regular worship service was held that afternoon and on *Annandag Jul* (Day after Christmas) when there was communion. The church was filled at every service. [13]

The first annual meeting was held on January 27, 1854. When

the church had been organized a year earlier, no minutes of the meeting were recorded, no constitution was adopted, and no officials were elected. The only record of the meeting was the date and a list of members preserved by C. J. Anderson. At the meeting in January 1854, it was decided that an attempt should be made to provide as complete information as possible about the developments in 1853 in the minutes of this meeting. The basic item was the letter of Pastor Hasselquist, who had presided at the first meeting, under the date of January 17, 1853. There were only thirty-six of the original members of the congregation at the formal organization in 1854. All but Eva Charlotta Anderson, the future Mrs. Erl. Carlsson, had arrived in Chicago in 1852. Miss Anderson came there the previous year. The following church officials were elected at the first annual meeting: C. J. Anderson, John Nilson and Isak Peterson, deacons, and John Björkholm, Göran Swenson, and Gisel Trulson, trustees. [14]

The adoption of a congregational constitution was a far-reaching achievement of the meeting in 1854. The confessional position was clearly stated in the first section: "As Christians in general and particularly as Evangelical Lutherans, this congregation adopts not only the three oldest symbols, the Apostolic, the Nicene, and the Athanasian [creeds], but also acknowledges that the Holy Scriptures, as the Word of God, are the only sufficient and unerring norm for man's faith and life; and also that the Augsburg Confession is a brief but true summary of the fundamental doctrines of the Christian religion." [15]

Following the vital confessional declaration in the constitution was the section on membership. The individual seeking membership must make application to the pastor, "who in private conversation and also by counseling with the elders of the congregation, shall inform himself of the person's Christianity and moral character." Reception of new members could take place at an ordinary service, or preferably, at the preparatory service of the Lord's Supper. When the applicants were assembled before the altar, following a brief prayer, the pastor was to address them as follows:

> Dear friends, since you have asked to be received as members of this Evangelical Lutheran congregation, and since you were born and reared in the Lutheran Church, we will not require a new confession [of faith]; we only desire to know whether you will hold fast to our

old and abiding faith and doctrine in this country also.

The applicants were then asked these questions:

> 1. Will you with an upright heart faithfully remain in that confession which you have already made before the altar of God, and will you in accordance therewith also hold fast to the unaltered Augsburg Confession?
>
> 2. Do you also sincerely promise to observe the obligation which this confession in general, and membership in this congregation, imposes upon you?

If the answer was "Yes," they were declared "members of this our congregation and that, as such, you have equally with us, free and open access to the treasury of the Kingdom of God and the use of the Means of Grace."[16]

The constitution recognized realistically that the immigrants were the primary source of membership. They had been identified in various degrees of activity with the Church of Sweden since birth. There was no other formal requirement for membership, except the following: "With reference to the reception of members, it was decided that no one shall be received into the congregation who is known to live an unchristian and wicked life," and the provision for "private conversation with the pastor and also by counseling with the elders of the congregation." The constitution emphasized the concept of a *folk församling* (a people's church) in contrast with *ren församling* (a pure congregation of believers) that was organized by Pastor Olof Olsson at Lindsborg, Kansas, in August 1869. Membership in the latter church was conditioned upon a thorough examination of the spiritual life of the applicant by the pastor and deacons. The difference between "Carlsson's church" and "Olsson's church" reflects the separate views of each pastor and the change in emphasis in some quarters of the *läsare* (readers) movement in 1854 in contrast with 1869.[17]

The final section in the constitution dealt with the church discipline. Provision was made for congregational action in the event that members "should fall into a sinful and ungodly life, such as drunkenness, profanity, covetousness or anything else that causes general offense and grief to the congregation of God." The decision of the meeting of the Chicago-Mississippi Conference in early January 1854, was adopted:

> No one shall be excluded from the congregation before the charges have been carefully examined, and the offender, according to Matthew 18:15-18, has received tender and earnest warning and admonition both privately and publicly. But if this does not have the desired result, it will be of the greatest importance not to permit persons to remain in our congregation who are guilty of causing manifest offense by a wicked life. And yet, because of conditions in this country, one must not immediately become too severe . . . In every case, excommunication must be an act of the congregation together with the pastor.

The response of the pastor and his people to others in trouble truly showed a Christian spirit of concern and love. They were "to receive tender and earnest warning" before congregational action took place.[18]

When Erl. Carlsson reflected in 1881 on the early days of his Chicago experience, he wrote as follows: "Above all we find here the foundation which the entire Augustana Synod in this aspect followed faithfully and which provided a golden mean between the inclusiveness of the State Church of Sweden and the sect's attempts to establish on earth congregations of pure believers. The form is with few changes almost literally that which the Synod ten years later adopted at Rockford and has since been used in all our churches."[19]

The faithful efforts of Erl. Carlsson as pastor of the immigrant church were reflected in substantial growth of membership. There were thirty-six communicant members when the new pastor arrived in August 1853. Since the reporting period for congregations in the Synod of Northern Illinois was October, the first annual report includes information to October 1 of the following year. The results were as follows: New members by reception 114 and by confirmation 7, for a total of 121; losses by death 10, and by removal elsewhere 31, for a total of 41. The net gain was 80 with a total communicant membership of 116. Pastor Carlsson baptized forty-six children during the first year of whom there were sixteen whose parents were members of the congregation. Twenty children of members died during the year.[20]

The Swedish Lutheran work had been launched in Chicago. It was destined to be the focal point in subsequent developments for higher education and missions, and the mother church of other congregations in the area.

Pastor Carlsson began life in Chicago as a single man. This involved renting a room or rooms and having meals with cooperative families. But a decisive change took place which brought a new way of life. On May 25, 1855, Erl. Carlsson and Eva Charlotta Anderson were married in Chicago. She was born in 1829 at Timmele, Bohus *län*, Västergötland, the daughter of Mr. and Mrs. Anders Anderson. The Anderson family had emigrated to America in 1851. The bride was a charter member of Carlsson's congregation. Her parents, who had moved to Taylors Falls, Minnesota, had been charter members of the Geneva-St. Charles church which Erl. Carlsson also served as pastor. [21]

Pastor Carlsson's wedding plans were not widely known. Early in June 1855, Pastor Esbjörn wrote to him: "Especially surprising to us was an account of your marriage. The letter arrived on the day of your marriage. My wife and I and our children wish for your wife and you all grace, happiness, and blessing now and forever. We prayed on the day of your wedding and we continue to pray that God may bless you for the sake of His Son." [22]

In the following year, in a letter to Jonas Swensson, who was planning to emigrate to America, Erl. Carlsson congratulated him on his marriage and expressed gratitude for his own good fortune: "We congratulate you heartily that you have a faithful and pious wife because in a distant country where one is separated from friends and relatives it is often difficult to live alone and not have a confidant to rely upon but also because unfortunately it is difficult to find someone to whom one may become attached. I have experienced both of these difficulties, but I am thankful to the Lord who has given me a pious and devoted wife." [23]

Erl. Carlsson would have occasion across the years to be thankful for a "pious and devoted wife." His great career would not have been possible without the new resources which came to him for the rest of his life in the dedication, understanding, and talent of Eva Charlotta Carlsson.

FOOTNOTES

[1]Erl. Carlsson, "Svenska Evang. Lutherska Immanuels-församlingen i Chicago, Illinois," *Korsbaneret. Kristligt kalender,* 1881, p. 74. *Korsbaneret,* 1881-1882, provides a history of Immanuel congregation by Erl. Carlsson. For verification of authorship, see *Korsbaneret,* 1881, p. 100 and 1882, p. 146 and Nils Forsander, *Lifsbilder ur Augustana-Synodens historia* (Rock Island: Augustana Book Concern, 1925), I, 107. These articles have been erroneously attributed to Norelius. He used this material extensively in his classic history of the Swedish Lutheran churches and the Swedes in America.

[2]Erl. Carlsson, *Korsbaneret,* 1881, pp. 75-76.

[3]Erl. Carlsson, *Korsbaneret,* 1881, pp. 76-77; Nils William Olsson (ed.), *A Pioneer in Northwest America, 1841-1858. The Memoirs of Gustaf Unonius* (Minneapolis: Swedish Pioneer Historical Society, 1960), II, 171. Hereafter cited as *Memoirs of Gustaf Unonius.*

[4]The original constitution and a commentary by Nils William Olsson is found in *The Swedish Pioneer Historical Quarterly,* I (October, 1950), 18-22. After organizing the church, Unonius returned briefly to Wisconsin but moved his family to Chicago in April, 1849. Erl. Carlsson, *Korsbaneret,* 1881, pp. 77-78; *Memoirs of Gustaf Unonius,* II, 170-71.

[5]*Memoirs of Gustaf Unonius,* II, 321; Erl. Carlsson, *Korsbaneret,* 1881, p. 78.

[6]Erl. Carlsson, *Korsbaneret,* 1881, pp. 79-80.

[7]T. N. Hasselquist to Peter Fjellstedt, Chicago, January 17, 1852, *Augustana Historical Society Publications,* XI, 7-8. Erl. Carlsson, *Korsbaneret,* 1881, p. 80 identified Fjellstedt as the recipient of the letter.

[8]"Minutes of the Meeting of the Swedish Evangelical Lutheran Church, Chicago, January 27, 1854," *Augustana Historical Society Publications,* XI, 8.

[9]Erl. Carlsson, *Korsbaneret,* 1881, pp. 82-83.

[10]*Ibid.,* p. 82.

[11]Norelius, "Hälsningar," *Minneskrift-Immanuelsförsamlingen, 1853-1903,* pp. 77-78; Erl. Carlsson, *Korsbaneret,* 1881, p. 83; Eric Norelius, "Några hågkomster från året 1854," *Korsbaneret,* 1888, pp. 107-108.

[12]Erl. Carlsson, *Korsbaneret,* 1881, pp. 86-87.

[13]Norelius, "Hälsningar," *Minneskrift-Immanuelsförsamlingen, 1853-1903,* pp. 78-79.

[14]Carl A. Evald, "Historik," *Minneskrift-Immanuelsförsamlingen, 1853-1903, p.* 10; Erl. Carlsson, *Korsbaneret,* 1881, p. 86.

[15]"Minutes of the Meeting of the Swedish Evangelical Lutheran Church, Chicago, January 27, 1854," *Augustana Historical Society Publications,* XI, 8; Erl. Carlsson, *Korsbaneret,* 1881, p. 87-88.

[16]"Minutes of the Meeting of the Swedish Evangelical Lutheran Church of Chicago, January 27, 1854," *Augustana Historical Society Publications,* XI, 8-9.

[17]"Minutes of the Meeting of the Swedish Evangelical Lutheran Church, Chicago, January 27, 1854," *Augustana Historical Society Publications,* XI, 8. For the implications of *"ren församling"* and Olof Olsson, see Emory Lindquist, *Smoky Valley People. A History of Lindsborg, Kansas* (Lindsborg, KS: Bethany College, 1953), pp. 25-32.

[18]"Minutes of the Meeting of the Swedish Evangelical Lutheran Church, Chicago, January 27, 1854," *Augustana Historical Society Publications,* XI, 9. For the minutes of the meeting of the Chicago-Mississippi Conference, see I. O. Nothstein, "Selected Documents Dealing with the Organization of the First Congregations and First Conferences of the Augustana Synod and their growth until 1860," Part I, *Augustana Historical Society Publications,* X, 90-92.

[19]Erl. Carlsson, *Korsbaneret,* 1881, p. 111.

[20]"Statistical Table," *Minneskrift-Immanuelsförsamlingen, 1853-1903,* p. 19; Erl. Carlsson, *Korsbaneret,* 1881, p. 126.

[21]M. C. Ranseen, "Fru Eva C. Carlsson," *Korsbaneret,* 1912, pp. 235-39.

[22]L. P. Esbjörn to Erl. Carlsson, Andover, Ill., June 6, 1855, E. Norelius, ed., *Tidskrift för Svensk Ev. Luth. Kyrkohistoria i N. Amerika och för teologiska och kyrkliga frågor* (Rock Island: Lutheran Augustana Book Concern, 1899), p. 278. Hereafter cited as *Tidskrift.*

[23]Erl. Carlsson to Jonas Swensson, Chicago, September 18, 1856, J. Olson Anders, "Select Letters to Jonas Swensson," *Swedish-American Historical Bulletin* (St. Peter, Minn.) V (June 1932), 51-52.

Paddle-steamer *Gauthiod*
(from Kalmar to Lübeck)

Castle Garden, 1850

4

The Life of an Immigrant Pastor

When Erl. Carlsson came to Chicago in the late summer of 1853, he entered a new and different world. He has described the situation while writing in the third person: "The newly arrived pastor felt very lonely, a stranger in a strange world, but he started his work with confidence and trust, convinced as he was that God had called him to this difficult but important mission field, and he, whom the Lord calls, will receive strength and success."[1]

In April 1855 Pastor Carlsson sent a long letter to the *Nya Wexjö-Bladet,* the newspaper which circulated in his home area of Kronobergs *län.* He described in considerable detail his life in America: "If our work as pastors here were judged by the membership of our congregations, it might be thought that we are not very busy. But everything is new here. Congregations must be organized; constitutions adopted; by-laws drawn up; churches built, etc." Then he discussed the general nature of his activities:

> Besides, duties are increased tenfold by the multitudes who are carried with the stream of emigration through the city or who reside here a few months. They are unable to rent a room, obtain employment, consult a physician, etc., without assistance, and usually it is the pastor who is called upon. The reason for this is that they are unfamiliar with the language. . . . They are helpless when business is transacted, a contract drawn up, a bill of exchange sent to Sweden or cashed—in all such matters the pastor must stand ready to help.[2]

Other responsibilities involved extensive correspondence. Letters were sent to him from immigrants' relatives in Sweden with the expectation that he would deliver them. He wrote that he had brought as many as fifty letters to the church on a Sunday. Then there were scores of letters containing all kinds of questions concerning which the sender expected an answer. Although he announced office hours from 8 to 10 a.m. and 2 to 3 p.m. daily, except Sunday, people ordinarily came in a constant stream throughout the day. He wrote: "It is seldom that I am left alone at the other hours." In addition to six congregations under his care, he provided confirmation instruction at Chicago for twenty children and at St. Charles for twelve. He was teaching English to a class of children a few hours a week. The consequences of the heavy load were viewed by him with deep concern: "Under the weight of so many burdens not only does one become fatigued physically and mentally, but there is a danger that the life of the spirit will be destroyed." But in the midst of it all there were great signs of hope: "Our churches are filled with attentive listeners and the number of members has materially increased in recent times."[3]

A fairly typical example of his activities is found in his autobiographical account. One day he met a large party of immigrants at the Michigan Central depot. He arranged for the renting of vehicles to transport their trunks, boxes, sacks, and other possessions to a railroad station on the west side. When the vehicles were loaded, he climbed on the top of one and sat there to accompany the immigrants to their next destination. As they crossed the Lake Street bridge, an American friend saw Pastor Carlsson and yelled: "Hello! Pastor Carlsson! Have you changed your business?" The pastor answered: "No, sir, I am in my Father's business and follow my Father's example, who was among the poor, sick, and needy, to comfort and help them."[4]

On many occasions when immigrant groups reached the railroad station, before starting the journey into the unknown, he gathered the men, women, and children around him on the platform. He then read a brief passage from the Bible, prayed, and the whole group joined in singing a well-known hymn from the homeland. Then Pastor Carlsson pronounced God's benediction upon them as they gathered their hand luggage and silently entered the coaches.[5]

A new assignment was added to Carlsson's busy schedule in 1858. P. Carlson had been sent as a colporteur to Carver, Minnesota, and the response to him had been so positive that they desired to have him as their pastor. Church officials concurred but with the understanding that P. Carlson should study with Erl. Carlsson for several months. Beginning in January 1858, young Carlson moved in with the pastor's family for four months. He studied grammar, symbolics, and church history together with what constituted a pastor's work in a congregation. He also served as the pastor's assistant. P. Carlson later became a pastor and a well-known home missionary in the Pacific Northwest.[6]

The Chicago pastor often shared his feeling about developments with Pastor Jonas Swensson, Andover, writing to him in March 1858, as follows:

> The Lord has blessed us, in general, with good health, better than I have had for many years. . . . I should be more grateful because I had feared that my health was permanently broken. Now I desire and pray that my improved health will make me work even more faithfully in the service of my Lord. . . . The Lord has allowed me to see a special blessing from my labors. In Chicago I find a real desire on the part of the people to hear the Word of God, and we have several meetings each week, some in the church, some in the schoolhouse, and some in the homes of our members.[7]

The heavy burden of work did not diminish after the first years. In October 1865, in a letter to *Domprost* (Dean of the Cathedral), Peter Wieselgren, his longtime friend at Göteborg, he wrote: "I would gladly be in lively correspondence with our old and dear friends in Sweden. But overwhelmed with the many-sided tasks, which always fall to my lot, I must most often deny myself that pleasure, and scarcely ever write to friends at home, unless I have a special concern." The sensitivity and responsiveness of the busy pastor is indicated by the purpose of the letter in which he urged Wieselgren to try to assist J. O. Lindgren, an Uppsala student, who desired to come to America with the ultimate goal of becoming a pastor. The next month he wrote a short note in English to Pastor Hasselquist: "It is late. I am tired, very tired. Have been running with the immigrants the whole day. We try to send off as many and as soon as possible and still our schoolhouse is overcrowded. The many sufferings and the hot weather make a good many sick among them. I had three funerals yesterday and one today."[8]

The pace of Erl. Carlsson's work increased dramatically as the fulltide of Swedish immigration struck Chicago in the late 1860s. In another letter to Peter Wieselgren in March 1869, he wrote:

> It is a miracle of God that we do not collapse or that the congregations do not break up or are swept away by this huge flood of immigrants. More than 30,000 Swedes during the past year either have gone through Chicago or stayed here. We rejoice that we are able to preach the crucified Christ to them. Although many deniers, mockers, and separatists turn their back on our churches, our congregations are growing with unbelievable rapidity. . . . But where shall we find workers and the means to support them? When we look at present developments we are ready to cry out with the disciples: "We are so few and they are so many." But God is powerful. We must learn to see that there is help in His hands.[9]

C. F. Peterson, author and journalist, and a contemporary observer, has written vividly and accurately about this dedicated pastor in a crucial period:

> On Sunday he would preach to his countrymen; on Monday, he had to scurry about town trying to find work for them; on Tuesday, he would be called upon to help someone disentangle an intricate business affair; on Wednesday, there would be a party of immigrants arriving, whom he had to meet and assist; on Thursday, he might be in court, acting as the interpreter of some newcomers in trouble; on Friday, people might call him to act as private secretary with the duty of reading and answering their letters; and on Saturday, there would generally be any amount of things for him to do, and often no thanks, and no compensation. [10]

Pastor Carlsson identified himself fully with the members of his congregation in every aspect of life. His awareness of the poor economic situation of the congregation is evidenced by the fact that in the first three years of his ministry he had no fixed salary. His pastoral income was based largely on collections which amounted to $116 in 1854, $180 in 1855, and $240 in 1856. In the following year the congregation fixed the salary at $400 but the pastor refused to accept more than $350. He also provided his own lodging and food. [11]

An interesting anecdote about the efforts of Pastor Carlsson and his congregation to aid immigrants is related to Nils Person, the custodian of the church. In order to assist the poor immigrants Person occasionally used his milk cow, known as the *express ko* (express cow) in transporting trunks to railroad stations. Regular haulers objected to this kind of competition, so the police allegedly charged him with hauling express without a license. The church custodian turned to Swedish Consul L. P. Hawkinson for help. He was asked if he had driven express with the use of a horse, mule, or ox. "No," he replied, "I have hauled express with my white cow." He was told to relax. There was no law against using a cow for such purposes. That was apparently also the decision of the judge.[12]

Sickness and suffering were well-known to Pastor Carlsson from the beginning of emigration to America. Sixteen of his fellow travelers died on the *St. Patrick* that summer of 1853 between Liverpool and New York. He brought consolation to the bereaved and frightened passengers as the ship slowly sailed the long miles across the Atlantic. Within a few months after arriving in Chicago, the new pastor, accustomed to life in a quiet rural parish in Sweden, was confronted with massive responsibilities and problems in the cholera epidemic of 1854.

In reporting on the dire situation, he wrote in December 1854, to the newspaper of his home area in the old country as follows: "No one can describe what misery and hardship there has been here. Sickness and death have raged frightfully and hundreds of our countrymen have died, especially among those newly arrived. Conditions among the survivors are deplorable. Here are scores of widowers and widows with no support for their children, without shelter, without money, and without friends and relatives."[13]

The editor of *Carlshams Allehanda,* after reprinting Carlsson's letter from *Nya Wexjö-Bladet* appended this comment: "On the basis of Pastor Carlsson's letter it is apparent that the general condition among the immigrants is tragic. How many must now regret that they disregarded all warning and advice and allowed themselves to be tricked into leaving . . . their homes in the fatherland and enter upon an adventure that for so many ended in misery."[14]

Nya Wexjö-Bladet published this account of the cholera epidemic from a Chicago letter:

> The cholera rages with fearful speed. In Chicago . . . people died like flies. During a two week period we have had hundreds of deaths a day and the cholera wagons carrying the dead go through the streets day and night. . . . Emigrants have suffered most. The number of dead have been so large that persons responsible were not able to find caskets, whereupon many corpses were hastily placed in coffins of rough-hewn lumber and buried in sheets or in the clothes they had on.[15]

When Erl. Carlsson reflected on this situation later, the impact was still overwhelming:

> The suffering and want among the immigrants in that year of testing transcends all attempts to describe it. . . . The hardest hit were those in Chicago. . . . Although we tried every possible means to arrange that as many as possible go elsewhere, it was nevertheless necessary that many stay there since they lacked the means to travel. No one can imagine what labor, sacrifice, and privation a pastor is subjected to in such a situation.[16]

Many of the immigrants were afflicted with cholera before they arrived in Chicago. When a group from Värmland, including a large number from Karlskoga and Bjurkärn, arrived at the Michigan Central Railroad station, six corpses were on the train. Seventeen were brought to a makeshift hospital where about one-half died during the night.[17]

Eric Norelius came to Chicago on October 2, in the great cholera year of 1854. He reported: "We arrived in Chicago toward evening. Here the dreaded cholera has raged and has not yet subsided. The streets are quiet and deserted while the people we have seen look more like ghosts than like human beings." Norelius went to the home of C. J. Anderson on Kinzie Street in search of information about Pastor Carlsson. He was informed that the pastor had suffered a severe attack of cholera and had moved to Geneva for the time being. When Norelius met Carlsson the next day he wrote: "I found him convalescing but still very weak and feeble. But his spirits are full of courage and joy." [18]

Although weak from his own bout with the cholera, Carlsson returned to a city where sickness and death visited almost every home. He constantly exposed himself to the contagion, ministering to the sick and dying from early morning until the late hours of the night. Where there was the greatest need, there one found the Swedish Lutheran pastor.[19] In a letter appearing in *Nya Wexjö Bladet,* Dec. 29, 1854, Carlsson reported: "No one can describe what misery and hardship there has been. Sickness and death have raged frightfully and hundreds of our countrymen have died, especially among the newly arrived. Conditions among the survivors are deplorable. Here are scores of widowers and widows with no support for their children, without house, without money, without friends and relatives."

Dr. W. A. Passavant has described some of the many demands upon Pastor Carlsson at this time including the fact that, "the pastor had to make coffins with his own hands in order to bury the dead." Many orphans were left with Pastor Carlsson who was now required to assume responsibility for them. On one occasion Passavant told Carlsson to send twelve orphans immediately to his children's home in Pittsburg, where they would have loving care. [20]

Other pastors faced the same hardships as Carlsson at this time. Pastor S. B. Newman, the Swedish Methodist minister, has recorded his experiences in his autobiography. He also describes the efforts and sacrifices of Carlsson. On one occasion the latter said to Newman as they planned joint efforts to raise money for the ill and survivors: "Brother Newman, let us each take one street and collect for the same pouch." [21]

Erl. Carlsson estimated that nearly two-thirds of the Swedish immigrants who arrived in Chicago during the sad cholera year of 1854 died from the illness. The attack was understandably more severe on the transients than on the people who were well-established and had better resources for fighting cholera. The epidemic continued to be serious also during the next year. Although complete statistics are not available, it is known that in October 1855 thirty-five Swedes who died in private homes were buried at public expense because of the destitution of their families. During the same period twice that number died in hospitals and in poor houses and were also interred at public expense. Large numbers of the dead were buried privately. [22]

On a comparative basis, the members of Carlsson's congregation were more fortunate than Swedish immigrants generally, although the rate of fatalities was still high. In 1854, when the communicant membership was 116, there were thirty deaths—twenty children and ten adults. It was not until 1865-66, twelve years later, when the communicant membership was in excess of 700, that the number of deaths approached the total of the cholera year of 1854. Twenty-two deaths were reported in 1855. [23]

Erl. Carlsson's close identification with the members of his congregation and his energetic activity were frequently interrupted by illness during the early years. Pastor Esbjörn warned him in October 1854: "You must take care of your health and not submit your body and soul to more than you can endure. You are needed in the vineyard in the future." In the great cholera year of 1854, during which he rendered ceaseless spiritual and physical aid to countless numbers of immigrants, the dreaded disease brought him to his sick bed. But he recovered in a surprisingly brief time and resumed his work. In December 1855, he informed Eric Norelius that he was seriously ill with what Dr. Walentin, a German physician, diagnosed as the effects of an enlarged liver. Although he was in great pain, he suffered courageously, and gradually recovered fairly good health. [24]

There was no permanent relief in the afflictions which came to the tired and overworked pastor. In December 1856, he told about being ill in bed for fourteen days as a result of overexertion, which was accompanied with a high fever and "a stitch in my left side." Then followed a bout with ague, which also afflicted his wife. But "the Lord blessed the medicine both for her and me so we are now, thanks to God, hale and hearty." In February of the following year he reported that, "my health has been unusually poor." In September he was in Geneva "on account of my poor health." He had left Chicago after Pentecost in order to recuperate, expecting to return to Chicago in November. [25]

The decade of the 1860s was intermittently a period of poor health for Pastor Carlsson. In May 1860 he confided to Peter Wieselgren, his friend in Sweden: "My health this spring has been frail. My liver is damaged and there is danger that I will not again be healthy. My life and health are in the hands of God." He was cared for over a period of three months in the hospital of his friend Dr. W. A. Passavant in Pittsburg. He recovered and resumed his busy life. But in March 1863, he was again afflicted, causing A. Andreen to write to Eric Norelius: "Reverend Carlsson is not well. I do not know what God will do with him." His recurring illness caused great anxiety among his friends in and out of the congregation. In August 1866 he was among the large number of members of his congregation who were stricken with cholera. In March of the following year, the future looked discouraging. T. N. Hasselquist wrote with great sorrow to Eric Norelius: "Brother Carlsson is ill. It isn't very ·far between him and death. There is great danger that he has brain fever."[26]

Although Erl. Carlsson experienced keenly the distress and interruption caused by illness, he was courageous in service and confident that God would provide the physical resources for his mission. The next decade brought much better health to the dedicated pastor.

FOOTNOTES

[1] Erl. Carlsson, *Korsbaneret,* 1881, p. 83.

[2] Erl. Carlsson in *Nya Wexjö-Bladet,* April 13, 1855, translated in George M. Stephenson, *The Religious Aspects of Swedish Immigration,* (Minneapolis: The University of Minnesota Press, 1932), pp. 172-73.

[3] *Ibid.*

[4] Norelius, *De Svenska Lutherska . . . historia i Amerika,* I, 433-34.

[5] *Ibid.,* I, 434.

[6] "Från P. Carlson," *Minneskrift-Immanuelsförsamlingen,* pp. 81-82.

[7] Erl. Carlsson to Jonas Swensson, Chicago, March 21, 1858, *Centennial Essays,* (Rock Island: Augustana Press, 1960), p. 153.

[8] Erl. Carlsson to Peter Wieselgren, New York, August 17, 1865, Westin, *Emigranterna och kyrkan,* pp. 119-20; Erl. Carlsson to T. N. Hasselquist, Chicago, September 15, 1865.

[9] Erl. Carlsson to Peter Wieselgren, Chicago, March 1, 1869, Westin, *Emigranterna och kyrkan,* pp. 222-23.

[10] Eric Johnson and C. F. Peterson, *Svenskarne i Illinois. Historiska anteckningar* (Chicago, 1880), p. 394.

[11] Erl. Carlsson, *Korsbaneret,* 1881, p. 117.

[12] *Minneskrift-Immanuelsförsamlingen, 1853-1903,* p. 66.

[13]*Nya Wexjö-Bladet,* December 9, 1854, Ulf Beijbom, *Swedes in Chicago. A Demographic and Social Study of the 1846-1880 Immigration* (Chicago: Chicago Historical Society, 1971, and *Studia Historica Upsaliensia,* 1971), p. 55.

[14]*Carlshamns Allehanda,* December 29, 1854.

[15]*Nya Wexjö-Bladet,* January 9, 1854.

[16]Erl. Carlsson, *Korsbaneret,* 1881, p. 116.

[17]Carl A. Evald, "Historik," *Minneskrift-Immanuelsförsamlingen,* 1853-1903, p. 14.

[18]G. Everett Arden (ed. and trans.), *The Journals of Eric Norelius. A Swedish Missionary on the American Frontier* (Philadelphia: Fortress Press, 1967), p. 139. Hereafter referred to as *Journals of Eric Norelius.*

[19]Ernst W. Olson, *History of the Swedes of Illinois* (Chicago: The Engberg-Holmberg Publishing Co., 1908), p. 476.

[20]Oscar N. Olson, "William Alfred Passavant and the Augustana Synod," *Augustana Quarterly* (Rock Island), XXIV (July, 1945), 232.

[21]S. B. Newman, *Sjelfbiografi* (Chicago: Svenska Metodist Bokladans Förlag, 1890), p. 152.

[22]Erl. Carlsson, *Korsbaneret,* 1881, p. 116; E. W. Olson, *History of the Swedes of Illinois,* p. 308-309.

[23]"Statistical Table," *Minneskrift-Immanuelsförsamlingen, 1853-1903,* p. 29.

[24]L. P. Esbjörn to Erl. Carlsson, October 24, 1854, *Tidskrift,* 1899, p. 268; Erl. Carlsson to E. Norelius, December 18, 1855.

[25]Erl. Carlsson to Jonas Swensson, Chicago, December 23, 1856, February 25, 1857, September 9, 1857, J. Olson Anders, "Select Letters to Jonas Swensson, 1856-58," *Swedish-American Historical Bulletin,* V (June, 1932), 53-56.

[26]Erl. Carlsson to Peter Wieselgren, May 7, 1860, Chicago, Westin, *Emigranterna och kyrkan,* p. 94; Erl. Carlsson to T. N. Hasselquist, January 2, 1861, G. Everett Arden, *The School of the Prophets. The Background and History of Augustana Theological Seminary, 1860-1960* (Rock Island: Augustana Theological Seminary, 1960), p. 130; A. Andreen to Eric Norelius, March 7, 1863; Erl. Carlsson to T. N. Hasselquist, August 30, 1866; T. N. Hasselquist to Eric Norelius, March 30, 1867.

5

The Pastor and His Congregation

Pastor Carlsson's first worship service in America was held in the Norwegian Lutheran church, Chicago, on August 28, 1853, the fourteenth Sunday after Trinity. The text for the day was that of a leper who had been healed by Jesus, and came again to him. Two important questions were asked by the pastor: "Were not ten [lepers] made clean? Where are the nine?" These were valid questions for Swedish immigrants who came from a nation in which they had received instruction in the Word of God and where the church was a central aspect of life. The pastor appropriately asked: "What has happened to such large numbers of these people?" Erl. Carlsson's mission was an attempt to find answers to that question.[1]

Erl. Carlsson is the prime source through his writings for information about the worship services in his congregation. Until 1856, when the Swedes acquired full possession of the Norwegian Lutheran church, the main service was held there at 2 p.m. each Sunday, when he preached on the text of the day. Bible study was conducted on Friday evening. After 1856, the main service was Sunday morning, Sunday School in the afternoon, and a worship service in the evening. At the morning service the basic liturgy of the Church of Sweden was used. In the informal evening service the epistle text for the day formed the basis for the sermon; the service opened and closed with a free prayer. Hymns were sung at all services. The Thomander and Wieselgren hymnal was used at the

51

services on Sundays, but at weekday services hymns were selected from *Hemlands-Sånger.* Prayer meetings were held on Tuesday evenings when the pastor conducted a brief Bible study, which was followed by prayers by members, "sometimes with some words of exhortation and solace." On Thursday evenings there was an informal service like that of Sunday evenings. All services were in the Swedish language.[2]

In a letter to Pastor Jonas Swensson in Sweden on September 18, 1856, Erl. Carlsson described items related to worship and study:

> I will mention that all of us use *Handboken* [service book] of 1811. But we have no scruples about an occasional divergence. For example, I usually close with the benediction from the pulpit. The hymnal of 1819 [Thomander and Wieselgren] is used everywhere. We usually read only Luther's *Small Catechism:* in explanation, an occasional section from Lindblom is used.[3]

The pastor later pointed out that when the new pericopes were introduced into the Augustana Synod on the first Sunday in Advent in 1865, the following order prevailed: Both older lessons were read from the altar, although the sermon was based upon the new text, and no hymns were sung between the epistle and the declaration of faith or between the texts. The hymn for the day was sung immediately after the Apostle's Creed. When hymn 24, v. 1, was sung, the congregation arose and remained standing during the collect and reading of the text, and the Apostle's Creed.[4]

The first confirmation service was held on April 17, 1854, when a class of seven members took their vows of faith in God at the altar. The instruction over a period of six months was based on Barth's *Bible History* and Luther's *Small Catechism.* The confirmands participated in Holy Communion the next Sunday. In a letter to a friend following the confirmation service, the pastor described the special meaning of the occasion to him:

> An oppressive feeling of alienation or a feeling that I was in a foreign country has followed me daily, even while in the church, but when we had confirmation yesterday, I forgot completely that I was in America. That was truly a holy day for my spirit and since it was the first confirmation service among our people here, it was also a real festive day for the congregation. The number of confirmands was seven, a holy number. May God save them for His heavenly kingdom.[5]

Pastor Carlsson considered confirmation instruction as a vital time in the life of a young person and in the future of the congregation. Nils Forsander has written about this phase of Carlsson's pastorate: "It was a pleasure to hear Carlsson *katekisera* [conduct confirmation instruction] with members of the confirmation class and Sunday School children. There is no doubt but that he had greater talent and skill than the majority of the synod's older pastors."[6]

Holy Communion was generally celebrated once a month when there was a sermon, confession of sin, and absolution preceding the distribution of the elements in accordance with the practice in the Church of Sweden. A change was made in the absolution during the first year whereby it read as follows: "Is this your unfeigned confession of sin so that you know and acknowledge yourself to be a poor, lost sinner before God, and is it your inner longing and desire that you be saved from all your sins and become free? Then I assure you, as God's servant, that God by His grace and for Christ's sake will forgive you all your sins and I declare to you the gracious forgiveness of your sins in the name of God, the Father, the Son, and the Holy Ghost. Amen." The Swedish *Church Book* was otherwise followed. The members of the church indicated in writing their desire to participate in the communion service.[7]

A central responsibility and a great opportunity in Erl. Carlsson's career as a Lutheran pastor was preaching the Word of God. He responded faithfully and diligently. The seriousness with which he regarded this aspect of his calling is apparent in letters which he wrote to Peter Wieselgren shortly before and after ordination. In June 1848 he confided to his friend and advisor: "I consider as an inescapable demand on a clergyman that he always studies, since otherwise he cannot keep up with developments nor achieve anything significant during his time on earth." In October of the next year, early in his pastorate at Lessebo, he wrote: "The Sunday services . . . are exacting. As a young pastor I need time and effort to prepare myself [for preaching]. Although I seldom write out my sermons, I must spend much time in study."[8]

Contemporaries have provided interesting information about Pastor Carlsson's preaching. Eric Norelius has written: "His motto as a preacher was: 'The law in all its sternness, and the gospel in all its glory.' He laid great stress on the preparation of the sermon and said that to the preparation belonged prayer, the study of the text, and a knowledge of the spiritual life of the congregation." He generally used only a brief outline in the pulpit. Norelius further observed that Carlsson "preferred the synthetic-analytical method. Therefore, he always had a theme that included material from the text, so that the Scriptures were expounded in keeping with the subject. He counted as goals of his preaching the glory of God, the conversion of the sinner, and the edification of the Christian. The most appealing thing in his preaching was simplicity and warmth of feeling; therefore, he was also gladly heard by all who had an ear for the Word of God."[9]

An interesting comparison between the preaching of two early leaders in the Augustana Synod is provided by Nils Forsander, former professor at Augustana Seminary: "Hasselquist and Carlsson both preached the Christian gospel purely and clearly in the power of the Holy Spirit; the former was more powerful in Biblical explanation, but the latter was greater by contrast in the practical application for his hearers; the former preached quietly and calmly without gestures and stories; the latter preached, in contrast, with greater feeling so that it happened occasionally that tears ran down his cheeks."[10]

The style of Erl. Carlsson in the pulpit has been described by the Reverend John Telleen as he recalled a sermon about Jesus and Zacchaeus based on Luke 19:1-10: "I never forgot the very eloquent and convincing fervor with which he spoke. I can yet see 'the shake of his holy head' as the tears flowed down his cheeks." In July 1859, newly arrived A. W. Dahlsten heard Pastor Carlsson preach on the text, "Jesus' Tears over Jerusalem": "The sermon was earnest and heart-searching. There were not many in the congregation who withheld their tears and even the pastor's eyes watered." [11]

Dr. Carl Swensson, son of Pastor Jonas Swensson, who had been a close friend of Erl. Carlsson, described a visit to Andover, late in Carlsson's career: "How wonderful it was to hear the large congregation singing to their hearts' content. There was none of that famous passiveness, that vacuum of indifference, which is so often protrayed in the faces of those who are in attendance at our American churches." The beautiful liturgical service moved on in an orderly fashion with full participation by the worshippers. "Then the sermon—warm, straightforward, truly Biblical, inspirational. It felt like a hungry man feels when he sits down at a rich and well-prepared table."[12]

Only two of Erl. Carlsson's sermons are known to be in print. One is found in the two-volume publication, *Korsets predikan af pastorer inom Augustana Synoden,* II (1885). It is based on the text for the second Sunday after Pentecost, John 12:44-50. The sermon is characterized by direct and simple style. Forty-two Bible passages are cited. The second sermon in print was preached at the opening meeting of the synod at Lindsborg in 1881. [13]

The Immanuel Church experienced times of revival. Erl. Carlsson has described "the autumn of 1857 and the winter of 1858 as times of special grace and joy." A powerful "wind of grace awakened souls to new consciousness and they received new life and peace through the crucified Saviour." This revival was rather general and deep-seated. Bible studies and prayer meetings were held almost every night in the church or in the homes of members. He wrote that, "At times tears flowed and on occasion people burst out in loud confession and prayers or in request for intercession in their behalf. The spiritual movement became quieter, deeper and more peaceful in nature. God's grace produced a distinction and a blessing for the congregation." The pastor reported that this was a time of song; there were some songs that they never tired of singing. [14]

Pastor Carlsson reported that there was no great and general revival until the early months and spring of 1870. The developments were described by him as follows:

> It started among the confirmation children. It spread from them to the rest of the young people in the congregation. There were special prayer meetings in which they sang, prayed, talked, encouraged one another, admonished one another, cried, and rejoiced. Many people attended other prayer meetings which were held for a long time every Sunday evening one-half hour before the regular service. That was a beautiful spring-time. The young trees stood in bloom, but summer with its heat came. The beautiful colors disappeared and the old proverb—"Fruit does not come from every flower"—described what happened ... The pastor warned often of the danger of taking only oil in the lamp and not the vessel, or about the seed that fell on solid rock.[15]

Erl. Carlsson came to America directly from the Church of

Sweden and was, therefore, accustomed to the clerical garb of that country. A meeting was held with a few members of the congregation shortly after his arrival in Chicago to plan for the first worship service. The question was asked if the new pastor planned to wear the *prästkappa,* a black flowing cape that hung down from the shoulders and touched the floor, and *kragen,* a white collar with tabs. Carlsson writes that when he indicated that this was his intention, the response was one of hearty approval. The members explained that since neither Esbjörn nor Hasselquist wore the *kappa* or *kragen* when they preached in Chicago, Unonius, the Episcopal pastor, and his followers declared that these Swedish pastors were not Lutherans and had abandoned the practices of the Lutheran Church. [16]

Erl. Carlsson participated in the meeting of the Mississippi Conference and dedication of the church at Andover, on Advent Sunday in December 1854. An individual in attendance reported that when Carlsson appeared in clerical garb "two aged farm women wept and one said to the other so loudly that we could hear her: 'Praise God that once again we are permitted to see and hear a pastor with a ministerial collar.' " [17]

Pastors Esbjörn and Hasselquist exercised their Lutheran freedom in the early years and at times used neither the *kappa* or *kragen.* They did not always use the entire *Kyrko-bok.* Norelius, in his biography of Hasselquist, points out that in his early American years, the latter would occasionally enter the church for a Sunday morning service dressed in a white linen suit, and walk down the aisle singing one of Oskar Ahnfelt's hymns, in which the congregation would join. The entire service would be informal and without liturgy. [18]

Erl. Carlsson understood the policy of the two pioneer pastors relative to clerical garb and so-called "unchurchliness." Conditions in the western frontier were important factors. Methodists in Andover and Galesburg, where Esbjörn and Hasselquist had their congregations, contended that the Lutheran preachers were so spiritually dead that they could not pray without using the *Church Handbook* and they were so popish and superstitious that they believed the *kappa* and *kragen* were essential if the Word and the sacraments were to be efficacious. The two pioneer pastors responded temporarily to the challenge of the frontier by adapting to current religious customs. It is interesting to note that Paul Andersen, the Norwegian Lutheran pastor and Erl. Carlsson's close friend, was opposed to wearing the *kappa.* He objected to the fact that Carlsson, at the outset of his ministry in Chicago, put on the *kappa* when he walked from his home to the church as well as using it in the service. Andersen said that if Carlsson left the *kappa* in the Norwegian church on some occasion, he would melt candle wax on it so that the mice would find it tasty and eat it. [19]

In a couple of years the three Swedish Lutheran pastors arrived at a compromise relative to clerical garb. Carlsson ceased wearing the *prästkappa* and Esbjörn and Hasselquist used the *prästkragen* and the *Kyrko-bok* regardless of what the Methodists said in criticism. In commenting on these developments later (1888) Norelius wrote: "I do not mourn the loss of the *kappa,* but I still believe that the fanatical cries of that time should not have been heeded in the least. But actually the strongest reason for dropping this garment was without doubt that at most places there was no church [building] and it was thought that without a church it was more proper to be without the *kappa.*" [20]

The clerical garb issue identified Erl. Carlsson as a pastor who believed in church order and tradition. But it also demonstrated flexibility and willingness to cooperate with associates.

The role of the Christian nurture of children was fully recognized by Pastor Carlsson. The Sunday School was an American institution which he supported from the beginning of his ministry. As long as the Swedes and Norwegians used the latter's church, the children of his congregation attended the Norwegian Sunday School. [21]

Instruction in the Norwegian Sunday School was in English. The Swedish children thus became accustomed to that language. Moreover, Pastor Carlsson reported that, "both parents and children at the outset placed such great emphasis on English that it is doubtful that a Sunday School could have operated in any other language." The Sunday sessions for children were held at Immanuel Church from 2:30 to 4:00 p.m. until 1890. Due to the lack of competent teachers in English, some Norwegians, who taught in their Sunday School in the morning, served as teachers of Swedish children in the afternoon. When Augustana Seminary was housed in the Swedish congregation's property (1860-63), the supply of

English teachers was substantially increased. English was used throughout the years except in 1873 when the congregation adopted a resolution authorizing the teacher, under certain circumstances, to decide which language should be used. One factor in using English was that there was no Sunday School material in the Swedish language. Carlsson reported that for several years the Sunday School used the series, *Lesson Leaves,* materials from the Old Testament and the New Testament, that was written and designed for children.[22]

The church on Superior Street and the congregation's nearby schoolhouse provided space for the Sunday School classes in the early years. Classes were held in both churches on Sedgwick Street. When the fire destroyed the church in 1871, classes were held in the Bethlehem Norwegian Lutheran Church on the west side. The first congregational report on Sunday School attendance was for the year 1872 when classes were held in the rebuilt church following the fire. There were 330 pupils and thirty teachers. [23]

The interest in home and foreign missions began with the organization of the congregation and continued across the years. Contributions were made regularly to missions. The Sewing Society and monthly mission prayer meetings provided substantial funds in view of the limited economic situation of the members. Mission cards were used by volunteers to enlist personal support. The year 1872, following the great fire, was a memorable one. Since organization meetings and auctions could not be held normally, recourse was had to mission cards. Forty-six members volunteered one Sunday to circulate cards. When they were handed out Pastor Carlsson spoke to the congregation:

> It may seem unsuitable to attempt to raise money among ourselves since we almost all are poverty stricken, live on charity, and inhabit wretched barracks [relief shanties]. But in the midst of our trying situation, we have many reasons to thank God and we should show our gratitude. It is true that now we are all beggars, but no beggar is so poor that he cannot share his crumbs with others. We hope, therefore, that this ingathering will be embraced with good will.

The response to the cards was inspiring. On the following Sunday $275 was brought to the church as an offering for missions. The leadership of Pastor Carlsson and the devotion of the members kept

Immanuel congregation in the forefront of mission support. [24]

Pastor Carlsson's ability to utilize the service of members of his congregation to spread the gospel of salvation was an important factor in the development of Immanuel Church. He first turned to the deacons who carried on their responsibilities faithfully. But a growing congregation in an expanding city required more personnel resources. Shortly after establishing the congregation with a program of regular services, Erl. Carlsson organized an Inner Mission Society. These dedicated people visited current and prospective members and others. A colporteur was engaged by the society to distribute books and tracts. Experiences with colporteurs were mixed. Two of them in the employ of the congregation became supporters of the separatist movement and consequently were asked to vacate their assignments. [25]

On the basis of the experience with colporteurs, Pastor Carlsson and the congregation established the Immanuel Church Tract Society. This group was to function under the direction of the pastor and deacons. No one was engaged as a colporteur; each member was pledged to give time and talent to this mission activity. A basic responsibility was that of visitation and delivery of tracts on Christian faith and life. These items were distributed to homes, hospitals, and other institutions. The degree of commitment is proved by the distribution of 20,000 to 25,000 tracts annually in a variety of languages to meet the needs of various people. Members of the tract society organized Sunday Schools and held prayer meetings in areas distant from a Lutheran church. Two devotional meetings were held each month in the church. Funds were raised for the purposes of the society at these meetings. The remarkable congregational life of Immanuel congregation owed much to the dedication of members through this and other organizations. [26]

Erl. Carlsson's leadership included provisions for organizations with specific functions. When Augustana Seminary was housed in the congregation's property, aid to students became a new responsibility. The Sewing Society was organized in 1860. The first projects were to make quilts for the students, to assist in mending clothing, and to maintain the rooms in an orderly fashion. When the seminary moved to Paxton, the women made articles which were sold at auctions in the church for the benefit of the students. The society adopted the name, the Mite Society in 1869, at the time the first church was built on Sedgwick Street. They raised money for the church windows, carpets, gas lights, and altar paraments. The minutes of the building committee include hearty commendation for the fine support which the church received from this group. At two festivals in 1873, the items made by members and friends brought in $1254 and $1400. Meetings were held every Thursday afternoon. [27]

An interesting organization, the Immanuel Society, made its appearance early in 1873. The men met in the church every Monday evening in order "to promote the spiritual and literary development of members." They discussed and debated such issues as the temperance movement and women's suffrage. J. A. Enander, the famous editor of *Hemlandet,* served as president. The group was reorganized in 1875 and continued an active program. [28]

The tradition of good music from the old country was a central part of the worship service from the beginning. At the meeting of the Mississippi Conference at Moline, in January 1853, a resolution was passed recommending that congregations establish a singing school. Although no musical instrument was available at the church the familiar hymns from Thomander and Wieselgren's *Psalmbok,* were sung a cappella under the leadership of shoemaker C. J. Anderson in the early years. A Hamline and Mason melodion was purchased for $45 in July 1856 when Johan August Andersson was serving as organist. In the years 1863-67, Jonas Engberg served as organist, as well as organizing a choir. This was the first Swedish church choir in America to sing a cantata. George E. Root's *Queen Esther* was performed at the opening of Augustana Seminary at Paxton, Illinois, in the autumn of 1863. [29]

Progress in the role of music in the life of the congregation was made steadily with great encouragement from Pastor Carlsson. During Jonas Engberg's tenure as organist, a large cabinet organ with bass and pedal was purchased for $400. This instrument gave valuable support to congregational singing. When the new church was built at Sedgwick and Hobbie streets, an organ committee was formed to raise funds for an instrument. On January 1, 1870, the new $3,000-organ, built by William Johnson, Westfield, Massachusetts, was dedicated. The great fire in the following October destroyed both church and organ. Since funds were not available for an organ when the new church was first used in 1872, Lars Lindberg, choir director, organized a brass band. This group led the congregational singing at the first service in the new church at *Julotta* (early Christmas matins) in 1872. The band provided the accompaniment at worship services until a cabinet organ was acquired. A pipe organ, built by Clark and Company, Indianapolis, was purchased in 1875. Pastor Carlsson reported that there were difficulties at times in presenting a good choir, but congregational singing was always on a high level.[30]

The story of the church structures of the Immanuel congregation provides an interesting record. The Chicago congregation held services in the Norwegian Lutheran church at the outset, as has been indicated previously. Since that congregation made plans to build a new church, the Swedes were able to purchase this property on Superior Street. On October 24, 1854, Carlsson's congregation took the following action: "Since the congregation is in need of a school for the Christian nurture of the children and also of a building for the common services of ·worship, a meeting was called for the purpose of counseling in regard to these matters so important to the congregation." At this meeting the trustees were authorized to purchase the old Norwegian church for $1500, including a lot adjoining the church. The trustees were also authorized to purchase a nearby lot for $900. [31]

The action by the congregation resulted in purchases in the amount of $2475, including the church, lot, and some interior fixtures in the church. Payments were to be made in installments with the final payment due when the church could be used exclusively by the Swedes. Necessary repairs were authorized in May 1855. [32]

The congregation now faced serious financial problems. The members were poor and unable to make substantial contributions. Various expedients were tried as recorded in the minutes of December 1855: "Since there is not much hope of receiving help from 'citizens' here in Chicago . . . the congregation ought to avail itself of the opportunity of meeting a portion of the necessary expenses through the renting of pew space in the church." Circumstances forced the congregation to seek an unusual solution. Since Pastor Carlsson had personally met all payments on the

Newberry lot and since C. J. Anderson and he agreed to make the other payments, it was decided to transfer the contract to them. The minutes expressed the feeling of members that, "It will be very pleasant to have the pastor reside near the church." [33]

Repairs were essential if the building was to survive. It was decided in August 1859 that the church should be raised ten feet above the ground and that brick walls nine feet high and one foot thick should be built. This construction added substantial space at the cost of $1047. Two large rooms were rented out to The Swedish Lutheran Publication Society, which for ten years had its printing shop and bookstore there. Three living rooms were available on the south end for a family. A pastor's study was also provided. The rent in time paid more than one half of the cost of the addition. [34]

The membership of the congregation increased to 305 in the period 1860-65. Early in the summer of 1865, the length of the church was increased by twenty feet. The schoolhouse, constructed in 1856, was moved to a vacant lot on Huron Street. The addition and painting cost $2,865. Lots west of the church were purchased for $1,050. Subscription efforts produced $1515, but the debt was increased by $2398. Annual contributions in the 1860s and early 1870s show the following pattern in ranges of personal giving: 1864, from $5.00 to $20.00; 1867, between $3.00 and $20.00; and in 1872, it varied from $1.00 to $10.00, reflecting the condition after the great fire. [35]

However, the continual growth in membership made the church too small. In February 1866, the decision was made to hold worship services also on Chicago's south side. Student P. Erickson was engaged to assist Pastor Carlsson. Immanuel Church purchased three lots at a cost of $1000 as a gift to encourage the newly organized Salem congregation. [36]

At the annual meeting in January 1868, the crowded condition of the church was described by Erl. Carlsson as follows:

> One thing, and that the most important . . . is what must be done for securing a larger church. The church we now have cannot house more than one-half of the congregation's members. It often happens that many, and at times, hundreds, must leave the church without finding a place, and generally the crowd is so large that it is not only disturbing for worship but threatens health. Something must be

done and we hope that the congregation will take this under serious consideration at this meeting. [37]

At a meeting in January 1869, the church council reported: "It is not only the extent of the need that is so demanding but likewise a holy duty to do all that is within our power, to build a church where we and our children as well as our newly arrived countrymen could assemble in prayer in the name of God, for the preaching of the Word, and the administration of the sacraments." The congregation then took action to build a new church on the southwest corner of Sedgwick and Hobbie streets. A committee of sixty members was designated to develop the project. Baurer and Company were selected as architects. The church was to be 68 by 118 feet . . . and 154 feet high, in two stories of brick. The work progressed rapidly after starting on April 14. On October 31, the first worship service was held in the new church. [38]

Following an impressive farewell service conducted by Pastor Carlsson at the old church on Superior Street at 8:30 a.m., the congregation moved in procession, to music by L. E. Lindberg's band, to the new structure, preceded by the pastor and the deacons carrying the church Bible and chalice. Pastors Hasselquist and Jonas Swensson preached at the festive dedication service. The total cost of the church and organ was $34,000. The indebtedness was $22,600. [39]

The year 1870 witnessed another development in which the Immanuel congregation was involved. In May of that year a new congregation, Gethsemane, was organized. The individuals who were interested in forming a church in another area of Chicago petitioned the Immanuel congregation for permission to use the old building on Superior Street, which was soon to be vacated. This request was willingly granted. After the Chicago fire, the Gethsemane Church was relocated at the corner of May and Huron streets. This was the first west side congregation of the Augustana Synod in Chicago. [40]

Grim tragedy struck Chicago in October 1871 when practically every building in an area of more than three square miles in the heart of the city was destroyed by a raging fire from the early evening of Sunday, October 8, to the early morning of Tuesday, October 10. Paul M. Angle, in an authoritative history of this shocking occurrance, writes that, "Property valued at $200,000,000 was turned into rubble, 90,000 people were left homeless, and 300 lost their lives. The common designation, the 'Great Chicago Fire,' is an understatement: it was the most destructive fire in American history." This devastating fire started in the O'Leary cowbarn at the rear of 137 De Koven Street and spread rapidly.[41]

Erl. Carlsson conducted services in Immanuel Church on Sunday, October 8. At the morning service he preached on the St. Michael's Day text, Matthew 18:1-11, "A True Christian." The church was filled. There was also good attendance at the evening service. Fortunately, he has written a full account of the developments that followed:

> On the way home from church, fire sirens were heard and a red glow in the sky was seen in the distance. The fire was more than three English miles from Immanuel Church and no one feared any danger. But before sunrise the following morning, most of Chicago was in ashes. Early Monday morning the fire flashed across the river to the north side where the ravaging element like an ocean of fire spread out from the river to the lake and soon swept everything in its path.[42]

Pastor and Mrs. Carlsson and some members of Immanuel congregation were present when their recently dedicated church caught fire and they watched with deep anguish as the flames played around the high tower and soon engulfed the entire structure. The pastor later recorded his feelings: "It is impossible to describe the sorrow and pain that was experienced at that moment." Only the church records and the clock that hung on the front of the gallery could be saved. A. P. Montén rushed into the church, gathered up the church records and brought them out in a pushcart. The old church on Superior Street was also destroyed. [43]

Members of Immanuel Church suffered tremendous losses with thousands of other Chicago residents. Out of a congregation of 340 families, 320 were "burned out" as it was described. Only seventeen families on the west side and three on the north side had their homes left according to the pastor's report. The Carlsson home was among those ravaged by the flames. Many members rented property but almost all personal belongings, clothes, and furniture were lost. Homelessness, poverty, unemployment, and concern about missing relatives and friends created anxiety which the pastor emphasized was "beyond description." It has been pointed out that the disaster struck with special force upon the Swedes since it is estimated that two-thirds of them lived on the north side between Chicago Avenue and Division Street on Market, Sedgwick, Townsend, Bremer, Wesson, and Larrabee streets and in great numbers below Division Street and North Avenue. [44]

Pastor Carlsson wrote to a friend less than two weeks after the fire: "Our homes are gone and our churches are gone as well as all our earthly things. But God reigns and He will not forsake us." He informed his friend, in thanking him for a generous gift of $100.00, that he had only $9.00 when the fire struck. However, the Carlssons were more fortunate than the vast majority of the victims of the fire. The home of the Swedish Consul, P. L. Hawkinson, had been spared the flames. The Carlssons were invited to live with them on East Kinzie Street. [45]

Erl. Carlsson was active in promoting the large meeting of Swedish people on Wednesday afternoon, October 11, in an open space on Division Street in order to discuss ways of providing relief in the distressing situation. The Swedish Relief Committee was organized and showed great energy in assisting persons in greatest need. In the absence of newspapers, it was agreed that there would be a meeting every afternoon for several days at this place to provide information and to serve as a clearing house for bringing together lost people. Relief efforts continued at an accelerated pace. At these meetings Pastor Carlsson announced that members of the Immanuel Church would meet next Sunday, October 15, in the Norwegian Trinity Lutheran Church on the west side. [46]

Pastor Carlsson reported that a large and sad crowd of people gathered for worship service that Sunday. They sang with deep feeling the opening hymn, "Hear your Zion's bitter lament, O Lord, Hear our prayer." The pastor observed that, "The song was almost choked by crying." Then he continued:

> It was a reassuring experience for the pastor and congregation to see one another and assemble in the name of the Lord and His Word. In many cases we did not know how many had been overcome and died. In families who were separated, all members had not yet been reunited. We could not meet without crying and tears. But in many faces joy shown forth like the clear rays of the sun between clouds.

> We had learned quite clearly to see the vanity of all temporal things. More than one declared: "I am poorer today than the first time I came to Chicago; but I thank God that I own treasures that no fire can destroy."

In a short time there was special cause for joy and thanksgiving: Not a single member of Immanuel Church died in the flames. [47]

The church council met on the following day, Monday, October 16. The tremendous loss of homes, jobs, and personal effects created a desperate situation. Moreover, the congregation had an indebtedness of $22,600 and the ashes of a burned church. Although there was $10,000 insurance on the structure, the likelihood of payment was small, and, in fact, amounted to only $428 because of the heavy losses of the insurers. Some members of the church council saw the prospect as hopeless. One member proposed that the congregation be dissolved and that the mortgage holders be permitted to take the lot, the ruins, together with the insurance, and that a new congregation be organized. After momentary silence, a firm voice was heard. Pastor Carlsson spoke out so all could hear: "If you intend to go into bankruptcy, I will no longer be your pastor. But if you will be honest and put your trust in the Lord, I will do my utmost that we may both build a new church and pay our debt." [48]

Pastor Carlsson stood silently and prayerfully before the members of the church council. Then, as he reported later, after an hour of reflection and prayer, the following resolution was passed for transmission to the congregation: "That the Immanuel congregation, in Jesus' name, will and shall continue its existence and its work under her legal name, constitution, and incorporation, and together with God's help, will and shall honorably pay her debt to the last penny." [49]

The Immanuel congregation met Sunday afternoon, October 22, in the Norwegian church. Dr. W. A. Passavant and the pastor spoke. The former gave a consoling talk saying, "Your church and homes have burned up, but God's kingdom has not burned up." A business meeting followed the service at which Pastor Carlsson read the resolution passed by the church council. By a standing vote the proposal to rebuild the church and pay the debt was endorsed unanimously. The clean-up work was to begin the next day. [50]

Erl. Carlsson recounted that a large crowd of people assembled in and around the ruins of the church at 9 a.m. the following day. A hymn was sung from *Svenska Psalmboken.* Pastor J. P. Nyquist of Salem congregation and Dr. Passavant presented brief meditations. Carlsson spoke briefly on Psalm 128:8, "Our help is in the hands of God, who created heaven and earth," followed by another hymn. Carlsson's wagon in the midst of the ruins served as a make-shift pulpit. The work to clear the site started immediately by men, women, and children.[51]

At the annual meeting in January 1872, the congregation decided to build a new church with the same size and style as the former structure on the old location. Pastor Carlsson then started the arduous task of raising $10,000 before building could begin. He worked hard in the area; in April he began to travel to raise money, largely among English and German Lutheran churches in Pittsburg, Philadelphia, New York, and Jamestown. The response was good and when he returned almost $10,000 had been raised.[52]

The work on the new church started in July 1872, the cornerstone was laid in August, and on Christmas Day the first service was held. Pastor Carlsson has written about that festive day: "It is impossible to describe with what feelings the congregation assembled on Christmas Day in the new gas and candle-lighted church after fifteen months of great hardship and sacrifice." The church was packed. There was a mixture of memories of the homeland and the joy of the new day as the Swedish Cornet Band led the singing *Var hälsad sköna morgonstund* (All Hail to Thee, O Blessed Morn), the traditional hymn of *Julotta* (early Christmas matins). The church had not been painted and benches had not yet been provided. But the Immanuel congregation had its own place of worship again. The church was completed in 1875 except for the spire. The dedication occurred on April 4, 1875, at which time Pastor C. A. Evald was installed as successor to Erl. Carlsson. [53]

The final financial report showed the following sources of funds for the new church: within the congregation $17,633.05; other Augustana churches, $4,177.05; English and German Lutheran Churches, $9,429.61; churches in Sweden, $2,954.45; special gifts and offerings, $3,349.66 for a total of $37,544.41. The church, without steeple, organ, or bell cost $31,845.68. The balance was applied to the old debt, which was $21,558 in 1875.[54]

On May 26, 1873, Erl. Carlsson boarded the *Celtic* at New York for a trip to Sweden in order to raise money for payment of the debt on the new church, to make contact with prospective pastors, and to identify the work of the Augustana Synod. [55]

The principal reason for the Sweden trip was to have an audience with King Oscar II and to request authorization of a collection in Swedish churches for the building fund of the Immanuel congregation. His Majesty responded cordially. The sum of $2,954.45 was later collected and sent to the congregation. The kindly monarch, who was greatly impressed with Carlsson's ministry among the Swedes in America, offered to arrange for him a pastorate in a good congregation if and when he wished to return to the homeland. Pastor Carlsson expressed great appreciation but declined and stated: "Where the young man has given his strength and life for the heavenly King, there the old man wishes to lay down his pilgrim's staff." Then, King Oscar, with tears in his eyes, bade him Godspeed for the remainder of life's journey. [56]

Erl. Carlsson spent several days at Kalmar where he visited his daughters, Annie and Emmy, students in Rostad School, and with the rektor, *Mamsell* Cecill Fryxell. A beautiful communion set was presented to Immanuel Church by *Mamsell* Fryxell to replace the one destroyed in the fire. She also wove and presented an attractive communion cloth. A baptismal basin for the Chicago church was provided through gifts from students of the school. They also contributed money for the organ as did students at *Mamsell* Hall's school in Göteborg. [57]

Visits with Peter Wieselgren in Göteborg renewed an old friendship and inspired the Chicago pastor. Later Carlsson wrote to his friend: "Heartiest thanks for all the love and friendship shown to me and my children during our stay in Göteborg and for the generous gift to Immanuel congregation." He was warmly received by Bishop E. G. Bring, his former Lund teacher, now bishop in Linköping. He attended the *prästmöte* (Pastor's meeting) in Uppsala, the *kyrkomöte* (Church convocation) in Stockholm, and the annual meeting of *Evangeliska Fosterlandsstiftelsen* (National Evangelical Foundation) in the same city. He was disappointed when his expectation for receiving support for Immanuel Church from this organization was not realized. [58]

It was with a heart beating fast and with eyes encompassing familiar scenes that he returned for a visit with relatives and friends in Älghult. The temple of memory had many dear portraits as he visited his parental home in Suletorp and Älghult church, with its spire and cross rising above the meadows and forests. He preached to a large and attentive congregation one Sunday morning.

But the Sweden experience must now yield to the demands of his adopted country. After a brief stay in England, the father and two daughters boarded the *Polynesian* at Liverpool in the last part of October for the return journey to America. The daughters had accompanied Pastor Hasslequist to Sweden in 1870 where they had shared a fine educational experience for three years at Rostad, *Mamsell* Fryxell's well-known school. On November 13, 1875, they were again in Chicago. [59]

Developments in Immanuel Church during the pastorate of Erl. Carlsson are clearly reflected in the growth of membership. The large increase in communicant membership from 36 in 1853 to 116 in the following year showed that Pastor Carlsson had effectively launched the congregation. Pastoral duties mounted decisively. In the following year he baptized ninety-four children of whom only thirty-eight are listed in congregational records. The communicant membership increased to 191. This is surprising in view of the distress and toll of the cholera epidemic. In 1860, the year of Augustana Synod's organization, there were 220 communicant members. There were 816 Swedes in Chicago that year according to the U.S. Census. At the end of the 1860-65 period, the church reported 525 communicant members. The fluid character of the membership is indicated by the fact that in that five-year period, 399 persons had been received by letter and 65 by confirmation but 140 had moved.[60]

The next five-year period witnessed the greatest growth as the communicant membership increased from 525 in 1865 to 1260 in 1870. The late 1860s brought record numbers of Swedes to America. The statistics are dramatic in portraying the transient nature of the immigrants. Confirmation added 136 members but 1285 members were received as adults. This figure is twenty-five more than the entire 1260 communicant members on the rolls in 1870. The number of persons moving from the congregation was 538. Deaths numbered 143 children and 59 adults during this period. The busy pastor baptized 447 children and conducted 220 weddings. The total membership, children and communicant, was 1790. The total Swedish-born population in Chicago that year was 6,154. The congregation continued to grow in numbers during the last five years of Carlsson's pastorate, 1870-75. The reception of new members was 932 but 630 moved during those years. The number dropped from the rolls was 313. There were 268 confirmands, 800 baptisms, and 258 marriages. In 1875, the total membership was 2185, with 1446 adults. [61]

A summary of Pastor Carlsson's ministry in Chicago 1853-75 shows the following: baptized, 1667; confirmed, 558; marriages, 606; members received, 2958; members who moved, 1549; deaths— children, 410, and adults, 169; excommunicated or dropped, 415. The statistical data was influenced by the organization of the Salem Lutheran Church with the assistance of Immanuel Church in 1868, but the effect was only modest in the parent church's member- ships. [62]

Dr. W. A. Passavant, noted Lutheran leader, evaluated the importance of Immanuel Church over and above the impressive membership statistics: "The amount of good which has been accomplished through the establishment of this church cannot be estimated. Thousands upon thousands of immigrants have passed through Chicago and have received counsel and assistance and spiritual direction for their new and untried American life . . . Hundreds who were unable to proceed further have been provided with employment, and have afterwards gone on their way rejoicing."[63]

FOOTNOTES

[1] Karl Hildebrand and Axel Fredenholm, *Svenskarna i Amerika* (Stockholm: Historiska förlaget, 1924), II, 98.

[2] Erl. Carlsson, *Korsbaneret,* 1881, pp. 101-102.

[3] J. Olson Anders, "Select Letters to Jonas Swensson," p. 51. The Lindblom *Catechism* was based on Luther's *Small Catechism.*

[4] Erl. Carlsson, *Korsbaneret,* 1881, pp. 101-102.

[5] Erl. Carlsson's letter to an unidentified friend, in *Korsbaneret,* 1881, pp. 93-94.

[6]Forsander, *Lifsbilder*, I, 111.

[7]Erl. Carlsson, *Korsbaneret*, 1881, p. 104.

[8]Erl. Carlsson to Peter Wieselgren, Lund, June 3, 1848, and Åry, October 26, 1849.

[9]Clifford Ansgar Nelson, *Centennial Essays*, p. 176, in Norelius, *De Svenska Lutherska . . . historia i Amerika*, I, 420.

[10]Forsander, *Lifsbilder*, I, 106.

[11]John Telleen, "A Memoir of Erland Carlsson," in Augustana archives (5 pages); A. W. Dahlsten, "Några minnen från Immanuelsförsamlingen i Chicago, åren 1859-1860," *Minneskrift-Immanuelsförsamlingen, 1853-1903*, pp. 83-84.

[12]C. A. Swensson, "Rostad," *Förgät-mig-ej, Fosterlandsk och Luthersk ungdomskalender för jubelåret, 1893* (Rock Island), p. 88.

[13]*Korsets predikan af pastorer inom Augustana-Synoden* (Rock Island: Augustana Book Concern, 1885), II, 387-401; *Augustana och missionären*, July 20, 1881, pp. 452-57.

[14]Erl. Carlsson, *Korsbaneret*, 1882, pp. 163-64; Forsander, *Lifsbilder*, I, 107-108.

[15]Erl. Carlsson, *Korsbaneret*, 1882, p. 165.

[16]*Ibid.*, p. 101.

[17]Sam Rönnegård, *Prairie Shepherd. Lars Paul Esbjörn and the beginnings of the Augustana Lutheran Church*. Translated by G. Everett Arden (Rock Island: Augustana Book Concern, 1952), p. 231.

[18]Eric Norelius, *Tuve Nilsson Hasselquist. Lefnadsteckning* (Rock Island: Lutheran Augustana Book Concern, n. d.), p. 52.

[19]E. Norelius, "Några hågkomster från året 1854," *Korsbaneret*, 1888, pp. 108-109.

[20]*Ibid.*, p. 109.

[21]Erl. Carlsson, *Korsbaneret*, 1882, p. 160.

[22]*Ibid.*, pp. 160-61.

[23]*Minneskrift-Immanuelsförsamlingen, 1853-1903*, p. 117.

[24]Erl. Carlsson, *Korsbaneret*, 1882, pp. 170-71.

[25] Erl. Carlsson, *Korsbaneret*, 1882, pp. 166-67; *Minneskrift-Immanuelsförsamlingen, 1853-1903*, p. 139.

[26] Erl. Carlsson, *Korsbaneret*, 1882, pp. 167-69; *Minneskrift-Immanuelsförsamlingen, 1853-1903*, p. 139.

[27] *Minneskrift-Immanuelsförsamlingen, 1853-1903*, pp. 141-43.

[28] *Ibid.*, p. 149.

[29] Erl. Carlsson, *Korsbaneret*, 1881, pp. 102-103; Evald B. Lawson, "Music, Art, and Architecture in Our Church," *After Seventy-Five Years* (Rock Island: Augustana Book Concern, 1935), p. 127.

[30] Erl. Carlsson, *Korsbaneret*, 1881, pp. 103-104.

[31] Erl. Carlsson, *Korsbaneret*, 1882, pp. 132-33; "Minutes of the Meeting of the Immanuel Congregation, October 24, 1854," Nothstein, *Selected Documents . . .*, Augustana Historical Society Publications; Part 2, XI, 10.

[32] "Minutes of the Meeting of the Swedish Lutheran Church, Chicago, January 26, 1855," *Augustana Historical Society Publications*, XI, 10-11.

[33] "Minutes of the Meeting of the Swedish Lutheran Church, Chicago, December 30, 1855, January 11, January 18, 1856," *Ibid.*, XI, 14-15.

[34] "Minutes of the Meeting of the Swedish Lutheran Church, Chicago, August 19, 1855," *Augustana Historical Society Publications*, XI, 26-27; Erl. Carlsson, *Korsbaneret*, 1882, p. 133.

[35] Erl. Carlsson, *Korsbaneret*, 1882, p. 134; Ulf Beijbom, "The Oldest Swedish Parish Records of Chicago," *The Swedish Pioneer Historical Quarterly*, XX (April, 1969), 63.

[36] Erl. Carlsson, *Korsbaneret*, 1882, p. 135; C. O. Bengtson, *The Story of the Immanuel Lutheran Church, Chicago. Seventy-fifth Anniversary Celebration, January 8-16, 1928*, (Chicago: Immanuel Lutheran Church, 1928), p. 16.

[37] Erl. Carlsson, *Korsbaneret*, 1882, p. 135.

[38] *Ibid.*, pp. 136-40.

[39] Erl. Carlsson, *Korsbaneret*, 1882, pp. 140-41; C. O. Lindell, "Axplockning mellan kärfvarna," *Minneskrift-Immanuelsförsamlingen, 1853-1903*, p. 86; Bengtson, *The Story of the Immanuel Lutheran Church, Chicago, Ill.*, p. 17.

[40] Bengtson, *The Story of the Immanuel Lutheran Church, Chicago, Illinois*, p. 17.

[41]Paul M. Angle, *The Great Chicago Fire* (Chicago: The Chicago Historical Society, 1946), pp. 11-12. *The Magazine of the Chicago Historical Society,* Fall, 1971, pp. 196-244, presents information about this great Chicago tragedy.

[42]Erl. Carlsson, *Korsbaneret,* 1882, p. 144.

[43]Erl. Carlsson, *Korsbaneret,* 1882, p. 144; C. O. Bengtson, *Lutheran Companion,* No. 56, April, 1948, quoted in Daniel A. Nystrom, *A Family of God* (Rock Island, 1962), p. 188.

[44]Johnson and Peterson, *Svenskarne i Illinois,* pp. 242-43; Erl. Carlsson, *Korsbaneret,* 1882, pp. 144-45.

[45]Erl. Carlsson to J. A. Seiss, Chicago, October 21, 1871.

[46]Erl. Carlsson, *Korsbaneret,* 1882, pp. 145-46. The congregation at the outset rented the Norwegian Lutheran Church on Sangamon St., near Milwaukee Ave. When it was too small, the congregation later met at the large Norwegian Lutheran Church located on West Indiana and Peoria Streets. See *Minneskrift-Immanuelsförsamlingen,* p. 71.

[47]Erl. Carlsson, *Korsbaneret,* 1882, p. 146.

[48]Erl. Carlsson, *Korsbaneret,* 1882, p. 151; C. O. Bengtson, *Lutheran Companion,* No. 56, April, 1948, quoted in Daniel Nystrom, *A Family of God,* pp. 188-89.

[49]Erl. Carlsson, *Korsbaneret,* 1882, p. 151.

[50]*Ibid.,* pp. 151-52.

[51]*Ibid.,* pp. 152-53.

[52]Erl. Carlsson, *Korsbaneret,* 1882, p. 153-54; "Minutes of the Meeting of Immanuel Congregation, January 1, 1872."

[53]Erl. Carlsson, *Korsbaneret,* 1882, pp. 154-55.

[54]Erl. Carlsson, *Korsbaneret,* 1882, p. 155; Bengtson, *The Story of the Immanuel Lutheran Church, Chicago, Seventy-fifth Anniversary, January 8-16, 1928,* p. 20.

[55]Erl. Carlsson to T. N. Hasselquist, en route to Sweden, May 26, 1873.

[56]Erl. Carlsson, *Korsbaneret,* 1882, p. 155; *Lutheran Mission World* (Philadelphia), XX (September, 1917), 34; Dahlén, "Bondpojken från Suletorp . . . ," p. 64.

[57]Erl. Carlsson, *Korsbaneret,* 1882, pp. 155-56.

[58]Erl. Carlsson to Peter Wieselgren, en route to USA, October 31, 1873,Westin, *Emigranterna och kyrkan,* pp. 346-47; Forsander, *Lifsbilder,* I, 120-21.

[59]Forsander, *Lifsbilder,* I, 121.

[60]"Statistical Table," Erl. Carlsson, *Korsbaneret,* 1881, p. 126; *The Eighth Census. Population of the United States in 1860.* Washington: Government Printing Office, 1864, p. 613.

[61]"Statistical Table," Erl. Carlsson, *Korsbaneret,* 1881, p. 126; *The Ninth Census (June 1, 1870) of the United States. A Compendium.* Washington: Government Printing Office, 1872, p. 449.

[62]"Statistical Table," Erl. Carlsson, *Korsbaneret,* 1881, p. 126. The figure 415 excommunicated includes only 14 in the years 1853-1869. The large number after that were not "excommunicated" in the strict sense of the word. They were "struck off" in connection with the Mission Friends conflict. See *Minneskrift-Immanuelsförsamlingen,* p. 29 for a full explanation.

[63]Editorial in *The Missionary* by W. A. Passavant, cited in G. H. Gerberding, *Life and Letters of W. A. Passavant, D. D.* (Greenville, Pa.: 1906), p. 615.

6

Outreach in Service

When Erl. Carlsson came to America in 1853, it was on a joint call to the Swedish Lutheran churches at Chicago and St. Charles, Illinois. He served the latter congregation until 1863 although his period of active regular service concluded four years earlier.

Swedes at St. Charles in 1852 subscribed money for a Scandinavian Lutheran meeting house. On January 21, 1853, Pastor T. N. Hasselquist organized the congregation with forty charter members. Erl. Carlsson's first sermon was delivered on October 2 of that year. Two factors soon required a new church building on the basis of Carlsson's statement: The church was too small, with the result that at the morning worship service large numbers were forced to stand outside. Differences about ownership relating to a deed resulted in the loss of the property. Norelius writes that when members appeared at the church for a *Julotta* service, they found the door nailed tight, but Jonas Peter Magnuson opened it. No Easter service could be held because the church had been placed on rollers and moved from the site.[1]

The Swedes of the area, including those at St. Charles and nearby Geneva, responded effectively. In November 1854, with encouragement from Pastor Carlsson, they purchased a stone house on a large lot in Geneva for $2,000. The structure had been designed for a courthouse but was never occupied for that purpose. The renovation proceeded forthwith so that the first worship service was

75

held the last Sunday in December. Carlsson wrote: "One can truly be amazed by the sacrifices which this poor and newly established congregation made in such a short time for their church . . . When I think of it my eyes are filled with tears." The church was officially dedicated following additional renovations in December 1856. The structure had a more characteristic Swedish architecture than most immigrant churches because of semi-circular windows and a high gallery. The seating capacity was 300.[2]

Erl. Carlsson served the congregation faithfully, devoting as much time as circumstances permitted. When he could not conduct services, A. Andreen, or someone else would do so. A congregational school was established in 1857. Mary Swensson, known as *"Skol-Mary,"* was a well-known teacher for many years. The growth in church membership was substantial. When Pastor Carlsson turned over the responsibility of the church to the second pastor, P. A. Cedarstam in August 1863, the financial condition was excellent, the debt being only $40.[3]

Erl. Carlsson owned a house and a lot in Geneva, but he lived there only during periods when he was recuperating from illness and during the summer months of 1857. Daughter Emmy was born in Geneva in September 1857.

The spirit and dedication of a true missionary characterized the life of Erl. Carlsson. After establishing congregational life at Chicago and Geneva-St. Charles, he devoted an amazing amount of time to travel, preaching, and founding congregations among immigrants. This work began early in his American career. Following the Galesburg meeting of the Synod of Northern Illinois in October 1853, Erland went to Rockford. His first need was to establish contact with Swedes in that city. Although he had considerable knowledge of the English language, he had problems with pronunciation and vocabulary. Norelius reports that Carlsson was not clear in the pronunciation of the English words "folks" and "foxes." As he approached some Americans in Rockford, he asked them if they knew about any Swedish "foxes" in the city. The source of this anecdote observed that the "hunt" succeeded and the pastor was soon in contact with several Swedes.[4]

Later, when John Rundbeck from Rockford came to the meeting of the Chicago-Mississippi Conference at Chicago in January

1854, he was informed that Pastor Carlsson would visit Rockford on the third Sunday of the month for the purpose of organizing a congregation. On January 15, under leaden skies and below zero temperatures, he organized the Scandinavian Evangelical Lutheran Church of Rockford with seventy-seven members, including thirty-three children. The constitution of the Chicago church was used as a model. Arrangements were made for either Carlsson or A. Andreen, his assistant, to conduct services four Sundays a year and on the first Monday of every month. The Chicago pastor devoted much time to the Rockford congregation in the early years. He was responsible for the plans whereby a church was built at a cost of $775.[5]

Although the Rockford congregation was the first home mission outreach of Erl. Carlsson, a prior trip to Minnesota had been planned for the autumn of 1853. This projected trip was based on his promise to visit members of the large group of emigrants who left Kalmar with him in June 1853, with Chisago Lake the intended destination. Carlsson started his trip to Minnesota but because of navigational problems created by ice on the rivers, he was unable to carry out his mission at that time. However, in April of the following year he was enroute to Minnesota. This was in response to a letter from Daniel Peterson, urging him to organize a congregation in the Chisago Lake area.[6]

The first stop on Erl. Carlsson's journey to Minnesota was St. Paul, where a group of Scandinavians, without a pastor, had organized a congregation in February 1854. They assembled quite regularly for devotional services which included the reading of a sermon from a *postilla,* (book of sermons). Their urgent desire for a pastor had been set forth in a letter to Hasselquist in March. When Carlsson arrived in St. Paul he officially organized on May 6, the Scandinavian Evangelical Lutheran Church of St. Paul. Seventy-six Swedes and Norwegians were charter members. The group adopted as their constitution the document which Erl. Carlsson had proposed when he organized his Chicago congregation the previous August.[7]

When Pastor Carlsson arrived in Chisago Lake, he was greeted by friends who had shared the hardships of the twelve-week voyage on the *St. Patrick.* It was a time of great rejoicing as the immigrants assembled under the leadership of their pastor-friend to organize the Swedish Evangelical Lutheran congregation of Chisago Lake, Minnesota

Territory, on May 12, 1854. In a letter to Peter Fjellstedt on July 10, Carlsson wrote: "I traveled from St. Paul to the Swedish settlement at Chisago Lake, fifty miles from that city and ten miles from Taylors Falls on the St. Croix River. I stayed here about a week." The minutes show that the members adopted the congregational constitution of the Chicago church. Plans were made for building an Evangelical Lutheran meeting house by next summer. This new congregation joined with the St. Paul church to call Pastor C. M. Swensson of the Växjö diocese. Approximately one hundred members formed the new congregation. Pastor Carlsson was able to stay only briefly at Chisago Lake. Eric Norelius arrived about a week later to join relatives in the area, at which time he conducted religious services. Norelius had a long and distinguished career as pastor and leader in Minnesota and in the Augustana Synod.[8]

One more congregation was organized by Carlsson before leaving the Minnesota Territory. A Swedish Lutheran congregation was formed on May 19 in the home of Daniel Nilson near Hay Lake, two miles south of present Scandia. No minutes of the meeting are extant. Carlsson wrote to Peter Fjellstedt: "On the way home [from Chisago Lake] I visited another Swedish settlement near Marine Mills between Chisago Lake and St. Paul, where a Swedish Lutheran congregation was organized with almost as many members as the congregation in St. Paul, namely, about fifty communicants and altogether eighty."[9]

Erl. Carlsson's trip to Minnesota Territory required six weeks. He was the first Swedish Lutheran pastor to visit that area. He had preached and presented Bible studies on thirty occasions. [10]

The ceaseless energy and dedication of Erl. Carlsson resulted in further missionary work. A sizeable number of Swedish immigrants had settled in Indiana at La Fayette, West Point, Attica, and elsewhere in the 1850s. The severe impact of the cholera epidemic had impeded church work. However, in the summer of 1854, Carlsson and his assistant, A. Andreen, visited the Swedish communities in Indiana. On February 18, 1855, the former organized the Swedish Evangelical Lutheran Church of Indiana, at a meeting which was held at West Point, Tippecanoe County. Members lived at Attica, Yorktown, La Fayette, and Milford or Montmorency as well as at West Point. The constitution proposed by Carlsson was adopted. It was an elaboration of the first constitution of the Chicago congregation with modest changes. Eric Norelius, famous pioneer pastor and long-time president of the Augustana Synod, has appropriately pointed out that the constitution adopted at West Point "contains the very source of the congregational constitution that has become common in all our Augustana congregations." [11]

The pattern of organizing congregations varied in Swedish communities. Immigrants settled in De Kalb, Illinois, in 1850, but it was not until December 25, 1858, that a congregation was organized by Pastor Carlsson. He had conducted services there on previous occasions. The organizational meeting was held in the public schoolhouse with members living as far away as Sycamore and Malta. Erl. Carlsson recommended that the forty members adopt the traditional constitution that traced its origin to his first year in America. He served the congregation until a permanent pastor was called. [12]

In September 1859, Carlsson made a missionary journey to eastern Michigan, where he made his headquarters at Sparta, Kent County, near Grand Rapids. On September 17, ten families shared in their first Swedish Lutheran service since coming to America. This important occasion was a communion service. The pastor recalled the occasion as "truly a festive day which will long live in my memory." He also baptized several children and conducted Bible studies for a few days. No congregation was organized at this time because of the small number of immigrants. [13]

When the Augustana Synod at its meeting at Princeton, Illinois, in June 1865, requested Pastor A. Andreen to take a leave-of-absence from his congregation at Baileytown (Porter) Indiana, to organize a congregation in New York City, Erl. Carlsson was asked to accompany him and assist in making preliminary contacts. He spent somewhat more than two weeks with Andreen, beginning August 10. In the *Missionstidning,* published by *Evangeliska Fosterlands-stiftelsen* (Evangelical National Foundation) in Sweden, co-sponsor with the Augustana Synod of the projected New York congregation, it was reported that, "This arrangement . . . had the effect that the cause attracted more attention and aroused interest. Through Reverend Carlsson's efforts several obstacles were overcome so that they obtained the right of admission to Castle Garden enabling them to meet emigrants as they landed." [14]

Andreen and Carlsson made several calls on their countrymen, including Captain John Ericsson, inventor and engineer of *Monitor* fame, who was cordial and later became a charter member and one of the original trustees of the congregation. The Illinois pastors had the good fortune to be able to use the St. James Evangelical Lutheran Church for meetings. Erl. Carlsson preached at a worship service and presided also at a meeting of 100 persons when there was discussion about the possibility of organizing a congregation. Carlsson wrote to Peter Wieselgren in August 1865: "It will gladden the hearts of the friends of our church that we finally in all earnestness have taken hold of the plans to found a Swedish Lutheran congregation in New York. One of our pastors, A. Andreen, has been sent by the synod to this place, and I have accompanied him hither to help him begin the work. The field here is both large and difficult . . . May the Lord in His mercy crown the undertaking with success." Andreen organized the Swedish Lutheran Church of Gustavus Adolphus in New York on September 22, 1865. [15]

Captain John Ericsson's relationship to the Swedish Lutheran church in New York was nominal and financial. He contributed $1,000 in response to an appeal for support in purchasing the church building on East Twenty-second Street in November 1865. He wrote on that occasion: "It will afford me great pleasure to forward the interests of the Swedish Lutheran church in New York. Please, therefore, use my name in the manner you propose. I will also cheerfully contribute means to a reasonable amount in furtherance of your important plan." William Conant Church, Ericsson's biographer, has written: "His relations to this church as a member do not appear, however, to have gone beyond pleasant responses to occasional applications from the good ladies of the congregation for help in carrying out the various enterprises requiring the issue of tickets, for which the brethren were expected to find sale. Brother Ericsson was always to be depended upon in this way, and if, as a trustee, he was not very punctual at attendance of board meetings, he was looked upon with confidence for advice and assistance when the occasion seemed to demand it." [16]

Erl. Carlsson shared intimately in the interest of the Augustana Synod in the attempt to establish mission work among American

Indians. Pastor Olof Olsson, founder of the Lindsborg community and later professor and president of Augustana College and Theological Seminary, in 1876, urged the Synod to begin a mission in Indian Territory. Later that year Carlsson made a plea for the support of such a project in *Missionären:*

> It is known that our synod plans to begin a mission among an Indian tribe in Indian Territory . . . May there be a contest among the people of this country to bring the Gospel to "the red man" whom we have so long and harshly scorned and oppressed unto this time. It is to us an encouragement that we walk in the steps of our fathers in New Sweden [Delaware Colony]. No people among the whites who have lived in the United States have dealt with them so well. May the whole Lutheran church lead the advance. [17]

Pastor Carlsson was chosen by the synod as chairman of a committee to consult with government officials in Washington about such an undertaking. Carlsson and Pastor John Telleen, who had made a journey in behalf of the synod to the Indian Territory in the spring of 1877, made an official visit to Washington in the autumn of that year. Senator Allison of Iowa introduced them to Commissioner of Indian Affairs Haas, who brought them to Secretary of the Interior Carl Schurz. He was the famous German immigrant who had been active in the revolution of 1848 in his homeland. The Swedish American visitors were cordially received by the secretary and the commissioner who promised them an agency in Indian Territory. A projected visit with President Hays did not develop because of his absence from the White House. [18]

Although no direct action was taken by Washington to authorize an agency, the synod continued to show interest in the project. In October 1878, Eric Norelius went on a missionary journey to Oklahoma Territory. His report concurred with the earlier recommendation of Telleen that the synod should begin work with the Comanches. At the synod meeting of 1879, Erl. Carlsson as chairman of the committee recommended that Mathias Wahlstrom be ordained as a missionary to the Indians. A variety of factors including inaction in Washington, Wahlstrom's poor health after his successful journeys among Indians, and other commitments of the synod combined to slow down and finally put an end to plans for a mission. An interesting approach is recorded in 1877-78 when three Delaware

youth—Simon Love, H. W. Goodtraveler, and T. W. Goodtraveler—
were selected by Chief Charles Journeycake, a friend of Pastor Olof
Olsson, for enrollment at Augustana College with the hope that they
could be educated for Christian service among their own people.
Financial support was received from Sunday Schools. This educational program did not achieve the expected results. [19]

Pastor John Telleen has written about Erl. Carlsson's great
interest in Indian missions:

> He grieved because the intended mission work among Indians
> came to naught. I can yet see him at the synodical meeting at
> Burlington, Iowa, in 1877, when he suggested that our synod take
> up work in the Indian Territory even if the government at
> Washington would not give us an agency. He spoke to me privately
> about it. I did not then favor independent work because we would
> have no guarantee to hold our field in the future, but I have often
> since wished that I had seconded Dr. Carlsson's views. [20]

The mission outreach of Pastor Carlsson went beyond the area of
concern only for the ministry of the Word and embraced fully the ministry of mercy. Pastor Carlsson was always closely identified with the
needs of people, always responding with Christian love and action. The
severe cholera epidemic of 1854 had dramatized the need for emergency
immigrant aid but there were also permanent problems that were met in
a variety of ways. Erl. Carlsson was always involved. Observers have
reported that periodically the Carlsson home was like a miniature
"Castle Garden," as the rooms filled with people. At times it served
as a kind of hospital for the ill. Emmy Evald, the Carlsson's daughter,
states that as many as sixty immigrants were cared for during certain
periods. When the traffic was especially heavy, the congregation's
schoolhouse served as a hospice. [21]

The impact of immigration decreased during the Civil War, but
when hostilities ceased the pace quickened and the influx became a
great tide. The problems could only be met through organized effort.
Erl. Carlsson, Paul Andersen, Victor Witting, a Swedish Methodist
pastor, and others associated with Scandinavian churches organized
the Scandinavian Emigrant Aid Society in the spring of 1866. The
annual dues were $2 per member. Financial support was developed
by subscription and by funds supplied by the immigration commissioner of Cook County. [22]

The first report by Fr. Nilsson, the director of the society, was presented on August 11, 1866. In the first month of service, 1590 Swedes, 600 Norwegians, and an unspecified number of Danes had arrived in Chicago according to his records. Nilsson and his associates helped many to move their possessions from one railroad station to another, aided them in arranging schedules and acquiring food, while some were able to find jobs through the assistance of society personnel. The first financial report showed income of $747.01 and expenses of $483.35. [23]

Nilsson's report in October indicated that in the last two months the society had been of service to 1,400 Scandinavians. Fortunately the organization had been able to arrange for housing many transients over a period of ten weeks in the freight depot of the Northwestern Railroad. Forty-nine families and twenty single persons had been supported over a long period of time with housing and food. Many immigrants had been similarly helped for shorter periods. Sixty permanent jobs had been found for them. In the two-month period fifteen persons had been provided with hospitalization and the society had provided ten coffins for burials. The income had been $1000.47 and expenses $957.80. [24]

The mounting stream of Scandinavian immigration produced ever increasing activity by Pastor Carlsson and his associates. In the spring of 1868, the society built a large building on the corner of Indiana and Michigan streets to house and feed the newcomers. The challenge that confronted the sponsors is reported in "An Appeal" to the general public in the *Chicago Daily Tribune* in June 1868: "All who come are poor, and a large proportion are entirely destitute. All of them need counsel and a very large number of them must have material aid or perish . . . The season is approaching when the emigrants will come in large numbers. Our funds are exhausted." The article stated that 20,000 Scandinavians had come through Chicago during the previous year. In addition to Fr. Nilsson, Erik Stone and Fr. Brown served as directors. [25]

Erl. Carlsson was responsible for resolutions by the Augustana Synod in 1867 which urged support of the society. The minutes record this action: "That we regard it as a duty to extend a helping hand to our poor and needy emigrants and especially through gifts and contributions to support the emigrant aid society." Each pastor on his return home was requested to arrange for sending contributions. [26]

The Svea Society, which was founded in 1857, entered the area of aid to Scandinavian immigrants shortly after action by the churches. Leaders included Herman Roos, O. G. Lange, and Charles Eklund. A cooper's shop at Franklin and Ohio streets was leased and remodeled into a hospice. S. Trägårdh was engaged as the society's representative. Later a $4,000 building was constructed at 120 Illinois Street where 200 immigrants could be accomodated. In July 1868, the *Tribune* reported that in the previous two weeks, 800 newly arrived Scandinavians had been cared for. The Svea Society rendered helpful service to many people. [27]

In the early years of the new decade, the urgent need for immigrant aid was not as critical as during the high tide of the late 1860s. Moreover, the resources of the societies had been strained to the breaking point. Both societies soon ceased operations. The Svea Society immigrant home was sold in September 1871 for the benefit of creditors at $6,000. The great fire next month reduced to ashes the properties of both groups. [28]

The immigrant aid outreach among Scandinavians might have been substantially greater if there had been cooperation between the two societies. Philosophical differences between the church-focused society and Svea were such that this was not possible. This situation reflects the "two worlds" among the Scandinavians of Chicago at this time.

The earliest formal attempt to provide a hospital for Swedes in Chicago was the result of action at the annual meeting of Immanuel Church in January 1864, when it was decided "to establish a Christian home for the sick, and a treasury for the sick and needy." Funds would come from annual dues of fifty cents per member, money from the monthly collection at communion services, and gifts. The income during the first year was $430 in cash plus *in natura* gifts and services. At the annual meeting in 1865, the report showed that a suitable house with four patient rooms on Larrabee Street had been rented as a hospital. The services of two physicians had been contracted by Pastor Carlsson at modest cost. A widow and her daughter, plus volunteers, had responsibility for patient care. [29]

The initial project of Immanuel Church was merged in 1866

with the hospital founded by Dr. W. A. Passavant at Dearborn and Huron streets. In sixteen months, 140 patients had been admitted, including 90 Scandinavians. The chief physician was Dr. Schoetzer who had served the Immanuel Church hospital. Passavant's Hospital of Mercy was a modest-sized structure with twelve beds. Pastor and Mrs. Erl. Carlsson were active supporters of the institution. Passavant was disappointed at the slow rate in which the hospital developed: "I regret to say that with the exception of what was done by the ladies of the Swedish and Norwegian churches in Chicago, there was little or no assistance from the churches of the Augustana Synod." The hospital building was destroyed in the 1871 fire. It was later rebuilt and its present successor is known as the Passavant Hospital. [30]

Erl. Carlsson later became a leader in founding the institution that became the well-known Swedish Augustana Hospital. He was the first chairman of the Board of Directors. [31]

FOOTNOTES

[1] Erl. Carlsson, *Hemlandet*, November 12, 1856, quoted in *Illustrerad minneskrift af Sv. Ev. Luth. församlingen i Geneva, Ill. 50-års jubileum*, p. 8; Norelius, *De Svenska Lutherska . . . historia i Amerika*, I, 446; *Geneva Lutheran Church, Geneva, Illinois, 1853-1963*, p. 13.

[2] *Illustrerad minneskrift . . . Geneva, Ill.*, 1903, pp. 8-10.

[3] *Ibid.*, pp. 14-15.

[4] Norelius, *De Svenska Lutherska . . . historia i Amerika*, I, 456-57.

[5] Norelius, *De Svenska Lutherska . . . historia i Amerika*, I, 457-59; *Centennial. The First Evan. Lutheran Church, Rockford, Illinois, 1854-1954* (Rockford, 1954), pp. 1-5; *Minnes-Album. Första Sv. Ev. Lutherska församlingen i Rockford, Ill. Femtio-Årsfest, 1904* (Rock Island: Lutheran Augustana Book Concern, 1904), pp. 8-9.

[6] *Minneskrift, 1858-1908. Minnesota konferensen* (Minneapolis: 1908), p. 14; Norelius, *De Svenska Lutherska . . . historia i Amerika*, I, 559.

[7] Norelius, *De Svenska Lutherska . . . historia i Amerika*, I, 613-14.

[8] Emil Lund, *Minnesota konferensens av Augustana synoden och dess församlingarnas historia* (Rock Island: Augustana Book Concern, 1923), I, 341-44; "Minutes of the Meeting of the Swedes of the Evangelical Lutheran

confession living at Chisago Lake, Minnesota Ter., May 12, 1854,"
Augustana Historical Society Publications, XI, 50-52. Carlsson's letter to
Fjellstedt is cited in Lund, I, 344. Norelius, *De Svenska Lutherska . . . historia i Amerika,* I, 562.

[9]Lund, *Minnesota konferensens historia,* I, 354-55; *Minnesalbum. Sammandrag
af Sv. Ev. Luth. Elims-församlingens i New Scandia, Minn. historia*
(Scandia: Församlingen, 1904), p. 17.

[10]Norelius, *De Svenska Lutherska . . . historia i Amerika,* I, 430.

[11]"Minutes Kept at the Meeting held in West Point, Tippecanoe Co., Indiana,
February 18, 1855, with the Swedes living in this town and many places
round about," *Augustana Historical Society Publications,* XI, 80-82;
Norelius, *De Svenska Lutherska . . . historia i Amerika,* I, 490-94.

[12]"Minutes Kept at a General Meeting with the Swedes of DeKalb, Sycamore,
and Malla in the Public School House in DeKalb. December 25, 1858,"
Augustana Historical Society Publications, XI, 128.

[13]Norelius, *De Svenska Lutherska . . . historia i Amerika,* I, 765-66.

[14]Gustav Andreen, "The Early Missionary Work of the Augustana Synod in New
York City in 1865-66," *Augustana Historical Society Publications,* II, 4-5,
11-15.

[15]Andreen, "Early Missionary Work in the Augustana Synod in New York
City," pp. 10-11, 13. A graphic account of Andreen's experiences with
Swedish immigrants is found in two letters to *Hemlandet* in 1865. See
George M. Stephenson, "Hemlandet Letters," *Year-Book of the Swedish
Historical Society,* 1922-23, pp. 126-28.

[16]William Conant Church, *The Life of John Ericsson* (New York: Charles
Scribner's Sons, 1907), II, 255-56. Church discusses Ericsson's religious
beliefs, pp. 249-59.

[17]*Augustana synodens protokoll,* 1876, pp. 26-28; *Missionären. Svensk
Luthersk missionstidning* (Rock Island), I (November, 1876), 276.

[18]*Augustana synodens protokoll,* 1878. p. 17; J. Telleen, "Indianmissionen,"
Jubel-Album, 1893, p. 198. John Telleen's description of his visit to
Indian country in April, 1877, is found in *Jubel-Album, 1893,* pp.
195-201. Telleen indicates that Eric Norelius was also in Washington for a
part of the sessions with public officials.

[19]*Augustana Luthersk kyrkotidning* (Rock Island), December 9, 1878; *Augustana synodens protokoll,* 1879, p. 42; 1877, p. 25; 1878, p. 18; 1880. p.
64; *Augustana,* June 5, 1930.

[20]J. Telleen, "Rev. Dr. Erland Carlsson," *My Church* (Rock Island), VII, 49-50.

[21] Forsander, *Lifsbilder,* I, 113; Hildebrand and Fredenholm, *Svenskarna i Amerika,* I, 261; Norelius, *De Svenska Lutherska ... historia i Amerika,* I, 434.

[22] Beijbom, *Swedes in Chicago,* pp. 302-303; Norelius, *De Svenska Lutherska ... historia i Amerika,* I, 434.

[23] *Hemlandet,* August 28, 1866.

[24] *Ibid.,* October 23, 1866.

[25] *Chicago Daily Tribune,* June 16, 1868; Forsander, *Lifsbilder,* I, 113; Norelius, *De Svenska Lutherska ... historia i Amerika,* I, 434.

[26] *Augustana synodens protokoll,* 1867, p. 30; 1868, p. 20.

[27] *Chicago Daily Tribune,* April 8, July 12, 1868; Johnson and Peterson, *Svenskarne i Illinois,* p. 263.

[28] E. W. Olson, *History of the Swedes of Illinois,* p. 891; Johnson and Peterson, *Svenskarne i Illinois,* p. 263; *Justitia* (Chicago) March 25, 1874.

[29] Erl. Carlsson, "The Beginnings of Our Benevolent Work," *The Alumnus* (Rock Island) I (April, 1893), 172-74.

[30] Gerberding, *The Life and Letters of W. A. Passavant, D. D.,* pp. 421-22; *Hemlandet,* Nov. 20, 1866; E. W. Olson, *History of the Swedes of Illinois,* p. 531; Beijbom, *Swedes in Chicago,* p. 254, Robert W. Holmen, "The Ministry of Mercy," *Centennial Essays,* p. 241.

[31] See Ch. XIII, "The Last Years," p. 185 for a description of Erl. Carlsson's role in the early history of Augustana Hospital.

First Immanuel Church, 1855

Second Immanuel Church, 1871

Immanuel Church School, 1856

Erl. Carlsson Home on Lincoln Ave.

7

The Church Beyond
the Parish

When Swedish Lutheran pastors came to the Middle West they
had been preceded by other Lutherans who had begun a pioneer
ministry. The Synod of Northern Illinois had been founded
September 18, 1851, in Cedarville, Stephenson County, Illinois. It
included German, Norwegian, and American congregations.

Pastor L. P. Esbjörn came late to the organizational meeting,
but he joined the synod when it was agreed that the official minutes
would include a statement that the Swedish congregations joined
with the understanding that, "the symbolical books of the Lutheran
Church contain a correct summary and exposition of the Divine
Word, wherefore we declare and adopt them as the foundations of
our faith and doctrine, next to the Holy Scriptures." Esbjörn felt
that the original reference in the constitution to the Augsburg
Confession, as "mainly correct," was too vague. This development
was a portent of the conflict that in less than a decade would result
in withdrawal by the Scandinavians from the synod.[1]

Erl. Carlsson in 1853 shared the feeling of Esbjörn and
Hasselquist that fellowship with other Lutherans would be helpful in
the adaptation of the immigrant church to the American scene and in
learning from older Lutheran groups. The Chicago pastor attended
synod meetings regularly and participated quite actively in the
proceedings. At the synod meeting at Waverly, October 4, 1855, he
was the Swedish representative on a committee of three persons who

89

presented a report advocating the establishment of a Scandinavian professorship at Illinois State University, Springfield, the synod's institution. The report, adopted by the synod, also recommended that Esbjörn collect funds among Swedish Americans for this purpose.[2]

Erl. Carlsson was present at the synod meeting at Geneva, May 8, 1856, when the principal business was defining the nature of the professorship and endorsing a provision which reflected the thought of the Swedes especially, "that said Professor be required solemnly to promise to teach according to the Word of God and the Augsburg Confession before he shall be installed in his office or entitled to the rights and privileges of such professorship." At the meeting of the synod at Dixon, October 8-13, 1856, Erl. Carlsson was appointed as one of three members on the Scandinavian Professor Committee. It was at this meeting, as has been pointed out that, "The English speaking element of the synod, at least a considerable portion of it, began to oppose the professorship plan openly because they feared it would put the confessional party in control in the school and synod."[3]

At the meeting of the synod at Cedarville, September 23-October 4, 1857, the synod confirmed the election of Esbjörn as Scandinavian professor based upon the nomination by the United Chicago and Mississippi Conferences a few days earlier at Rockford. In due course, Erl. Carlsson presented the report of the Scandinavian Professor Committee at the synod meeting at Mendota September 15-20, 1858, and indicated that Esbjörn was prepared to begin his duties at Springfield by the end of that month. The decision to petition the King of Sweden for help in financing the position was also presented by him.[4]

While action had taken place within the Synod of Northern Illinois to identify clearly the Scandinavian role in its educational plans, developments occurred in Minnesota which ultimately played a part in the dissolution of the synod. In the spring of 1858 plans were being discussed about the possibility of forming a Lutheran synod among German, American, and Swedish congregations. Eric Norelius, in a letter to Erl. Carlsson, explained the situation: "When I was requested by Rev. Thompson, Heyer, and Passavant to join them in a synod of Minnesota, I thought that it would have its advantages, which anyone who has any power of judgment must see,—and in this nothing new of my own was implied because there was just such a one to be found in the Synod of Northern Illinois." He also pointed out that the location of Minnesota and the great difficulty of travel made it impossible for the pastors there to participate actively with the brethren of Illinois. Moreover, Norelius was not satisfied with the doctrinal position of the Synod of Illinois.[5]

Erl. Carlsson's response to prospective developments in Minnesota is found in his long letter to Norelius June 28, 1858, in which he could not help "deploring and lamenting the approaching separation." He regretted that Norelius had "proceeded from the assumption that it is already decided that the Scandinavian element in our church from the very beginning shall be fused together with the American and as a result thereof it is proper to build a synod in Minnesota which will include Scandinavians, Germans, and Americans in our confession. But such a situation does not appear to me to be correct."[6]

Carlsson felt strongly that a synod of this kind in Minnesota would be divisive: "But how will it be if we separate? Will not the devil mockingly say: 'Now I have won my old game, *divide et vince* . . . ' How should we be able to take care of the interests of our church among our people if we be divided among separate synods of Germans and Americans? . . . But it is not enough that we would lose much through a divorce, but I fear something much worse. Think, Brother, if on account of one or another condition the devil would be permitted to come between us, think if an unfortunate strife should arise sooner or later. How would not our church suffer and how unfortunate would it not be!" Carlsson then concluded with an admonition: "Throw not away my letter and your old friend. After you have read the letter go to your chamber and pray."[7]

Norelius responded immediately (July 1, 1858) to Carlsson's plea. He denied the assumption that he was the initiator of the plan to organize a synod in Minnesota by citing his articles in *Minnesota Posten* to prove his point. He made his position clear: "I said therefore if it was the intention of the Scandinavians to remain in that union [the Synod of Northern Illinois] and not think of founding their own particular organization, it would therefore be a great advantage for us to act in the same manner and we would not have to travel so far for the solution of the one thing that could easily be settled among us." He then emphasized his principal objective: "But I also urged that we ought to organize our own Scandinavian synod, in order that we might then justly and in an undisturbed fashion be together, and I said in case such a synod was formed that I would prefer to connect myself with such a one."[8]

Four days after Norelius' reply to Carlsson, on July 5, 1858, a meeting was held in the Swedish Lutheran church, Red Wing, Minnesota, then under the care of Norelius, to discuss the formation of an Evangelical Lutheran Synod of Minnesota. The Swedish representatives were not ready to vote for this proposal because, "We wish to hear the full discussion of the question by our Swedish brethren in Illinois." The matter was discussed at a meeting of the United Chicago-Mississippi Conference at Princeton, Illinois. At the meeting of the Synod of Northern Illinois, Mendota, Illinois, September 15-20, the formation of the Minnesota Conference, consisting only of Swedish pastors and congregations as distinct from the proposed Minnesota synod, was authorized.[9]

The gratitude of Carlsson for Norelius' reply and the subsequent action was expressed in the former's letter on July 29 in which he stated, "Your explanation appears to me to be fully satisfactory." But he could not refrain from citing the reasons for the concern expressed in his letter of the previous month: "The starting of your own newspaper [Minnesota Posten], now the organization [proposed organization] of a new synod, and then additional talk about building a new school in St. Paul, I could not consider as anything else but opposition and the beginning of a division."[10]

A series of events, including the impact of the proposed Minnesota synod in stimulating Swedish nationalism and cohesiveness, produced a change in the relationship of the Swedish Lutherans with the Synod of Northern Illinois. Esbjörn's professorship at Illinois State University, the synod's institution, was an unhappy experience for him and others. Included among his laments at Springfield were the following: The congregation there did not fully acknowledge the Augsburg Confession and hence Esbjörn and his family could not join such a congregation; he was so occupied in teaching non-theological subjects with the result that he could not give adequate time to his principal assignment of theology and assistance to Scandinavian students; he was not allowed to conduct Swedish communion services as he desired; the Scandinavian students favored leaving the school. In October 1859, he wrote to Norelius: "We live here in a kind of Babylonian captivity, and no one feels it as deeply as I do. . . . I entertain—almost against my will—plans about how we can establish our own school in Chicago." The Esbjörn family spent Christmas 1859, in Attica, Indiana, as guests of the Norelius family. The question of a separate school was discussed at that time.[11]

The conflict reached a climax on March 30, 1860, when Esbjörn suddenly sent his resignation to the Board of Directors and left Springfield. Erl. Carlsson invited Esbjörn and his family to move to Chicago where they lived with the Carlsson family. Seventeen of the twenty Scandinavian students followed Esbjörn to Chicago. Carlsson arranged for students to live in his congregation's schoolhouse. A room in Immanuel Church and the lecture room of the Norwegian Lutheran Church were used also for classes. Augustana Seminary was soon to come to birth. [12]

Erl. Carlsson supported Esbjörn who was the key figure in these developments. When the latter wrote to Norelius, March 19, 1860, shortly before leaving Springfield, he stated: "Carlsson writes that general opinion is more in favor of moving than in not moving." This was not an aggressive declaration for action, but Carlsson's cautiousness was not unusual. An important factor, in addition to his strong confessional position, was undoubtedly the firmness of Pastor Paul Andersen, pastor of the Chicago Norwegian Lutheran congregation, whom Erl. Carlsson esteemed highly. Andersen was an ardent supporter of the pure confessional position. In the controversy over doctrine at the Dixon meeting in October 1856, Norelius reported: "Andersen distinguished himself by a powerful defense of the confession and showed himself inflexible towards any concession in which he had the support of all the Scandinavian members." [13]

There is no doubt that Hasselquist supported Esbjörn in the crisis although as Norelius, a close associate of both men, has stated: "The relationship between Esbjörn and Hasselquist was not real good at that time. . . . They possessed two different temperaments and personalities, which even under the best conditions would have made it difficult for them always to agree. There was a certain aggressiveness on one side and a certain apprehensiveness on the other. But it must be acknowledged that Hasselquist had not come to the firmness in confessionalism that came later." In his biography of Hasselquist, Norelius wrote: " . . . he was no more unionist than the others."[14]

The controversy between certain leaders of Illinois State University and Esbjörn and broader issues were fully aired at the Chicago united meeting of the Chicago-Mississippi and Minnesota conferences, April 23-27, 1860. This meeting brought to a crisis the latent differences between the Scandinavian Lutherans and an influential group within the Synod of Northern Illinois. The doctrinal controversy was closely related to the ideas of Dr. S. S. Schmucker, a spokesman for the "New Lutheranism" who has been described as being "of the opinion that the Lutheran Church of America should cast off the historical confessions and work out its doctrinal position independently of any European historical influences." Schmucker's volume, *Definite Synodical Platform*, 1855, provided basic material for the controversy. The Reverend Francis Springer, former president of Illinois State University, was a leader of the "Definite Platform" people some of whom wished to withdraw from the synod and form an "anti-Augsburg Confession" synod. [15]

When the time came at the united meeting of the Chicago-Mississippi and Minnesota conferences for considering Professor Esbjörn's resignation from the faculty of the synod's school at Springfield, Erl. Carlsson and members of the committee who had been elected to report on the matter recommended, and the conferences supported, the following resolution:

> Since we are fully convinced, that there is found in our synod a decided difference of opinion in regard to doctrine; and since there is in reality a rupture instead of a union in the synod and since contentions and quarrels serve to diminish confidence, weaken our strength and prevent our progress; and since we are exposed to the danger that at any time through a sufficient majority of votes against us, a change in our doctrinal position may be forced upon the synod, and since it is our most holy duty to protect and defend our confession of faith unpolluted both in our congregations and in the teaching of theology which our students receive, and in the influence which is exerted by those who shall become the preachers and pastors of our congregations; and since our experience clearly shows

us that in these respects we have no security in the connection in which we have hitherto stood, therefore Resolved, 1st that we approve of Prof. Esbjörn's resignation as our Scandinavian professor at Illinois State University, and that we give him our thanks. . . .[16]

The above resolution set the stage for two resolutions which went far beyond the immediate controversy. The result was not only separation of the Scandinavian members from the Synod of Northern Illinois, but a new, independent Augustana Synod was established.

Resolved, that we Scandinavian pastors and congregations, who have hitherto been united with the Evang. Lutheran Synod of Northern Illinois, herewith peacefully withdraw from our churchly union with said synod, and that the officers of our Conference respectfully inform the president of said Synod of our withdrawal.

Resolved, that we hereby decide to meet on Tuesday the 5th of next June in the Norwegian Evang. Lutheran Church at Jefferson Prairie, near Clinton, Wisconsin, in order to organize a synod and that a committee of three be appointed to work out a constitution, which is to be presented at the said meeting for adoption. [17]

Carlsson had been a supporter of the Synod of Northern Illinois prior to the developments of 1860. In the spring of 1858 he had written to Norelius: "We now have, God be praised, our synod's [Synod of Northern Illinois] doctrinal platform so complete that we can, with good conscience stand upon it." In July 1859, at a meeting in Our Savior's Lutheran Church, Chicago, between representatives of the Norwegian Lutheran Synod and Scandinavian members of the Synod of Northern Illinois, Carlsson had strongly defended the doctrinal position of the latter synod against the bitter attacks and the extremism of Pastor H. A. Preus. [18]

The conflict within the synod of Northern Illinois which came to a head in 1860 over the Scandinavian professorship unfortunately tends to obscure the importance of that relationship for Swedish Lutherans. Conrad Bergendoff has pointed out in an interesting and important article that " . . . the original Augustana Synod constitution is to a very large extent a copy of the constitution of the Synod of Northern Illinois, which had been adopted in 1851, and amended at various times before 1860 and with which the members of the newly organized synod were very well acquainted." In assessing this situation he concluded: "It is evident from a comparison of the constitution of the Synod of Northern Illinois and of the Augustana Synod how much the Augustana founders had learned from their brethren in the English-speaking congregations. At the same time, it is just as clear that on certain points they differed." [19]

The relationship of the Augustana leaders with the Synod of Northern Illinois had other important implications. It gave them a feeling of solidarity in their Lutheranism as strangers in a strange land. They gained a sense of belonging that would not have been possible if they had attempted to carry on in isolation. Membership in the Synod of Northern Illinois for almost a decade was an important aspect in their Americanization. It is readily understandable for these reasons that Hasselquist and Carlsson were somewhat reluctant to sever their bonds of fellowship with other Lutherans. It was a matter of alternatives and after these years of experience and learning they were in a fairly good position to face the world independently.

Although the Swedish pastors and congregations were active in the Synod of Northern Illinois, the effective forum for discussion leading to action was the Mississippi Conference which was authorized by the synod in 1852. Norwegians were organized into the Chicago Conference. Erl. Carlsson, a resident of Chicago and the pastor of a Swedish Lutheran congregation, was considered a member of both conferences, although his principal activity was with the Mississippi Conference.

The first meeting of the Mississippi Conference was held at Moline, Illinois, January 5-9, 1853. In the nineteen meetings until April 1860, Carlsson was absent on only two occasions. In the pattern of rotating chairman he served in that capacity and as secretary.

The scope of the activity of the Mississippi Conference is apparent in a chronicle of Erl. Carlsson's following committee assignments, when he often served as chairman: To draw up a statement to assist newly arrived immigrants; to examine credentials for the ministry; to prepare for publication the form and content of congregational record books; to negotiate for the transfer of *Hemlandet,* Swedish newspaper, to control by the churches; to arrange for the establishment of a publication society and bookstore; to regulate the activities of colporteurs; to draw up calls to pastors in

Sweden; to draft the official congregational constitution; to prepare circular letters for congregations; to prepare forms for baptism, confirmation, wedding, and membership certificates; to write resolutions for the establishment of a Scandinavian professorship; to present recommendations of aid for needy students; to petition for aid from the King of Sweden, churches in Sweden, and friends; to draft resolutions for the creation of the Augustana Synod; to draw up resolutions for the founding of Augustana Seminary; and transmit resolutions to other Lutheran groups setting forth the reasons for withdrawal from the Synod of Northern Illinois. [20]

The founding of the Augustana Synod in 1860 changed the role of the conferences. The new situation is described in a resolution of the Mississippi Conference in August 1861: "Since we have organized our own synod, the affairs of our congregations to a large extent will be the concern of our synod, hence the conference's mission in the future will be principally to encourage and stimulate the congregations to new and more earnest life so that . . . members may be cheered and become more steadfast in the faith." Synodical activities engaged leaders like Erl. Carlsson with the result that for several years the conference played a lesser role. [21]

However, a change took place in 1870 when circumstances, related to growth in membership and emergence of latent regional interests, produced a new situation. These regional interests are reflected in the creation of five conferences by synod action in 1870. L. G. Abrahamson has written: "The nature of our own work was changed substantially by this action. Much of the work which heretofore had been done by the president and designated committees of the synod, now fell into the hands of conferences. . . . One responsibility after another, which previously was that of the synod, was now turned over to the conferences." [22]

The Illinois Conference, one of five, included congregations in Illinois, Indiana, Michigan, and the southern part of Wisconsin. Erl. Carlsson was elected the first president, a position which he held until 1882, shortly after his election as president of the synod. The role of the conferences was further strengthened by action of the synod in 1879 which made the conferences into districts, synods in some aspects of their responsibilities. Support of institutions, except Augustana College and Theological Seminary, home missions, and pastoral discipline became a conference responsibility. [23]

Erl. Carlsson was an able and energetic conference president. He worked hard to promote missions and evangelism. He was known and loved as "a pastor's pastor." Although he had supported the new role of the conferences, he had some doubts about their impact on the support of missions. In his report to synod in 1872 as chairman of the Central Mission Board, he expressed his concern: "We cannot avoid thinking with anxiety about how it will be for our thousands of countrymen living in Dakota, Nebraska, Missouri, and Kansas, if the Illinois Conference will be only concerned about mission work in Illinois, the Minnesota Conference with Minnesota, and the Iowa Conference with Iowa. . . . If they had stayed in Illinois or Iowa or if they had gone to Minnesota, we would take care of them." In 1874 he informed synod with great regret that only $576.96 had come to the Central Mission Board for the support of general missions and all of that had come from the Illinois Conference. [24]

An appraisal of Erl. Carlsson's service as Illinois Conference president for eleven years has been made by L. G. Abrahamson:

> His sensitive care for all congregations, which always character-
> ized him, his keen insight into all that affected the church's welfare,
> his well-known administrative skill, his ability to give counsel in all
> troublesome situations, all of these qualities, combined with his
> indomitable courage, which had its source in his child-like trust in
> God and a life completely dedicated to God, made him admirably
> suited to hold the top leadership position in this important area of
> our church.[25]

Erl. Carlsson's leadership experience as president of the Illinois Conference was another fine credential for his later position as president of the Augustana Synod.

The outreach of Erl. Carlsson's devotion to the church went beyond conference and synod and embraced co-operative relationships with other Lutheran denominations. His support for the General Council of the Evangelical Lutheran Church of North America is evidence of this interest.

The Lutheran federation known as the General Council had come into being in 1866 as a conservative protest against the General Synod. At the 1867 synod meeting, Carlsson was elected as an Augustana delegate, although the synod had not yet joined the council. Hasselquist and he reported favorably following their attendance at the Pittsburg meeting that year. At the synod meeting of 1870, Carlsson reported for Peter Colseth and himself as Augustana representatives at the General Council meeting which had been held the previous autumn in Carlsson's church. In his report he gave the following endorsement:

> The General Council has not only taken its stand wholly and unconditionally on the confessional basis of the Lutheran Church, but it has also called forth new activity, greater liberality, more interest in higher education, greater zeal for organizing and maintaining new congregations, and also a greater interest in foreign mission work—in brief, a greater zeal for home and foreign missions.

The Chicago pastor also declared, "There is new life-energy at work and a new day is dawning for our Lutheran Zion in this land." Carlsson's recommendation that the Augustana Synod become a member of the General Council was discussed and a resolution approving membership was passed. [26]

Erl. Carlsson attended the annual meeting of the General Council fourteen times during the period 1867-86. In 1869 he was elected "Swedish Corresponding Secretary" for the council thus serving as the liaison official with the Augustana Synod. He held this position until 1875 when he moved to Andover. He was the channel of information from the council to leaders of the synod and he reported the council's activities through the church press. He also kept officers of the council informed about synodical activities. This assignment is a further indication of his commitment to the General Council. Erl. Carlsson's relationship to the council has been described as follows: "He was for many years the synod's most influential representative at the meeting of the General Council . . . " He also was active in this organization during his years as president of the Augustana Synod. [27]

FOOTNOTES

[1] "Minutes of the First Session of the Synod of Northern Illinois, Sept. 18-21, 1851," Arden, *Augustana Heritage*, p. 37.

[2] "Minutes of the Meeting of Synod of Northern Illinois Oct. 4, 1855," *Augustana Historical Society Publications*, X, 107-108.

[3] "Minutes of the Meeting of the Synod of Northern Illinois, May 8, 1856, and October 8-13, 1856," *Augustana Historical Society Publications*, IX, 25, 33. See comment *Ibid.*, p. 112 and reference to articles in *Ibid.*, IX, pp. 96-103, 103-105, 106-110. Also, George M. Stephenson, *The Founding of the Augustana Synod, 1850-1860*, pp. 55-57.

[4] "Minutes of Meeting of United Chicago and Mississippi Conferences, Rockford, Sept. 28-29, 1857," *Augustana Historical Society Publications*, X, 128, 132 and "Minutes of Meeting of Synod of Northern Illinois, Mendota, Sept. 15-20, 1858," *Ibid.*, X, 148-49. Hasselquist favored the appointment of Peter Fjellstedt as professor rather than Esbjörn. See Stephenson, *The Founding of the Augustana Synod*, pp. 60-61.

[5] Eric Norelius to Erl. Carlsson, Red Wing, Minn., July 1, 1858, O. Fritiof Ander, "Some Letters Pertaining to the Proposed Minnesota Synod," *The Augustana Quarterly*, XII (Oct. 1933), 366.

[6] Erl. Carlsson to Eric Norelius, Chicago, June 28, 1858, Ander, "Some Letters Pertaining to the Proposed Minnesota Synod," pp. 362-63.

[7] Erl. Carlsson to Eric Norelius, Chicago, June 28, 1858, Ander, "Some Letters Pertaining to the Proposed Minnesota Synod," pp. 363-65; Nothstein, "Selected Documents . . . Congregations and Conferences of the Augustana Synod," *Augustana Historical Society Publications*, XI (1946), Part 2, 134-36; Norelius, *De Svenska Lutherska . . . historia i Amerika*, I, 840-50.

[8] Eric Norelius to Erl. Carlsson, Red Wing, Minn., July 1, 1858, Ander, "Some Letters Pertaining to the Proposed Minnesota Synod," p. 366.

[9] Nothstein, "Selected Documents of Organization . . . First Congregations and Conferences of the Augustana Synod," *Augustana Historical Society Publications*, XI (1946), Part II, 137; Nothstein, *Ibid.*, X (1944), Part I, 150.

[10] Erl. Carlsson to Eric Norelius, Chicago, July 29, 1858; Ander "Some Letters Pertaining to the Proposed Minnesota Synod," p. 367.

[11] See comment in *Augustana Historical Society Publications*, X, 178 and L. P. Esbjörn to E. Norelius, Springfield, Ill., October 26, 1859, *Tidskrift, 1899*, cited in Arden, *Augustana Heritage*, p. 65. For an interesting interpreta-

tion of the issues and the role of Esbjörn, see O. Fritiof Ander, "Augustana-Kyrkan vid sitt sekelskifte," *Kyrkohistorisk årsskrift* (Stockholm), LXI, 152-55; 161-66.

[12]Erl. Carlsson, "Augustanasynodens läroanstalter. Inledning," *Jubel-Album, 1893,* pp. 123-24.

[13]Norelius, *De Svenska Lutherska . . . historia i Amerika,* I, 801-802, 809.

[14]See Norelius' comment in *Tidskrift,* 1899, pp. 291-92; Norelius, *T. N. Hasselquist. Lefnadsteckning,* p. 70.

[15]"Minutes of the Meeting of the United Chicago-Mississippi and Minnesota Conferences in Chicago, April 23-27, 1860," *Augustana Historical Society Publications,* X, 179-88, and comment in note, p. 149 for background material. O. Fritiof Ander, in his biography, *T. N. Hasselquist. The Career and Influence of a Swedish-American Clergyman, Journalist and Educator* (1931) pp. 43-44, has written: "A letter from Rev. Erland Carlsson indicates in a startling manner that he had been won by the 'New Lutheranism'." This statement is based on Carlsson's letter to Norelius Dec. 15, 1855. But neither the letter itself nor Carlsson's entire career gives evidence of attraction to S. S. Schmucker. Certainly the unorthodox Gettysburg professor would not appear to Carlsson as Gideon, in the biblical reference. Rather, Carlsson, the writer of the letter, hoped for a leader not among "the Amalekites and Midianites who dwell in the land."

[16]"Minutes of the Meeting of the United Chicago-Mississippi and Minnesota Conferences in Chicago, April 23-27, 1860, *Augustana Historical Society Publications,* X, 183.

[17]*Ibid.*

[18]Erl. Carlsson to Eric Norelius, Chicago, June 28, 1858; Ander, "Some Letters Pertaining to the Proposed Minnesota Synod," p. 363.

[19]Conrad Bergendoff, "The Sources of the Original Constitution of the Augustana Synod, 1860," *Augustana Historical Society Publications,* V (1935), 86-87. In another important article Bergendoff has emphasized that "from the Church of Sweden the Augustana Synod inherited its faith and cultus; from American Lutheranism it has acquired its polity." See Conrad Bergendoff, "The Cultural Heritage of the Augustana Synod," *The Augustana Quarterly,* XIV (October, 1935), 352.

[20]The Minutes of the Chicago and Mississippi Conferences have been translated and printed in *Augustana Historical Society Publications,* X (1944), 87-190.

[21]*Illinois-Konferensen, 1853-1903,* p. 25.

[22]Abrahamson, "Augustana-Synoden," *Jubel-Album, 1893,* pp. 75-76; *Augustana synodens protokoll,* 1870, pp. 41-42.

[23] Abrahamson, "Augustana-Synoden," *Jubel-Album, 1893,* p. 76; *Augustana synodens protokoll,* 1879, contains the constitution pp. 60-69. Eight articles in Section 8 of the constitution specify the role of the conferences, pp. 68-69.

[24] *Augustana synodens protokoll,* 1872, p. 50; 1874, p. 26.

[25] Abrahamson, "Augustana Synoden," *Jubel-Album, 1893,* p. 95.

[26] *Augustana synodens protokoll,* 1868, p. 27; 1869, pp. 38-39; 1870, p. 27. The latter reference is translated in Arden, *Augustana Heritage,* p. 152.

[27] S. E. Ochsenford, *Documentary History of the General Council of the Evangelical Lutheran Church in North America* (Philadelphia: General Council Publication House, 1912), pp. 510, 538; Evald B. Lawson, "The New York Conference of the Augustana Synod. Its Place of Founding," *Swedish Pioneer Historical Quarterly,* V (1954), 49; Abrahamson, "Doktor Erland Carlsson," *Minneskrift-Immanuelsförsamlingen,* p. 45.

8

Champion of Education

The three pioneer pastors and leading spirits in founding Swedish Lutheran congregations in America and in organizing the Augustana Synod were university graduates—T. N. Hasselquist and Erl. Carlsson from Lund and L. P. Esbjörn from Uppsala. The implications were far-reaching. Their study of theology, philosophy, languages, and related subjects had developed their intellectual resources and resulted in continuous demonstration of faith in the worth of learning. Although their university education was sometimes criticized by those who believed that the "spirit" was the primary source of power, their definite evangelical commitment, combined with intellectual strength, created respect and high level achievement.

Although Erl. Carlsson was confronted by manifold problems when he arrived in Chicago in August 1853, he initiated plans for a school within a month. On September 18, 1853, Eric Norelius, at that time a student at Capital University in Columbus, Ohio, and temporarily living with Carlsson, recorded in his diary that the pastor and he were discussing the establishment of a parochial school. Carlsson suggested that Norelius should be the teacher until his relatives arrived from Sweden. Young Norelius wrote: "Carlsson is quick in making decisions." After teaching one week he reported on October 1st that he had been teaching "a motley crowd of students." Most of them knew only one language so the young teacher at the

103

outset was confronted with using Swedish, Norwegian, and English in the classroom. He reported that, "They are an undisciplined lot, some of them are real hellions."[1]

The classes were held for several weeks in the little Norwegian Lutheran Church of the Hauge Synod, located on Chicago Avenue between Sedgwick and Townsend streets. There were about twenty students, each paying a dollar a month. The subjects included *Luther's Catechism,* Bible history, and the New Testament. Classes were held for about two months when Norelius' illness and the non-availability of space in the church interrupted the program. Early in December 1853, Norelius rented a room from a Norwegian merchant on Kinzie Avenue which served both as school room and teacher's residence. Furnishings consisted of a long table with benches on both sides, a stove, a chair, and a bed. The salary was meagre. Norelius said he lived on tea and crackers with the occasional luxury of syrup.[2]

Norelius reported in January 1854 that with Erl. Carlsson's encouragement he had decided to stay in Chicago. A new course, English for older students, was introduced. The instruction for the first ten students lasted from early morning until 5 p.m. Emphasis was devoted to Goodrich's, *Third Reader,* a simple summary of the history and geography of the United States. He described the instruction: "We read and translated every word, over and over again, carefully memorizing every detail."[3]

When Norelius left Chicago in the latter part of March 1854, he was succeeded by A. Andreen for a brief period. Andreen's successor, *Magister* Munter, West Point, Iowa, then taught the Immanuel Church school for several years. Norelius was quite likely the first school teacher among the Swedish-Americans.[4]

The early efforts to establish and maintain the school had been based on the personal initiative of Erl. Carlsson. At the congregational meeting of September 16, 1855, the church elected a school board of four members. This action was preceded by the following preparatory note: "Considering the great importance attached to the early instruction and nurture of the children in Christianity, therefore, although two previous attempts have been made to have a school, and that at great sacrifice on the part of the pastor without corresponding cooperation, the congregation is nevertheless called to meet and to consider this very important matter." The definite involvement of the congregation resulted in the construction of a two-story schoolhouse, 25 x 32 feet, in the autumn of 1856 at a cost of $600. The upper part was rented, which aided substantially in paying for the structure. This building, located near the church, later housed Augustana Seminary, 1860-63, and the Swedish Lutheran Publication Society for several years.[5]

The Immanuel Church parochial school continued to function satisfactorily, with substantial progress occurring in the late 1860s. A. P. Montén, later an Augustana pastor, was the principal teacher from 1867 to 1873. In the fall term of his first year the enrollment was thirty-five children, increasing to 150 in 1870 and 219 in 1873. The staff increased to four teachers. There was considerable difficulty in arranging instruction in English. When the evening school was established on a firm basis to provide adult education in English, a competent teacher was employed who also taught in the parochial school.[6]

Erl. Carlsson and the other supporters of the school wished to broaden the curriculum to include instruction in music, especially in piano and organ. Montén reported that it was with some fear that he approached the deacons for permission to use "the little room" for music lessons. One deacon was skeptical and said to him: "I have thought that Montén was a brother in Christ, but now, since he wants to start a music school, I do not know what to believe." But the music school became so popular that more students enrolled than could be accommodated. The doubts of the deacon had been turned to faith in the project when he urged Montén to permit his daughter to enroll. It is undoubtedly true that this early instruction in music was responsible for the acquisition of an organ, and later a piano, in many Swedish homes in Chicago.[7]

The parochial school developed by Erl. Carlsson was a response of the church to provide elementary education for the lower grades and instruction in the Bible. The addition of instruction in English for adults was a fine service to immigrants. Music instruction provided new opportunities for enriching life and was a pioneer venture for a pastor and congregation. The Immanuel School continued beyond Erl. Carlsson's pastorate in Chicago.

Leaders among the Swedish Lutheran immigrants showed their

belief in education. When the delegates to the organizing convention of the Augustana Synod, in June 1860, had completed their task, they turned immediately to the first order of business. Symbolic for the future as well as an expression of their current commitment was the founding of a Christian school to be known as Augustana Seminary.

At the sessions of the Augustana Synod on Friday, June 8, the center of interest focused on Pastor Erl. Carlsson, chairman of the committee elected in April at the meeting of the Chicago-Mississippi Conference, to prepare a constitution for the proposed Christian educational institution. Carlsson and his associates had planned effectively and worked conscientiously in writing the document which contained thirteen articles. They believed that the Christian faith which they cherished must be supported and enriched in the years ahead by a spiritual and intellectual center, which would also be a constructive influence throughout the church and play a decisive role in educating Christian pastors and teachers. Although more than two centuries separated them from the Swedish colonies founded in the era of Queen Christina in Delaware and Pennsylvania, they knew what had happened to the Lutheran faith among the descendents of their countrymen when no native source of Lutheran leaders was available.

Erl. Carlsson read carefully and explained thoroughly the articles of the proposed constitution. This was a decisive time for generations yet unborn and for the religious life of many Swedish Americans. The first three articles set forth the goals of the new institution:

> Article I. The Augustana Synod shall establish and support a theological seminary, to be called Augustana Seminary and for the present to be located in the city of Chicago.
>
> Article II. The purpose of this institution of learning shall be to educate youth for the office of the sacred ministry in the Lutheran Church, especially for those congregations that belong to the Augustana Synod, as well as to educate school teachers.
>
> Article III. This institution shall be divided into two departments, namely a preparatory and theological.

After ample discussion, the proposed constitution was unanimously adopted without change.[8]

Pastor Carlsson then proposed, and the synod adopted, a series of motions relating to the school: Since the resignation of L. P. Esbjörn as Scandinavian professor at Springfield in no way terminated the professorship, that he be elected to that position at the Chicago location; that the board of directors arrange for additional professors and tutors; that a committee be appointed to consider various aspects of financial support; that each member of the congregations be admonished to contribute twenty-five cents annually to assist needy students.[9]

When Erl. Carlsson initiated the first official action that created the institution to be known later as Augustana College and Theological Seminary, neither he nor anyone else could have foreseen the leading role that he was destined to have for more than a quarter of a century. In addition to continuous membership on the Board of Directors from 1860 to 1889, he was chairman of the board, 1860-70, 1878-82, and 1884-87. He served as treasurer 1860-68 and 1887-89, and during this latter period he was full-time business manager. In addition, he was a member and often chairman of important committees. [10]

When Esbjörn left his professorship at Springfield in March 1860, he and his family lived with the Carlssons in Chicago, Esbjörn and his host worked on plans for the new school at that time. When the Chicago-Mississippi Conference met in April, Carlsson, as indicated above, was designated as chairman of a committee to draw up a constitution for the school. His election as chairman of the Board of Directors two weeks after the organization of the synod placed him in a key position. Moreover, Carlsson's church was the "campus" of the school. When classes began in September, they met in the basement of the church. A. W. Dahlsten, a student, recounts that he lived with other students in four rooms above the schoolhouse back of Carlsson's church. A little frame house had been built near the schoolhouse where meals were provided for students. The supplies were sent in by Lutheran congregations in the conference. [11]

In an interesting report in May 1862, Carlsson tells the story of the first two years of the seminary. The first term began on September 1. Twenty students enrolled during the year but only sixteen remained to the end. Instruction was given principally by

Professor Esbjörn, assisted by Pastor Jacobsen of Chicago, and by some of the more advanced students. The curriculum included Latin, Greek, Hebrew, English, German, Swedish, and Norwegian languages; history and geography; New Testament Greek and exegetics; church history, dogmatics, symbolics, and practical theology. Five of the students were ordained at the Galesburg meeting of synod after the first year. The second school year began September 2, 1861, with seven Norwegian and six Swedish students. Only two studied theology, the others being in the preparatory department. Due to Professor Esbjörn's leave-of-absence and trip to Sweden, instruction was terminated in March. Carlsson concluded the report on an optimistic note: "With reference to the future of our institution the prospects are good and hopeful." [12]

In August 1860, before the classes had met, arrangements had been made to send Pastor O. C. T. Andrén to solicit funds in Sweden. An appeal was made to the king, to the church, and to the people. Hasselquist and Carlsson prepared a lengthy appeal which included the following:

> During more than ten years no small numbers of Sweden's children have left your shores to seek a new opportunity in the great West of America ... As newcomers we have to begin with every-thing ... But whence shall we expect this encouraging help which we in our circumstances are in such dire need, if not from brethren in the homeland to whom we can say: "We are bone of your bone, and flesh of your flesh" ... In the wide stretches of America, both in cities and in the country, are Swedes from all parts of our homeland. May we not also expect a general participation by the Swedish people in this cause? Natural love assures us of it; the importance of the cause gives us reason to hope. But we turn to you, not only as fellow countrymen, but also as brethren in the faith.

The long communication was printed in its entirety in *Wäktaren, Tidning för stat och kyrka* and in *Lunds Missions-Tidning.* Carlsson's urgent plea for the cause which Andrén represented in Sweden resulted in a four-page extra number of *Wäktaren* in November 1860, which was devoted exclusively to the needs and plans of Augustana Seminary. [13]

Carlsson wrote many letters to friends in Sweden urging support for Andrén's mission. Among those who responded enthusiastically was his good friend, Peter Wieselgren, Göteborg, where the congregations influenced by him subscribed substantial sums. When Erland in July 1861, wrote to thank Wieselgren, he described clearly the role of Augustana Seminary: "Our school is of the greatest importance for our church's future in America. If we get it well-established it will contribute mightily to the performance and future of our work." [14]

O. C. T. Andrén's fund raising in Sweden was eminently successful. The sum contributed was $10,846. One phase of the appeal had been for books, an urgent need for the new institution. The response was excellent, including about 5,000 volumes from the king's own library, containing many precious volumes that now are rare books. The collection was cataloged by Esbjörn and housed in the basement of Carlsson's church. [15]

The location of the seminary in Chicago was viewed at the outset only as a temporary arrangement. The constitution made this clear when the document stated that the school "for the present is to be located in the city of Chicago." Moreover, Erl. Carlsson, at the organizational meeting of the synod, carried a motion that provided for the appointment of a committee to select a permanent site for the seminary in an area where land would be available to establish a supporting farming community. Several possibilities were explored by Carlsson and Hasselquist—Iowa, Wisconsin, and a few places in Illinois—before the decision was made to locate at Paxton, Illinois. This action produced a division between Esbjörn who insisted on Chicago and his two associates, Carlsson and Hasselquist, who preferred Paxton and the proposed colonization project based upon an arrangement with the Illinois Central Railroad Company. Esbjörn also opposed the colonization project. [16]

When Esbjörn resigned as the only professor at the seminary in the spring of 1863 and returned to Sweden, Erl. Carlsson, chairman of the board, was faced with a serious problem. At the meeting of the Board of Directors in June 1863, Esbjörn's resignation from the faculty was accepted "with feelings of sorrow and regret and with gratitude to him for his faithful service rendered our institution and church." In the crisis situation, Pastor T. N. Hasselquist was persuaded to leave his congregation at Galesburg and agreed to become pastor at Princeton and professor at the seminary. Hasselquist's great ability and unflagging dedication was a precious resource for Augustana during his service as professor and president of the college.[17]

As chairman of the Board of Directors of Augustana Seminary, Carlsson sought diligently to engage theologians in Sweden to serve as professors. At the meeting of synod in 1861, he was authorized to contact P. P. Waldenström at Uppsala University about joining the faculty. In the following March, Carlsson and Hasselquist jointly issued a call to him "for the purpose of teaching the dead languages and such other scientific branches as may be mutually agreed upon, and, if needed, also serve our Church with the preaching of the Gospel." [18]

This invitation to a young theologian would be of only passing importance except for the fact that the call was to Waldenström, who later became famous for his theological position on the atonement which split many Augustana congregations in the 1870s and stimulated the development of Mission Friends and the Mission Covenant Church. Waldenström declined the call, at least in part, at the request of his father whose wife had passed away just prior to this time. [19]

In 1863 Erl. Carlsson wrote a long letter to Sven Libert Bring, subsequently a professor of theology at Lund University, in which was enclosed a call to become a professor at Augustana Seminary. Carlsson was again in contact with a promising theologian. He challenged Bring with the opportunity "in laying the foundation which made the assignment of incalculable significance for coming generations. . . . Our Lutheran denomination has a great future in this nation but that future will depend principally on how the foundation is built and that in turn requires that we have the right people." Carlsson emphasized that Bring's evangelical spirit and piety as well as his keen intelligence and great learning would be great assets for the seminary and church. The chairman of the board confidently described the bright prospects for the seminary in the midst of a prospective, flourishing Swedish community in the Paxton area. But he was disappointed again since Bring declined the call. [20]

Later, in August 1875, Carlsson made an earnest plea to Pastor Olof Olsson, Lindsborg, to accept the call to become a professor at Augustana. He emphasized clearly that no one else in the synod stood in the same high esteem among pastors. He suggested that if

Olsson could not accept a permanent call, he should do so for at least one year in the great emergency. He pleaded: "We need you and we want you. May the Lord give you grace to accept the call for His sake, for our school's sake, and for our Zion's sake." Olsson accepted on a one-year basis which was extended to a permanent call. [21]

The course of events proved that Paxton was not a good choice for the seminary's location. There was poor response to the sale of land with the result that the hoped-for supporting community of substantial size would not be forthcoming. After much agonizing and consultation a new beginning was made at Rock Island in 1875. This change and attendant developments involved Carlsson and his associates in time-consuming negotiations. Although there were many problems, the institution was stabilized and steady progress was achieved.

Erl. Carlsson attended hundreds of meetings of the Board of Directors and committees during his long and faithful commitment to Augustana Seminary, which in 1868 became Augustana College and Theological Seminary, reflecting broader objectives and greater academic outreach. Matters of finance were always a matter of great concern and Carlsson worked hard personally and with others to achieve greater financial stability for an expanding program. His reports to synod were complete and detailed. There was a constant theme which emphasized the critical role of Augustana in the present and future. Typical is the thrust of his opening words in the report of 1879: "The college at Rock Island is the synod's most important institution since it is from this place of learning that our pastors will go forth to serve our congregations and where our people generally will acquire their higher education and insight for right living and thinking across the years." [22]

The chairman of the board always recognized the role of good teaching as related to capable faculty members. In 1879 he announced with pride that Dr. Joshua Lindahl had joined the faculty during the past academic year as teacher of mathematics and natural science. Lindahl, a doctor of philosophy, had been a docent at Lund University, had participated in important scientific expeditions and had resided in the United States since 1875 as secretary of the Swedish section of the World's Exposition in Philadelphia. He reported to the synod that Dr. Lindahl had already "won the esteem of his colleagues and students." [23]

Carlsson fully understood the supreme importance of Augustana as the center for the religious, cultural, and intellectual life of Swedish Americans as they sought to make their contribution to the great symphony of American life. Study of his reports as chairman of the Board of Directors indicate clearly his respect for learning and his urgent concern to provide the best possible faculty. The board cooperated effectively with President Hasselquist and the faculty in providing a fine course of study that emphasized the best in the classical tradition of the homeland while also responding to changes in rapidly developing America.

The need for instruction related closely to the American scene is interestingly shown in Carlsson's report to synod in 1879: "The directors have established the principle for the future to engage teachers as far as possible who have been educated among us here in this country. Such people already know our situation and our conditions and with intimate ties and warm interest are attached to our people, our denomination, and our school." He cited what the board had in mind in the case of C. M. Esbjörn, a talented person who would study at the University of Pennsylvania, and then return as a teacher at Augustana. [24]

The involvement of Erl. Carlsson in the physical development of the college was continuous and extensive. In October 1875, he participated in the dedication of the not yet completed first building on what was called "the gentle slope" of the new property in Rock Island. "Jubilee Hall," dedicated in 1883, although largely the creation of Olof Olsson and the Oratorio Society, had the hearty support of Carlsson. He was chairman of the board during the years of great discouragement and struggle that resulted finally in 1889 in the dedication of "Memorial Hall," the majestic and excellent multi-purpose building which still graces a widely expanded campus with all that the name "Old Main" means to generations of Augustana students and friends. [25]

Erl. Carlsson's last official service to Augustana College and Theological Seminary was as business manager and treasurer from 1887 to 1889, following his resignation as pastor at Andover for reasons of poor health. In spite of physical handicaps, he carried on effectively and courageously in managing and developing finances, planning for buildings and the campus, and the many other demands of the position. In the midst of an uncertain future for the struggling institution, he had written, in November 1862, to Eric Norelius: "I love Augustana Seminary. I have worked and sacrificed for it joyfully and I will do so as long as the Lord grants me life and strength." His love for Augustana College and Seminary never lessened and his devotion never faltered. His name is written large in the annals of Augustana's history. [26]

The uncertain future of Augustana was translated into magnificent achievement because of the dedication and action of the founders and their associates. Dr. Conrad Bergendoff, distinguished president emeritus, theologian and college historian has accurately described the situation:

> Only the faith and persistence of Hasselquist as professor and Erl. Carlsson as chairman of the board explain the vitality of the hope that carried the school through the pioneer days. They saw it not as a struggling college and seminary but as an indispensable part of a church which was seeking to gather thousands of Swedish immigrants into a strong and living community of faith. Only a living Lutheran church could hold the immigrants together and make them a healthy contribution to American society.[27]

Moreover, Dr. Bergendoff has emphasized an issue that was decisive in the struggle by Carlsson, Hasselquist, and their associates in behalf of Augustana: "Leadership for such a church would have to be created in this country. Augustana was the instrument by which the spiritual culture of the homeland could be translated and transfused into the life of the new nation. The resources of these latter-day Pilgrims must be concentrated on the building of a strong intellectual center."[28]

Erl. Carlsson's contemporaries also recognized the results of his constant labor and devotion to higher education and the church. One notable occasion was commencement at Augustana in 1892. There was deep and abiding love—and a flood of memories and gratitude—as three distinguished pioneer pastors and leaders were presented for honorary degrees of Doctor of Divinity. Erl. Carlsson was the oldest in point of service—four decades, followed by Eric Norelius and Olof Olsson. This was indeed a festive occasion. Never before or since in the annals of the Swedes in America have a trio been simultaneously recognized for such distinguished achievements. The real meaning of their individual and aggregate contribution is known only in the sure knowledge of God. [29]

A final and singularly important testimony of Erl. Carlsson's contribution to Christian education received eloquent expression in a resolution passed by the Augustana faculty at the time of his death in 1893. "We record our sincere conviction that Augustana College and Theological Seminary has lost one of its best friends, one to whom more than to any other single individual this institution owes its success and prosperity."[30]

FOOTNOTES

[1] Arden, *Journals of Eric Norelius*, p. 129.

[2] Erl. Carlsson, *Korsbaneret*, 1882, p. 157; Norelius, "Dr. E. Norelii hågkomster från 1853," *Minneskrift-Immanuelsförsamlingen, 1853-1903*, p. 78; Arden, *Journals of Eric Norelius*, p. 130-131.

[3] Arden, *Journals of Eric Norelius*, p. 131; Norelius, "Dr. E. Norelii hågkomster från 1853," p. 79.

[4] Erl. Carlsson, *Korsbaneret*, 1882, p. 158.

[5] "Minutes of the Meeting of the Swedish Lutheran Church, Chicago, September 16, 1855," *Augustana Historical Society Publications*, XI, 12; Erl. Carlsson, *Korsbaneret*, 1882, p. 158.

[6] "Brev från A. P. Montén," *Minneskrift-Immanuelsförsamlingen, 1853-1903*, pp. 89-90; Beijbom, *Swedes in Chicago*, p. 257.

[7] "Brev från A. P. Montén," *Minneskrift-Immanuelsförsamlingen, 1853-1903*, p. 90; Beijbom, *Swedes in Chicago*, p. 257.

[8] Conrad Bergendoff, *Augustana. A Profession of Faith*, p. 20; *Augustana synodens protokoll*, 1860, p. 5. A copy of the original constitution of Augustana Seminary is found in *Augustana synodens protokoll*, 1860, pp. 24-25.

[9] *Augustana synodens protokoll*, 1860, pp. 5-6.

[10] Norelius, *De Svenska Lutherska . . . historia i Amerika*, I, 435-36.

[11] G. A. Andreen, "The Story of Augustana College and Theological Seminary," *"After Seventy-Five Years, 1860-1935* (Rock Island: Augustana Book Concern, 1935), pp. 30-31.

[12] Erl. Carlsson, "The Scandinavian Lutheran Augustana Seminary in Chicago

Illinois," Oscar N. Olson, *Olof Christian Telemak Andrén: Ambassador of Good Will*, Augustana Historical Society Publications, XIV (1954), pp. 92-95. This report was sent to the minister of ecclesiastical affairs in Sweden as information at the suggestion of Andrén.

[13]O. N. Olson, *O. C. T. Andrén*, pp. 87-88; *Wäktaren. Tidning för stat och kyrka* (Stockholm), November, 1860; *Lunds Missions-Tidning* (Lund), December, 1860.

[14]Erl. Carlsson to Peter Wieselgren, Chicago, July 12, 1861, Westin, *Emigranterna och kyrkan*, p. 104.

[15]*Augustana synodens protokoll*, 1864, pp. 12-13; *Augustana Historical Society Publications*, V, 134.

[16]Bergendoff, *Augustana. A Profession of Faith*, pp. 25-26.

[17]Bergendoff, *Augustana. A Profession of Faith*, pp. 26-29; "Minutes of the Board of Directors, June 23, 1863."

[18]*Augustana synodens protokoll*, 1861, p. 30; G. Everett Arden, *The School of the Prophets. The Background and History of Augustana Theological Seminary, 1860-1960*, p. 127; *The Augustana Journal* (Rock Island), October 1, 1902. This journal printed an English translation of the call which had been sent to Waldenström.

[19]"Minutes of Board of Directors, December 10, 1862;" Bergendoff, *Augustana. A Profession of Faith*, p. 33.

[20]Erl. Carlsson to S. L. Bring, Chicago, October 7, 1863; "Minutes of Board of Directors, June 14, 1864;" Bergendoff, *Augustana. A Profession of Faith*, p. 33.

[21]Erl. Carlsson to Olof Olsson, Andover, Ill., August 25, 1875.

[22]*Augustana synodens protokoll*, 1879, p. 21.

[23]*Ibid.*, p. 22.

[24]*Ibid.*, p. 23.

[25]Bergendoff, *Augustana. A Profession of Faith*, pp. 49, 65-67.

[26]Erl. Carlsson to Eric Norelius, Chicago, November 26, 1862.

[27]Bergendoff, *Augustana. A Profession of Faith*, p. 32.

[28]*Ibid.*, pp. 32-33.

[29]Forsander, *Lifsbilder*, I, 124.

[30]Bergendoff, *Augustana. A Profession of Faith*, p. 91.

First (1875) and Second (1888) Old Main
Buildings, Augustana College

Carlsson Hall (1928) Augustana College

9

Promoter of the
Printed Word

Erl. Carlsson's varied areas of service to the church included his devotion to and belief in the importance of the printed word. The first discussion of the possibility of publishing a newspaper among the Swedish immigrants in Illinois apparently occurred at the meeting of the Synod of Northern Illinois at Galesburg in October, 1853. On the basis of a letter from Hasselquist to Erl. Carlsson in November of that year, this preliminary discussion envisaged Chicago as the place of publication and Carlsson as the editor and publisher: "Have you given any thought to the proposed Swedish newspaper? I hear many express a longing for such a one, especially for complete news from the home country. You must not put the matter out of mind, for we must seek to free our people from immoral and unchurchly papers. May the Lord send you courage." Late in December, Hasselquist wrote again to Carlsson: "Have you given further thought to the publication of a newspaper? We must risk a sample issue, but I am sure it will carry itself. I still maintain that if you do not take the journalistic field, someone of the proselyting power will do so, to the detriment of our congregations."[1]

The projected responsibility of publishing a newspaper was thrust upon Erl. Carlsson after a residency in America of less than three months. Events showed that he could not carry out the assignment. But the expectation continued, largely because Chicago seemed to be the most logical place. On January 30, 1854,

Hasselquist once more implored Carlsson to take action: "Have you got the paper (*Svenska Posten* it might be named) started yet? There is such a constant inquiry for it, that you would hardly believe it. . . . But I must now close with a loud call for the paper."[2]

In March Esbjörn was also urging Carlsson to act: "If there is anything over from the collection [Hasselquist and Esbjörn had each collected $5 for printing the Conference Minutes], use it for a specimen copy of *Svenska Posten.* We must arrange to get it started while there is time. If we delay, the opportunity will slip out of our hands." Esbjörn in this letter also referred to the possibility that the proposed Swedish paper might be published in conjunction with the Norwegian *Kirketidende,* but he believed that a supplement to that publication would not be pleasing to the Swedes. Esbjörn's concern was further apparent when he wrote to Hasselquist: "How is that prospect getting along? Is it about ready? You must force Carlsson to issue a specimen copy of *Svenska Posten.* It should not be delayed longer."[3]

Some uncertainty as to what might happen is apparent from a letter that Esbjörn wrote to Carlsson on October 6, 1854: "It is fine that you are thinking about the Swedish newspaper. May it have success! But Hasselquist is in the process of publishing a specimen issue. By all means write to him about the matter, so that competition and confusion will not occur. If your strength permits, Chicago will be a more suitable place than Galesburg."[4]

Apparently some understanding was reached between Hasselquist and Erl. Carlsson whereby the former would assume responsibility for the first issue of the Swedish newspaper. It is understandable that it was not possible for Carlsson to do it. The immense demands upon him as a new pastor in Chicago were augmented by pressing problems during the cholera epidemic in 1854. Moreover, he had been afflicted with the illness and had been forced to retire to Geneva for several weeks. In any event, when Esbjörn wrote to Norelius on December 23, 1854, he stated: "About *Svenska Posten* I know as little as you do. Hasselquist had not returned at the time of the Conference [He was on a trip to New York]. . . . Hopefully he has fortunately returned and immediately proceeds with *Posten* so that it can come out at New Years."[5]

Esbjörn's wish became a reality, on January 3, 1855, when the first issue of the Swedish paper appeared with the name *Hemlandet, det gamla och det nya* (Homeland, The Old and The New), published and edited by Hasselquist at Galesburg. It is reported that Carlsson suggested this more appropriate and distinctive name to replace *Svenska Posten.* Several issues were printed at Knoxville, before Hasselquist was able to set up a little print shop in his home at Galesburg in March 1855.[6]

On February 2, 1855, Hasselquist wrote a long and interesting letter to Carlsson about the newspaper. He had been expecting a few lines from the latter, especially after the first issue of *Hemlandet* had reached him. Moreover, Hasselquist was disappointed that the Chicago pastor had sent no material for publication in *Hemlandet.* He then wrote frankly, declaring: "I cannot possibly single-handed write all that is required for the paper, although it is not large." He lamented the fact that the type, which he purchased in New York, had not yet arrived, with the result that the cost of printing was twice as much as he had expected: "So here I stand helpless, not knowing what to do. You must exert yourself to the utmost to get an issue printed at Chicago. I have plenty manuscripts on hand."[7]

The above correspondence indicates that Hasselquist was not trying to dominate the publication of the Swedish newspaper and that he actively sought the cooperation of Erl. Carlsson. The latter was not able to respond affirmatively. The crisis for the present was met. Hasselquist continued to publish the newspaper in Galesburg until 1858, and Carlsson cooperated with him. *Hemlandet* was launched and served Swedish Americans well and faithfully until it was merged with *Svenska Amerikanaren* in 1914, thus losing its identity.

A development took place in 1858 which was destined to involve Erl. Carlsson in publication activities for many years. Background information is found in the minutes of the meeting of the Mississippi Conference at Galesburg in April 1858: "Since Pastor Hasselquist, in consequence of his many pastoral duties, wishes to be relieved at least from the chief management of the paper, and as the Conference wishes that both the paper and the printing plant might be not only of permanence for the future, but also more inclusive and fruitful for our church and people, therefore, resolved that a regular publishing society under the name of the Swedish Lutheran

Publication Society of the United States be organized." The next paragraph stated the following: "The purpose of the society shall be not only to continue the newspaper, *Hemlandet,* but also to enlarge the printing plant and to handle and circulate useful books in general and especially Christian books, preferably of the Lutheran confession."[8]

The prime-mover in this development, in view of Hasselquist's wish to be relieved of the publication responsibility, was Erl. Carlsson. He was designated chairman of the committee to draw up a permanent constitution and to provide for legal matters under the laws of the State of Illinois. *Minnesota Posten,* a newspaper started by Norelius in Red Wing in 1857, was merged with *Hemlandet* in 1858. *Det Rätta Hemlandet* (The True Homeland) a monthly religious journal, founded by Hasselquist in 1857, also became the responsibility of the society. The new publication society started business the first week in January 1859. The society was incorporated in February of that year. The school room in Immanuel Church and a room in the second story of the congregation's schoolhouse were rented for $100 during the year. When the church was enlarged, two rooms in the basement were used.[9]

When Eric Norelius withdrew as editor after nine months, full responsibility for the management of all of the affairs of the society fell upon Erl. Carlsson. Jonas Engberg served as editor until November 1864, when A. R. Cervin, Hasselquist's brother-in-law, assumed editorial responsibilities. His successor was P. A. Sundelius who held the position until 1869 when John A. Enander began his long and distinguished career as editor. In 1860, when the Augustana Synod was founded, the publication society membership consisted of all Swedish clergy of the synod and all lay delegates to the synodical convention. [10]

Erl. Carlsson rendered great service to the publication society for a decade beginning in 1858. The printing office was housed in the basement of Immanuel Church until 1870, when it was moved to rented quarters at 139 North Clark Street. Carlsson never received compensation for his many services to the society. Although the publications were not numerous, the list indicates their great importance: Luther's *Catechism, Psalmbok, Kyrko-handbok* and *Hemlandssånger.* Erl. Carlsson's leadership as chairman of the catechism committee as well as principal editor of the *Catechism* and the great popularity of this edition has been discussed in the context of his direct contribution to the Augustana Synod. [11]

A lasting contribution to the Augustana Synod was made by Carlsson's decisive contribution in providing the official *Psalmbok* which established a permanent pattern of worship and hymnody with only modest changes across the years. As early as 1854, in his *Emigrant Guide,* he wrote for those planning the journey to America: "When buying Psalmbooks, the Thomander-Wieselgren edition (1849) is preferred, especially since here in this country it is beginning to be used with predilection by our countrymen and it is very likely that it will displace the one generally used in the homeland."[12]

The reference in the last part of the sentence above is to the *Psalmbok* by Johan Olof Wallin, published in 1819. Ardent *läsare* and other evangelicals sharing their view felt that the Wallin *Psalmbok,* although containing many fine hymns, was too rationalistic. Erl. Carlsson's close identification with Peter Wieselgren was undoubtedly a factor in his preference for the Thomander-Wieselgren volume. Moreover, Arvid Arvastan, who has written a classic volume on the Thomander-Wieselgren *Psalmbok,* pointed out: "In Chicago, Pastor Carlsson became pastor of a small immigrant congregation who consisted in a large part of disciples of *Smålandsläsare* (Småland pietists) of the Sellergren type and Hoovianer [followers of Jacob Otto Hoof] from Västergötland. He found from the outset that the aforesaid Thomander-Wieselgren *Psalmbok* was well-suited to disarm the opposition and distrust which both groups held towards the Wallin psalmbook." [13]

Carlsson as chairman of the Board of Directors of the Swedish Lutheran Publication Society was in a strategic position to influence the choice of the official *Psalmbok* of the Augustana Synod. In 1863 the synod decided to print the Thomander-Wieselgren volume and adopted it for use within the synod. This action pleased Erl. Carlsson, although he was faced with several problems before the project was completed. In a letter to Norelius in December 1864, he expressed regret about delays in the binding of the book: "If our friends knew how much work and worry I have had they would not only excuse us, but they would all the more sympathize with us. I cannot tell you how much trouble and distress I have had relative to the *Psalmbok* and how much embarrassment and annoyance the wretched bookbinder has caused." It was not until 1865 that he could report that the books had been received from the bookbinder. He had advanced $1,000 of his own money to make possible the printing of the volume. A second edition was published in 1871. [14]

Arvid Arvastan has written that the decisive role of the Thomander-Wieselgren *Psalmbok* in the worship services of the Augustana Synod is in a high degree due to Erl. Carlsson: "He stands out as the one who made the impact of greatest importance. He had at that time a firmer churchly attitude than Hasselquist or Esbjörn and was animated by a stronger feeling for the traditional. He, moreover, of the four founders [Esbjörn, Hasselquist, Jonas Swensson, Erl. Carlsson] had the liveliest relationship with Wieselgren." [15]

Although the *Psalmbok* constituted the principal source of hymns for worship services, additional publications were also available. As early as 1856 Hasselquist published at his Svenska Boktryckeriet at Galesburg, fifty of Oskar Ahnfelt's *Andliga Sånger*. The need for a more comprehensive collection of hymns was soon recognized. This became a project of the publication society. *Hemlandssånger* (Songs of the Homeland) containing 240 hymns was published in 1860. [16]

Arvid Arvastan has written about the planning of this hymn book: "Although several people it appears were involved in gathering material for this book, it was Erl. Carlsson and T. N. Hasselquist, who finally assembled the hymns and decided what should be included." This scholar has also pointed out that the publication of *Hemlandssånger* the same year as the founding of the Augustana Synod was of monumental significance: "The free and deeply spiritual hymns which this collection presented were destined to give a permanent color to the Augustana Synod." In 1866 a second edition with 413 hymns was published, and a third edition in 1892 contained 500 hymns. [17]

The promotion of good literature was another service emphasized by Erl. Carlsson as manager of the Swedish Lutheran Publication Society. He has been described appropriately in this context: "Erl. Carlsson stands out among the founders of the Augustana Synod as the one who worked hardest in order to provide suitable Swedish literature for the immigrants." One important factor was his acquaintanceship from university years with C. W. Gleerup, Lund, the famous bookseller and publisher. Gleerup assisted Carlsson in contacting other bookmen in Sweden, who also supplied books under favorable terms. Pastors served as agents in selling books without commission on sales. Henry Ludwig, a book dealer in New York, served as commissioner for the society. [18]

The problems confronting Carlsson in his responsibility with the publication society were many and he described them in a letter to a friend in January 1866:

> That our friends are tempted to impatience and dissatisfaction with the management of the affairs of our society does not surprise me. . . . I have reason to be annoyed to death. We are almost out of books. We have only a few copies of the catechism in Esbjörn's translation. We need nothing as much as a catechism. *Hemlands-sånger* [the second edition] was set in type in March, so the type can [now] be set for the catechism. . . . But we need money. I have advanced $1000 for the *Psalmbok;* have not received half of it in repayment. The *Psalmbok* has been sent out but not half of the brethren paid for their copies. In order to publish *Hemlandssånger* at least the same sum will be required. I cannot any longer advance money. The brethren must help. [19]

The affairs of the society seemed to be developing favorably in the next few years. A fine building on North Clark Street was rented in 1870; it provided for the bookstore in the front and the printing plant in the rear. But the prospects were dramatically changed in October 1871, when the bookstore, printing plant, and all contents were destroyed by the ravaging fire. The assets at that time were listed as $18,000 with $10,000 insurance. Only $5,000 was recovered since the insurance company went bankrupt as the result of the multitudinous losses in the Chicago fire. Carlsson and his associates arranged to have *Hemlandet* printed temporarily at a German print shop in Aurora. Twelve large boxes of books were in New York and escaped the fire, thus furnishing the nucleus for a new bookstore. It was temporarily located on Milwaukee Avenue and then moved to Chicago Avenue. [20]

However, difficult times were ahead for the society. Dr. E. W. Olson has identified the problems: "The great losses caused by the

Chicago fire; the limited market for Swedish newspapers and books; conflict between the church and non-church elements; discontent because the society had not produced adequate profit; and the attack by individuals." [21]

At the meeting of the synod at Galesburg in October 1872, it was decided to turn over the assets and activities of the publication society to the Board of Directors of Augustana College and Theological Seminary. *Hemlandet* was sold to John A. Enander and J. A. Bohman in 1872 for $10,000, payable in semi-annual installments of $750. It was also agreed that the Board of Directors would not publish another political newspaper as long as *Hemlandet* was published as specified in the bill of sale. This agreement was ratified by the synod. The board sold its publications, copyrights and stock of books in 1874 for the sum of $17,000, payable in semi-annual installments, to Jonas Engberg, Charles P. Holmberg, and Rev. C. O. Lindell. The new firm took over a stock of books valued at about $12,000, debts totalling $11,000, and book accounts of $4,700. [22]

Eric Norelius has described these developments as they relate to Erl. Carlsson:

> What meanwhile made Erl. Carlsson tired and sad was the criticism of the Publication Society, which did not cease until the goal had been achieved—its dissolution. *Hemlandet, det gamla och det nya* was sold in 1872 and the bookstore in 1874 for a sum of $27,000. One must realize that this was the fruit of Carlsson's long, non-salaried and persevering work; but he has received little recognition for it.

Pastor P. Sjöblom of Minnesota was the leader of the agitation against the publication society. [23]

The dissolution of the publication society eliminated direct ownership and control by the Augustana Synod until 1889. What transpired is a long and involved story which is beyond the scope of this study. Erl. Carlsson never served on the Board of Directors of successor publication companies. [24]

Erl. Carlsson, champion of higher education, had the satisfaction of knowing that the assets of the defunct publication society went to Augustana College and Theological Seminary at a critical time in its history. In the decade beginning with 1873, Augustana

College received an annual income of $1,000 from the sale of *Hemlandet.* Additional funds were made available when the bookstore was sold. Dr. E. W. Olson provides an interpretation of the importance of this development: "It is fair to assume that without substantial income for the school secured by the sale of *Hemlandet* and the bookstore, printing office and publishing rights of the Synod, its college and seminary could hardly have been maintained and would have been still less likely to establish itself in Rock Island during the financial crisis of 1873 and the following years." Although this may be an overdramatization of the facts, it is nevertheless true that the income from the assets of the publication society provided substantial financial assistance to the institution at a critical time. [25]

Carlsson had early understood the need of providing information for prospective immigrants. While in Liverpool, enroute to America, he had addressed a letter to "My Countrymen," which was published in *Borås Tidning, Nya Wexjö-Bladet,* and elsewhere, in which he made several suggestions. He received many letters in America from people in the homeland who asked many questions. In August 1853, Jöns Swensson, from Stora Beddinge, listed eleven specific questions. In March 1854, *Komminister* S. Stenwall in Berga had written: "I should like to read a true description of America. Why don't you Swedish ministers get together and put down the actual facts and a full account of conditions and send it here?" In January 1854, at a meeting of the Chicago-Mississippi Conference at Chicago, Erl. Carlsson had been appointed member of a committee "to draw up a statement which might serve as a guide for emigrants in regard both to spiritual and temporal matters." [26]

The earliest publication by Erl. Carlsson, "Some Advice and Information for Immigrants to the United States," appeared in 1854. It was dated April 24 and was published in *Nya Wexjö-Bladet,* May 26-June 2, 1854. It also was published in *Norrlands-Posten,* August 7-17, and *Hwad Nytt,* June 9-13, in the same year. The background of the publication is described in a letter from H. S. Cederschiöld, editor and publisher of *Nya Wexjö-Bladet,* to Erl. Carlsson, October 22, 1854: "I at once published your communication in my newspaper and in addition I had the account printed in the form of a small brochure, copies of which I sent to Kalmar, Karlshamn,

Göteborg, and Jönköping, so it has been widely circulated. Pre-
sumably it has already been shown to you by arriving immigrants." 27

Since "Some Advice and Information for Emigrants to the
United States of America" by Erl. Carlsson, and translated by O. V.
Anderson, is included in an appendix to this volume, only a brief
summary is presented at this point. Carlsson took no sides in the
matter of immigration: "Concerning immigration, I believe that one
cannot endorse nor advise against it unconditionally." He was
concerned that, "It is undertaken by the great majority so
thoughtlessly and without plans." Several aspects of immigration
were discussed: The route or possible routes to be taken to America;
food that should be purchased for the trip across the Atlantic;
clothing that should be acquired; the time of year best suited for the
voyage; activity on the ship during the trip; Swedish books that
should be purchased before leaving Sweden; the exchange of money;
the best routes beyond New York to settlements in the western
states; etc. Carlsson's guide was published in an expanded edition at
Karlshamn, also in 1854. 28

The title of the new edition was "Detailed Advice and
Information for Immigrants to America." The four sections were: I.
Advice and information. II. Announcements about money, food,
weights, provisions for the trip, etc. III. Excerpts of letters from
resident Swedes in America. IV. Word list. The first section was a
verbatim reproduction of the first Erl. Carlsson guide. The publisher of the new forty-eight page guide was Ludwig Lindgrens
Bokhandel, Karlshamn. New and comparative information was
provided for money exchange, weights and measurements, food
requirements, etc. The word list included approximately 200 items.
The Swedish words, English equivalents, and the English pronunciation based upon Swedish sounds were provided "so that one can
learn upon arrival in America to make himself understood when one
needs food, drink, housing, medicine, work, etc." Two letters from
Swedes in America in 1853 were presented: one from La Fayette,
Indiana, the other from Feliciana, Kentucky. The latter described in
considerable detail the conditions and opportunities in America. 29

FOOTNOTES

[1] Norelius, *T. N. Hasselquist. Lefnadsteckning,* p. 43; T. N. Hasselquist to Erl. Carlsson, Galesburg, Ill., November 15, 1853 and December 22, 1853, Ernst W. Olson, "Early Letters of Erland Carlsson," *Augustana Historical Society Publications,* V (1935), 111.

[2] T. N. Hasselquist to Erl. Carlsson, Galesburg, Ill., January 30, 1854, E. W. Olson, "Early Letters of Erland Carlsson," p. 112.

[3] L. P. Esbjörn to Erl. Carlsson, Andover, Ill., March 7, 1854, *Tidskrift,* 1899, pp. 260-61; L. P. Esbjörn to Erl. Carlsson, Andover, Ill., April 20, 1854, *Ibid.,* p. 262.

[4] L. P. Esbjörn to Erl. Carlsson, Andover, Ill., October 6, 1854, *Ibid.,* p. 267.

[5] L. P. Esbjörn to Eric Norelius, Andover, Ill., December 23, 1854; *Ibid.,* p. 271.

[6] Ernst W. Olson, "Augustana Book Concern: Publishers to the Augustana Synod. History of Activities Since 1889, with an Introductory Account of Earlier Publishing Enterprises," *Augustana Historical Society Publications,* III, 4; Ernst W. Olson, *En bokhandels historia,* p. 7.

[7] T. N. Hasselquist to Erl. Carlsson, Galesburg, Ill., February 2, 1855, E. W. Olson, "Early Letters to Erland Carlsson," pp. 127-28.

[8] "Minutes of the Meeting of the Mississippi Conference, Galesburg, Ill., April 21-24, 1858," I. O. Nothstein (ed.), "Selected Documents . . . ," *Augustana Historical Society Publications,* X (1944), Part 1, 137-38.

[9] "Minutes of Meeting of Mississippi Conference, Galesburg, Ill., April 21-24, 1858," *Ibid.,* X, 138; E. W. Olson, "Augustana Book Concern," *Ibid.,* III (1933), 7-8.

[10] E. W. Olson, *En bokhandels historia,* pp. 29-30; E. W. Olson, "Augustana Book Concern," *Augustana Historical Society Publications,* III (1933), 8; E. E. Ryden, "Early Publication Ventures," Nystrom, *A Family of God,* pp. 88-89; Nystrom, *A Ministry of Printing,* pp. 11-12.

[11] E. W. Olson, "Augustana Book Concern," *Augustana Historical Society Publications,* III, 8-9; *Missionären, Svensk Luthersk missionstidning* (Rock Island), January 1876-June 1878. Carlsson served with A. G. Setterdahl as co-editor of *Missionären* for two and one-half years from its founding in January 1876.

[12] O. V. Anderson (trans.), "Erland Carlsson's Immigrant Guide," *The Augustana Quarterly,* XXVII (April 1948), 155.

[13] Allan Arvastan, *Den Thomander-Wieselgrenska psalmboken* (Stockholm: Svenska kyrkans diakonistyrelses bokförlag, 1949), p. 185.

[14]Arvastan, *Den Thomander-Wieselgrenska psalmboken,* p. 192; Erl. Carlsson to Eric Norelius, Chicago, December 3, 1864, and January 19, 1865, E. W. Olson, *En bokhandels historia,* pp. 35-36.

[15]Arvastan, *Den Thomander-Wieselgrenska psalmboken,* p. 184.

[16]*Ibid.,* p. 183.

[17]Arvastan, *Thomander-Wieselgrenska psalmboken,* p. 183; Oscar N. Olson, *The Augustana Lutheran Church in America. Pioneer Period 1846 to 1860* emphasizes the role of Jonas Engberg in editing *Hemlandssånger,* p. 369; C. A. Swensson, "Augustanasynodens förlaggare verksamhet," *Jubel-Album 1893,* p. 245. Swensson points that 30,000 copies of *Hemlandssånger* were sold within a few years.

[18]Arvastan, *Thomander-Wieselgrenska psalmboken,* p. 183; C. A. Swensson, "Augustanasynodens förlaggare verksahmet," *Jubel-Album 1893,* p. 244; Nystrom, *A Ministry of Printing,* p. 11.

[19]Erl. Carlsson to a friend, Chicago, January 9, 1866. Carlsson's reference to a proposed catechism relates to the fact that plans, tracing their origin to 1862, to publish a catechism manuscript prepared by E. Norelius and G. Peters never materialized. It was not until 1868 that a translation by Peter Fjellstedt was printed. See E. W. Olson, *En bokhandels historia,* p. 40.

[20]C. A. Swensson, "Augustanasynodens förlaggare verksamhet," *Jubel-Album 1893,* pp. 244-45; Nystrom, *A Ministry of Printing,* p. 13.

[21]E. W. Olson, "Augustana Book Concern," *Augustana Historical Society Publications,* III, 8-9.

[22]E. W. Olson, "Augustana Book Concern," pp. 8-9; *Augustana synodens protokoll,* 1873, pp. 19-20; 1874, pp. 19-20; 1875, p. 40; Norelius, *De Svenska Lutherska . . . historia i Amerika,* I, 435. Norelius is in error when he states that *Hemlandet* was sold in 1873. Hasselquist states officially that it "was sold towards the end of last year [1872]." *Augustana synodens protokoll,* 1873, p. 19.

[23]O. V. Holmgrain, "Augustana-synodens förlagsverksamhet," *Minneskrift med anledning af Augustana-synodens femtioåriga tillvaro, 1860-1910,* pp. 298-99.

[24]For a discussion of these developments, see E. W. Olson, "Augustana Book Concern," pp. 12-80.

[25]*Ibid.,* p. 11.

[26]See Chapter II, pp. 19-20, Jöns Swensson to Erland Carlsson, Stora Beddinge, August 2, 1853, and S. Stenwall to Erland Carlsson, Berga, March 1, 1854, E. W. Olson, "Some Early Letters to Erland Carlsson," pp. 109-11 and pp.

113-17. The action by the Chicago-Mississippi Conference is found in *Augustana Historical Society Publications,* X, 95.

[27]O. V. Anderson, "Erland Carlsson's Immigrant Guide," *The Augustana Quarterly,* XXVII (April, 1948), 162; H. S. Cederschiöld to Erland Carlsson, Växjö, October 22, 1854, E. W. Olson, "Early Letters to Erland Carlsson," p. 125. *The Augustana Quarterly* includes an "Introduction" and a translation of Carlsson's immigrant guide by O. V. Anderson, pp. 149-63. See appendix of this volume.

[28]Anderson, "Erland Carlsson's Immigrant Guide," pp. 151-52 and *passim,* pp. 153-63. O. Fritiof Ander, *The Cultural Heritage of the Swedish Immigrant. Selected References* (Rock Island: Augustana Library Publications, no. 27, 1956), p. 38. The Swedish title of the first guide is: *Några råd och underrättelser för utwandrare till Amerikas Förenta Stater* (Wexjö: H. S. Cederschiöld, 1854).

[29]The Swedish title for the second edition is: *Tillforlitliga råd och underrättelser för utvandrare till Amerika* (Carlshamn: Ludvig Lindgrens bokhandel, 1854).

Eva Charlotta Carlsson

Eben, Annie, Samuel and Emmy Carlsson

Annie Carlsson

Emmy Carlsson Evald

10

Leadership in the
Augustana Synod

On Tuesday afternoon, June 5, 1860, in the frame Norwegian
Lutheran Church at Jefferson Prairie, near Clinton, Wisconsin, Erland
Carlsson was one of eighteen pastors and fourteen lay delegates who
signed the register at the meeting which organized the Scandinavian Evangelical Augustana Lutheran Synod. The meeting
had been called to order by Pastor T. N. Hasselquist who had
preached the sermon on Rev. 2:1-7: "Our Work, Our Fears,
and Our Victory." Following the election of Hasselquist as president, pastors and laymen of forty-nine Swedish and Norwegian
congregations, with 4,967 communicant members, adopted a synodical constitution and turned to the business of the day.[1]

The momentous consequences of this action for the future of
Swedish American culture is difficult to describe adequately in view
of the predominant influence of Augustana Lutherans among the
Swedish immigrants and their children. The time element was
crucial—continued involvement with groups in the American Lutheran church might have made this declaration of independence an
impossibility a decade later. In Minnesota, as early as 1858, there had
been considerable discussion about the possibility of the Swedish
churches in that area joining a newly created German Lutheran
synod. The passing of the years would have been accompanied
necessarily by accommodation to the dominant religious *ethos* and
organization. This early loss of identity would have had far-reaching,

limiting effects on the unique piety, congregational life, church polity, educational interests, and language of the immigrants and their children. An independent college and seminary, and later, other colleges, centers for creative spiritual and intellectual life, dynamic sources for perpetuating and enriching the tradition, would have been unlikely. The influence of the Swedish language church-press would have been curtailed. What is conveyed in the words, "the Augustana tradition" would never have attained its historic potential. Certain aspects of Americanization, like earlier use of the English language, might have been speeded up, but the resources of Swedish American contributions to American pluralism have offset this possible gain.

Although Erl. Carlsson may not have fully sensed the long-range implications of the formation of the new synod, he fully realized some of the vital consequences. In a letter to Peter Wieselgren a month prior to the events at Jefferson Prairie, but in full confidence that the synod would be founded, he wrote as follows: "We have taken an important step. The consequences will reach into future generations. We are in great difficulty presently. We will no longer have the temporal help which we heretofore have received from the Americans and we must attempt to establish a school for the instruction and education of our future pastors. Funds are required for that purpose and in our eyes it seems very dark. But the Lord in whose fear we acted and in whose name we work and struggle is mighty in opening doors, when we see no way out, as well as in building and supporting His kingdom and His truth among us."[2]

When Erl. Carlsson cast his vote for the organization of the Augustana Synod, he took the first step in his life-long dedication to this part of the Kingdom of God. The pages that record the history of the synod identify clearly his central role. He served as president, vice-president, and member of the synodical council as well as president of the Illinois Conference, an important unit in the synod. Thirty-five boards and committees of the synod shared in his dedication; twelve of them had the benefit of his leadership as chairman. Carlsson's magnificent leadership as long-time chairman and member of the Board of Directors of Augustana College and Theological Seminary has already been discussed. He was chairman of committees that had responsibility for such vital areas as home missions, foreign missions, preparation of the catechism, revision of the synod's constitution, publications, confirmation, and communion. He served for many years as a representative of the synod to the meetings of the General Council. He attended meetings of the synod with unfailing regularity.[3]

The union of the Swedes and Norwegians in the Augustana Synod came to an end in 1870. The detailed reasons for the division go beyond the purposes of this study. A variety of factors that transcended the fine personal relationship—the definite minority position of the Norwegians, nationalistic feeling, differences in certain aspects of theology, polity, and practices—produced the winds of change. Since division seemed almost inevitable, people of good will worked to achieve it in an orderly manner. At the synod meeting at Carver, Minnesota, in June 1868, Erl. Carlsson was a member of the committee of Swedes and Norwegians who presented a petition characterized by Christian understanding on the subject of division. Each group was to have its own synod and officers. The new group was to be known as the Norwegian-Danish Augustana Synod with the same articles of confession. The two synods should cooperate in one institution of higher learning. Moreover, it was agreed that they stood in a friendly and brotherly relationship to each other and that the two new synods considered themselves as sister synods which not only continued close ties in general but also through delegates would join together with each other in synod and conference meetings.[4]

The decision to separate was discussed at the synod meeting at Moline in June of 1869 but was postponed for another year at the request of the Norwegian delegates. The separation became a reality at the Andover meeting of synod in June 1870. The basis for the division was almost identical with the petition of 1868 which Erl. Carlsson had shared in drafting, except that the Norwegians would support their own school. A session for a brotherly farewell was held before the Norwegians withdrew. Pastor O. J. Hatlestad thanked the Swedes "for all the love they had showed them." President Hasselquist, officially, and Erl. Carlsson, personally, "wished the new synod success." There was a great quiet as the relationship came to an end. The minutes record simply these words: "With brotherly handclasps and deep feeling the brethren [the Norwegians] departed, whereupon the synod resumed its deliberations."[5]

Erl. Carlsson's role in the division of the synod identifies him as a man of peace and good will. P. J. Reinertsen suggests that Carlsson, Pastor Paul Andersen, his good Norwegian friend, and others were aware of the potential conflict in which "bitter strife and perhaps division would result." It was for that reason that they joined in the petition for separation in a peaceful, Christian manner. One issue, highlighted by Professor Weenas, a recent Norwegian immigrant, and a member of the faculty of Augustana Seminary, was related to the "congregational" in contrast to the "synodical" form of church government which prevailed. He was strenuously opposed to the latter. Several Norwegian congregations objected to the separation. Some persons felt that they were "overthrown by strangers," as Pastor Paul Andersen wrote.[6]

Erl. Carlsson's view of the organization of the immigrant church in the new world is interestingly described in his report to the synod at the Andover meeting in June 1870. As chairman of a committee to revise the congregational and synodical constitutions he provided interesting background information: "When we pastors and people came to this country we had little familiarity with how a free church should be organized. After much reflection and many prayers and deliberations, a decision was made concerning a constitution for our congregations and synod. The principles which guided us in our deliberations were:

> 1. To see to it that not too much power in the church was placed in the hands of a few, whereby the individual congregations' and members' freedom and wholesome development might be hindered or impaired; but also that there might be good church order and government, so that arbitrariness and individualism would not destroy everything.
>
> 2. To maintain the church's historic development and not create unrest and strife within congregations through changing too many practices and regulations."

The Chicago pastor concluded his report with these words: "Many years of experience have taught us that . . . we ought to observe Christian conservatism and not go down the radical path, lest more harm than gain result, and that which seemed an improvement, would soon need to be changed.[7]

The revised congregational constitution that Carlsson's committee proposed was adopted in 1870 with only modest changes. It was based upon the action of the Mississippi-Chicago conference in March 1857, which in turn owed so very much to the congregational constitution of Carlsson's own church. Basic elements were sustained throughout the entire history of the Augustana Lutheran Church.

At the meeting of the synod at Paxton in 1873, Erl. Carlsson, chairman of the committee on synodical constitutional revision, recommended that, "the synod be divided into district synods, but that these district synods should be associated and united most closely with each other through a general synod consisting of delegates from the district synods." Carlsson was named chairman of a committee to draft a constitution that would embody this proposal.[8]

The plan for establishing district synods was discussed at the synod meetings during the next two years. Oscar N. Olson has pointed out that both Carlsson and Eric Norelius favored this arrangement. The former, who was in Sweden during the summer of 1873, wrote from there: "It has become more and more clear to me the division into district synods neither can be or should be postponed." Norelius concluded: "No one ought to be surprised that Pastor Carlsson advocates division into district synods, and the latter united in a general synod. Anyone who has given the question serious thought must come to this same conclusion." In March 1875, Carlsson, who was chairman of the constitution committee, wrote to Norelius: "The committee was unanimous that the synod should be divided into three districts; north, east, and west of the Augustana Synod with the right to ordain and discipline pastors and to conduct their own institutions." The districts should meet annually for two years but the third year would provide for a meeting of the entire synod. At the meeting of synod in 1876, the delegates defeated the proposal which would have increased the power of the districts and decreased that of the synod. Apparently the fear of centralization was not great and was counterbalanced by the concern that the growth in power of district synods would be a divisive element in the church.[9]

Erl. Carlsson's service to the Augustana Synod was often in the form of special assignments. He was appointed a member of the

committee for revision of the *Catechism* in 1873. He served as
chairman from 1874 until the committee's report was adopted at
synod in 1879. Revision of Martin Luther's *Small Catechism* as
current in the church of Sweden was an assignment of highest
priority since this volume furnished the basis of instruction in
Sunday School, in the intense preparation for confirmation, and as a
frequent reference for church members. [10]

A variety of important issues were involved in the long and
painstaking labor of the committee. Consideration had to be given to
theological meaning, problems of interpretation, classification of
subject matter and changes in language for adaptation to Swedish
America. Carlsson's customary prudence and good judgment were
apparent in the broad participation before a final decision was made.
Many individuals were consulted, conferences within the synod were
asked to provide evaluation, and publication of the proposed revision
in a supplement to *Augustana och missionären* before final printing
brought general understanding of the revised catechism.

The scope of the revision is apparent in Erl. Carlsson's report to
synod: Eighty sections were more or less revised, thirteen sections
were eliminated, six new sections were added, resulting in a total of
230. The presentation and adoption of the revised catechism at the
meeting in 1879 was a cardinal event in the synod's history. The
language, structure, and form of the revision were admirably suited
to a new generation of Swedish American youth who still used the
language of their parents. Thirty years after the publication of *Dr.
Martin Luthers lilla katekes med förklaring* (Dr. Martin Luther's
Small Catechism with Explanation) by the Augustana Book Concern, 244,000 copies had been printed. This represents the greatest
publication effort in the history of the Augustana Book Concern. [11]

The key figure in the revision of the catechism was Erl.
Carlsson, the chairman during the entire period of constructive
achievement. Professor Nils Forsander, while describing Carlsson's
emphasis upon effective confirmation instruction, has written: "It
should be mentioned that he was the leading and driving force in the
committee's proposal which was adopted at the meeting of the
Synod in Chicago in 1879." Forsander points out that an important
source for the committee's work was a manuscript which Carlsson
had written and used at Chicago and Andover as an explanation of

the *Catechism* for members of his confirmation classes. Eric Norelius wrote: "Erl. Carlsson expended more work, anxiety, and effort on that book than any member of the Synod." [12]

When an English translation of the *Catechism* was first published by the synod in 1902, the text was based on the Swedish revision which Erl. Carlsson and his colleagues had drafted. He was selected as chairman of the committee as early as 1886 to plan for an English translation, a further demonstration of his interest in this important book for the Lutheran church as well as a manifestation of his concern that it should be available in the language of the land. He served as chairman of the committee. [13]

At the meeting of the Augustana Synod at Lindsborg in July 1881, Erl. Carlsson was elected president, after several ballots, to succeed Eric Norelius, who asked not to be re-elected for reasons of poor health. Carlsson was vice-president at that time.

A great contrast prevailed with the situation upon his arrival as a pastor in 1853. Then there were only three ordained pastors among the Swedish Lutherans in America, a half dozen congregations in Illinois and Iowa and a few hundred members. In 1881 there were 147 pastors, of whom only five were born in the United States, 332 congregations, 226 church buildings, a membership of 74,716, of whom 41,976 were communicants, a synodical college and seminary, and several other church institutions. [14]

Erl. Carlsson's presidential reports indicate his thorough understanding of the synod. His first report in 1882 emphasized the role of the conferences and expressed his pleasure in having worked closely with them. As he viewed the current situation he found that, "The greatest concern has been the shortage of workers [pastors]. It is therefore with great joy that I can inform the synod that after a long period of waiting and many prayers it seems as if the Lord in his great mercy understands our need and will send workers into the field." His basis for hope was a new spirit among some church leaders in Sweden who seemed to realize the great spiritual needs of their scattered countrymen in America. He reported that seven students from Fjellstedt's school in Uppsala and four from Ahlberg's school in Örebro would join the ranks of prospective pastors in the following year. In another area of concern he warned members of the synod that too much emphasis on the outer life of the church could displace commitment to inner spiritual life. He reminded them that Jesus, in the relationship of Martha and Mary, had clearly stated that the latter had chosen the better part. [15]

Carlsson's understanding of the American scene is clearly demonstrated in his second report when he emphasized the role of the English language in the future of the immigrant church. He had been largely responsible, as a leader of the Board of Directors, for a call to "an English professor" at Augustana Seminary. He rejoiced at the prospect that the synod would in time accept English Lutheran congregations as members, thus serving people other than those who understood Swedish. He argued pointedly that the two languages should be used side by side, and the language to be favored should be the one that the people understood better. He concluded: "We have God's pure Word and we can pray and praise him just as devotedly and faithfully and be just as pleasing to him in one language as in the other." Although he lamented the general indifference in the church of the homeland to the needs of the church in America, he was pleased to report that twelve new students from Sweden had enrolled at Augustana. He explained that there was heavy correspondence in the president's office. During the past year a 406-page book had been filled by copies of letters that he had written and two large volumes recorded the incoming correspondence. The delegates responded to the president's services by passing a resolution which declared, "The synod extends hearty thanks for the untiring efforts and unfailing energy that he has given to his official duties." [16]

The annual reports by Erl. Carlsson offered an opportunity not only to emphasize important business items on the agenda, but they also provided an insight into his view of the church and the nature of the Kingdom of God. In 1884 he reported to the synod:

> In appearance, the kingdom of God on earth is feeble and infirm. It possesses no standing armies to protect it, nor does it have emperors or kings to maintain its power and dignity. It has no central bank on which it can make requisition for its needs. Nevertheless, the kingdom of God alone is and remains secure. Its weapons "have divine power to destroy strongholds." Of its King it is said that "the government shall be upon his shoulders." Its national bank is God's glorious promises for time and eternity.

> Therefore this kingdom stands, firmly founded on Christ the Rock, ever strong and invincible through all the centuries of the world's history. The Word of God, which is its strength, abides forever; wherefore our proud era with its spiritual arrogance and unbelief can avail as little as any that has passed in actual harm to the church. Of the Christ-confessing church, its Founder and Head has said, "The powers of death shall not prevail against it." [17]

Carlsson's report to the synod reflected the concerns of conferences and congregations. A focal point was the difficulty of maintaining the interest of youth in the church following confirmation. A special complaint came from Minnesota that too many young people were involved in dancing and drinking. In other areas pastors were alarmed that adults were greatly interested in secret societies. However, the president was encouraged that many congregations were developing effective programs in music and literature as well as devotional emphasis in young peoples societies. On the whole, attendance at worship services was good and the general response to the church was satisfactory. Moreover, the observance of the four-hundredth anniversary of the birth of Martin Luther the previous year, which had been climaxed by a great Lutheran festival at Augustana College in newly constructed Jubilee Hall, had revived understanding of the church's tradition and stimulated interest in spiritual life.[18]

At this meeting Erl. Carlsson informed the synod that, "On account of my worsened health I ask to be relieved from the heavy and exacting assignment of the president's office which I have had for three years, and which, if it is properly conducted, requires full time and good health." The synod, however, was unwilling to accept his resignation. The election of Professor Olof Olsson as vice-president undoubtedly indicated the desire to have someone at the center of the synod's life available to assume the presidency in the event that Erl. Carlsson could not serve for reasons of health. [19]

In the twenty-fifth anniversary year of the synod's history (1885), Erl. Carlsson presented an interesting report comparing immigrants in the early years with those of the current era:

> Formerly, the newly arrived immigrants were dedicated Christians who were a great source of strength to the church. They gathered around the pastors with trust, prayerfulness, and joyous sacrifice.

> They supported them in their work. But other times came. . . . Most
> of the Christians, who have come from Sweden in the later years are
> characterized by having proud spiritual attitudes instead of being
> poor and humble in spirit. . . . They mock the creed of the church
> and hate the pastors, especially the earnest ones, and tramp all
> church order under their feet.

The pastor suggested the reason for this situation: "The spirit of the
times meets us in the libertinism of our era. . . . It is to be greatly
lamented that far too many of our dear countrymen, who were more
or less influenced by the spiritual revivals of the homeland, have thus
degenerated. But there is nothing new under the sun. What
Phariseeism and Gnosticism was during Christianity's early centuries
and the heavenly prophets and zealots in the days of the Reformation, so are these spiritual libertines, these separatists in our time." [20]

In identifying another concern, the pastor contended that the
"age-old problem of conflict" with the forces of the world continue.
"The enemies of the Kingdom of God—disbelief, denial, ungodliness,
persecution, mockery—seek ascendancy. . . . Our greatest danger lies
in making concession to the spirit of the times, that our light is
placed under a bushel and that the salt loses its saltiness." [21]

Evidence of the dire circumstances, according to the president
of synod, was to be found in the youth of the land and even in the
church. Once again he lamented the fact that young people too often
ceased to participate in the activities of the church following
confirmation. The family no longer served as an effective unit for
cultivating the spiritual life. In the public schools there was neither
Christianity nor education. Moreover, "The nurture of the whole life
of the person is no longer in the program of the school and they
[school personnel] do not know what it means." But the situation
among pastors according to the president of the synod was a
contributing factor to the sad situation: "We pastors have in a
strange manner understood our calling to be *preachers,* and we
preach a great deal, and I dare say, faithfully and with inspiration,
but we are poor *catechists* and even worse *educators* and *shepherds
of souls.* This one-sidedness—preaching—this failing in our religious
work, has unconsciously smuggled itself in among us, and is
characteristic of our spirituality almost everywhere." He argued,
therefore, that a greater responsibility rested upon the seminary to

provide education that will result in dedicated, educated, and deeply spiritual pastors. He also lamented the great independence of a large number of pastors and congregations, and of some conferences, as proven by their unwillingness to follow wholeheartedly the official regulations and resolutions of the synod. [22]

The president's report of 1886 was comparatively brief but it was filled with vital pronouncements. Erl. Carlsson was a pastor who believed wholeheartedly in education. This commitment is demonstrated in all his presidential reports, but it received special emphasis this year in the education of youth: "We cannot emphasize enough the need and the importance of the Christian nurture of the young, for if this is neglected we move toward the end of our denomination. What our congregations will be like twenty-five years from now will depend principally on the spiritual nurture that is given to the new generation of our time." He lamented that the action which had been taken by the synod the previous year, namely, that pastors in "visitations" throughout their congregations, should examine what was being done to develop the spiritual life of children, had gone largely by default. [23]

Carlsson's long years of service as chairman and a member of the Board of Directors of Augustana College and Theological Seminary gave him a special understanding of the role of higher education in the synod. In his presidential address of 1886, he spoke as a prophet. After expressing pleasure for the achievements of the institutions at Rock Island, St. Peter, Lindsborg, and Wahoo, he expressed great concern:

> All the great and fine educational work still suffers from a grievous fault which could expand and become a threatening danger. We are lacking in a definite plan, according to which our colleges ought to be organized and governed. The entire work in education should be the synod's responsibility. . . . I consider it to be my duty to awaken the synod's awareness of this matter and I venture to propose for the synod's consideration the practicality of establishing a large committee with the name, "The General Board of Education of the Augustana Synod," which will be instructed to consider seriously this urgent matter and present at the next meeting of synod a proposal about how our schools and educational efforts shall be organized within our synod. Through unity and cooperation

our schools, with the help of God, will be a mighty lever for our peoples uplift, progress, and blessing. [24]

The committee on the president's report heartily endorsed Carlsson's recommendation as "a word for our time" and proposed that a large and representative committee meet at Rock Island next August 24 for a consideration of this matter. But the divisiveness and parochialism which Carlsson described prevented the realization of the high hopes that he had expressed in 1886 for a General Board of Education of the Augustana Synod. The first report of such a board occurred in 1925, four decades later. [25]

When Erl. Carlsson surveyed the world and the church in 1887, he found cause for both hope and despair. Reports from conferences indicated that the Word was preached and the sacraments administered with greater receptivity than in recent years. The response to the needs of children and older youth had been encouraging as a result of "visitations" in ever larger numbers of congregations. His recommendation that a synodical committee be appointed to recommend a design for the organization of Sunday schools and the preparation of instructional material for the church's youth was heartily endorsed. The president argued convincingly that the demands upon pastors required that the course in the seminary be extended from two to three years. This proposal was also endorsed for consideration. [26]

Dark and threatening clouds were on the horizon of both church and state according to President Carlsson. Especially alarming were "anarchism, socialism, and the dangerous and calamitous restlessness among labor." Signs of the times indicated that, "The tortuous days of anti-christ were soon at hand, when all worldly order and government will be destroyed, and when no one will buy or sell without having the wild beast's mark on his forehead . . . " The committee responded to the president's statement by "most earnestly warning our members not to belong to, or in any way support such organizations, regardless of their names which oppress their fellow human beings by deciding under what conditions they shall be allowed to work or buy or sell." [27]

Erl. Carlsson, president of the synod, was not in good health when the delegates assembled in Galesburg for the annual meeting in 1888. Pastor C. A. Swensson read Carlsson's annual report to the synod, except the last few paragraphs. In this final report to synod, Carlsson spoke as a pastor who knew well the church which he had loved and served so faithfully but his words were those also of a prophet with stern warning about current trends and the possible shape of things to come. As chairman of the committee for revising the constitution in 1873, he had advocated the creation of district synods with considerable power, but joined together in a synod by united fellowship. But new forces had developed with the passing of the years which now threatened the unity of the Swedish Lutheran Church in America. In clear and precise language he forthrightly declared:

> Local and parochial interests, competing literary ventures, indeed, our several schools with their imperative needs and great demands— all threaten our inner unity, tend to chill our Christian comradeship, and unless remedies are applied will destroy those bonds which hitherto have held us together and contributed to the progress of our work for the Lord and his kingdom.

The outgoing president was fearful that the bonds of unity would be broken "if each and everyone persisted in being concerned only about his own interests, his own local ambitions, his own conferences, his own mission field, his own school, and his own publications." [28]

Erl. Carlsson then turned to the cause for this distressing situation:

> The chief reason for this regrettable situation ... is to be found in our outdated constitutional arrangements ... That our constitutional structure is altogether too loose and indefinite will doubtless be acknowledged by all. ... Many of us think that the synod should merely be an advisory body without any legislative power or authority. ... Individualism has altogether too large a place among us.[29]

The president turned to the American political tradition of that time to illustrate what had happened in the Augustana Synod: "In politics we are nearly all Republicans, decrying a strong centralized federal authority; but in the affairs of the church we have unwittingly become Democrats, desiring a weak decentralized synodical authority, having been unduly influenced by states rights' notions." In the midst of a situation which seemed fraught with critical problems he concluded: "May the Lord lead our synod on the golden middle way in the matter of our constitutional structure, so that we neither shipwreck on the Scylla of dictatorship or the Charybdis of selfish parochialism. . . . United we stand, divided we fall." [30]

Erl. Carlsson's report in 1888 is especially interesting in the context of a letter of October 21, 1887, from Pastor Carl Swensson, Lindsborg, to Pastor Peter Sjöblom of Minnesota, the principal advocate of conference independence. Swensson noted the emphasis that Sjöblom placed on the power of the conferences and then raised this question: " . . . but will not the practical result be that under your free-churchly and democratic viewpoint every leader, instead of an official governed by law, will become a lawless (not necessarily in a bad sense) demagogue, who deals and acts absolutely according to his own whims?" Swensson also made an interesting observation about Erl. Carlsson: "E. C. has a great deal of the European bureaucratic view, no matter how well-concealed it may be." [31]

There is no record of what the committee of twelve men, who had responsibility for recommending action on the president's report, discussed with reference to Erl. Carlsson's precise and passionate description of the evils of parochialism and disunity within the synod. The response was general and evasive. There was complete failure to recognize the importance of the issues as is clear by the following resolution which became the synod's action:

> In regard to the danger which the president names, the synod admonished everybody to take to heart earnestly his warning as a word for our times, urging all to greater concern for the inner life and greater faithfulness to the Holy Spirit, together with practicing brotherly love and harmony and to act not for their own advantage and local interests, so that the life of the denomination and the spirit of unity is suffocated, and if there are shortcomings in our constitution that we nevertheless permit our great purpose, the salvation of souls and the progress of the church, to hold us together with the bonds of love and peace. [32]

The controversy between centralization and decentralization continued until the synod meeting at Rock Island in 1893 when a compromise arrangement was provided. [33]

Erl. Carlsson, for reasons of poor health, presented his

resignation as president at the synod meeting in 1888. He expressed gratitude for the support which he had received across the years. The synod in a resolution of farewell expressed to him "hearty thanks for his faithfulness and concern, with which he had conducted the office of president during his long tenure and hoped to have him as an experienced and tested father of the denomination." [34]

Erl. Carlsson's dedication to the Augustana Synod is clearly revealed by contemporary observers and by the records. Pastors C. A. Swensson and Olof Olsson, editors of *Jubel-Album, 1893,* who knew Carlsson intimately, have described his outstanding leadership: "But in our denomination's history Pastor Carlsson has won the name as our leading man in church affairs. We can confidently say that without in the least discounting our other church fathers in this respect. . . . In our school, missions, and ministry of mercy he has always taken a leading role. *Broder Carlsson föreslag* [Brother Carlsson made a motion] appears again and again in our synodical minutes from the first and especially when it came to the important questions." Eric Norelius wrote in 1885: "The resolutions at the synod meeting 1860 dealing with the seminary in general were introduced and promoted energetically by Pastor Carlsson, who during the entire history of the synod was, so to say, the leading spirit in its leadership and laid down great services, especially in its organizational development." [35]

FOOTNOTES

[1] *Augustana synodens protokoll,* 1860, pp. 3-4; L. P. Esbjörn, "De Svenska Lutherska församlingarnas i N. Amerika uppkomst" (Norelius' address at pastor's meeting, Uppsala, June 14, 1865), *Korsbaneret,* 1885, p. 48.

[2] Erl. Carlsson to Peter Wieselgren, Chicago, May 7, 1860, Westin, *Emigranterna och kyrkan,* p. 95.

[3] A composite study from *Augustana synodens protokoll* provides the materials for Carlsson's service to the synod. See Ch. VIII pp. 111-14 for a discussion of his contribution to Augustana College and Theological Seminary.

[4] *Augustana synodens protokoll,* 1868, p. 48.

[5] *Ibid.,* 1869, p. 20, 1870, pp. 33-34.

[6]P. J. Reinertsen, "The Division of the Scandinavian Evangelical Lutheran Augustana Synod," *Augustana Quarterly*, XII (July 1933), 258-61.

[7]*Augustana synodens protokoll*, 1870, pp. 34-35.

[8]*Ibid.*, 1873, pp. 18-19.

[9]Oscar N. Olson, *The Augustana Lutheran Church in America, 1860-1910*, p. 47; *Augustana synodens protokoll*, 1876, p. 49; Erl. Carlsson to Eric Norelius, Chicago, March 10, 1875.

[10]*Augustana synodens protokoll*, 1874, p. 42; 1879, pp. 19-21.

[11]O. V. Holmgrain, "Augustana synodens förlagsverksamhet,"*Minneskrift med anledning af Augustana-Synodens femtioåriga tillvaro, 1860-1910*, p. 300.

[12]Forsander, *Lifsbilder*, I, 111; Norelius, *De Svenska Lutherska . . . historia i Amerika*, I, 436.

[13]*Augustana synodens protokoll*, 1886, p. 83.

[14]*Augustana synodens protokoll*, 1881, p. 87 and appendix; *Augustana och missionären*, July 20, 1881, p. 462.

[15]*Augustana synodens protokoll*, 1882, pp. 11-16.

[16]*Ibid.*, 1883, pp. 15-17, 33.

[17]*Ibid.*, 1884, p. 13

[18]*Ibid.*, 1884, pp. 14-22.

[19]*Ibid.*, 1884, p. 22.

[20]*Ibid.*, 1885, pp. 12-13.

[21]*Ibid.*, 1885, p. 12.

[22]*Ibid.*, 1885, pp. 19-22.

[23]*Ibid.*, 1886, p. 13.

[24]*Ibid.*, 1886, p. 16.

[25]*Augustana synodens protokoll*, 1886, pp. 17-18; *Minutes of the Augustana Lutheran Synod*, 1923, p. 57, 1924, p. 31, 1925, pp. 145-47.

[26]*Augustana synodens protokoll*, 1887, pp. 13-14, 18, 21.

[27]*Ibid.*, 1887, pp. 19-20, 22.

[28] *Augustana synodens protokoll,* 1888, pp. 20-21, quoted in Arden, *Augustana Heritage,* p. 192; *Augustana och missionären,* June 21, 1888, p. 296.

[29] *Augustana synodens protokoll,* 1888, pp. 21-22, quoted in Arden, *Augustana Heritage,* p. 192.

[30] *Augustana synodens protokoll,* 1888, p. 23; *Augustana Heritage,* p. 193. See analysis of later developments in Arden, pp. 193-194.

[31] Carl Swensson's letter is translated by Clifford Ansgar Nelson in "A Pertinent Historical Letter with Comments," *The Augustana Quarterly,* XIII (January 1944), p. 25.

[32] *Augustana synodens protokoll,* 1888, p. 26.

[33] Arden, *Augustana Heritage,* pp. 193-97.

[34] *Augustana synodens protokoll,* 1888, p. 25.

[35] Olsson and Swensson, *Jubel-Album 1893,* p. 42; Eric Norelius "Återblick på Augustana-synodens historia under dess första tjugufem år," *Korsbaneret,* 1885, pp. 13-14.

Pastor Erl. Carlsson during Early Years
in the Ministry

PETER CARLSON,
1822-1909

J. P. C. BOREN
1824-1865

P. A. CEDERSTAM
1830-1902

L. P. ESBJORN
1808-1870

M. F. HAKANSON
1811-1893

ERIC NORELIUS
1833-1916

PETER BECKMAN
1822-1915

ERLAND CARLSSON
1822-1892

ANDREW ANDREEN
1827-1880

O. C. T. ANDREN
1824-1870

JONAS SWENSSON
1828-1873

T. N. HASSELQUIST
1816-1891

PIONEER PASTORS PRESENT AT THE ORGANIZATION
OF THE AUGUSTANA SYNOD 1860

Pastors Present at the Organization of
the Augustana Synod in 1860

Pastor Peter Fjellstedt

Pastor Carl Olof Rosenius

11

Conflict and Criticism

The career of Erl. Carlsson involved a variety of relationships in differing situations. His firm principles in religion and conduct, although not as extreme as those of some of his contemporaries, were challenged by individuals and groups. Although he had many friends, he also had his share of critics and a few enemies.

Religious issues provided an area for conflict and criticism. Reference has already been made to his relationship with Gustaf Unonius in the early 1850s and the conflict which developed as this Swedish Episcopal pastor sought to enlist Swedish immigrants as members of his St. Ansgarius congregation under what Carlsson and his associates considered false pretenses. Esbjörn and Hasselquist were involved in conflict with Unonius far more than Carlsson although the latter declared that Unonius' "use of the name Lutheran would serve as bait on the hook since they wished to fish for Episcopalians among the new immigrants."[1]

Relations with the Episcopalians reached a more serious level after Unonius returned to Sweden in 1858. Episcopalian policy at high levels was devoted to reaching an agreement with the Church of Sweden whereby Episcopalian efforts among Swedish immigrants might receive official sanction from the homeland. Henry J. Whitehouse, bishop of the Protestant Episcopal Church of the diocese of Illinois, went on an official mission to Sweden in 1866. Archbishop Reuterdahl, Bishop Sundbärg, Bishop Bring, and others

149

were contacted by him. Whitehouse was successful in receiving a *Cleri Comitialis Circular* from the House of the Clergy in the Swedish parliament which gave a measure of official sanction to the Episcopalians, including a directive to Swedish pastors to give emigrants a certificate which recommended the person to the bishops and priests for spiritual care in case there was no Evangelical Lutheran congregation. Included in the proposed Episcopal plans was the appointment of a Swedish clergyman who would serve as a bishop in America for Swedish immigrants. Carl Henrik Lyttkens, in a scholarly study of the relationship of the Episcopalians with the Church of Sweden, has pointed out that Hasselquist disapproved strongly of the proposal "to place us under the King of Sweden as our *summus episcopus*."[2]

When Bishop Whitehouse returned to America he presented his findings in a Chicago address before a large crowd of Swedes in March 1867. He described "his cordial reception at the hands of the Archbishop and the Swedish clergy, how he communed at the Lord's table with them, and about the arrangements by which the bishops were to formulate letters of dismission to immigrants, which assured them of cordial admission into Episcopal churches in the adopted country. He also stated that the Anglican Church, the Episcopal Church in the United States, and the Swedish Church were identical, except for differences in liturgy." Pastor Carlsson was in the audience when Bishop Whitehouse presented his report.[3]

The Swedish Lutherans in America were heartily opposed to the activities of Bishop Whitehouse and his successors in Sweden. They felt that this was an attempt to cover up the differences between the Episcopalians and the Lutherans and that it would undermine the work of the Augustana Synod.

Svenska Amerikanaren, the rival newspaper to *Hemlandet,* the traditional supporter of the Augustana Synod, reviewed Bishop Whitehouse's address favorably, and in considerable detail. Herman Roos, the editor, was hostile toward Carlsson. He berated the pastor and Immanuel congregation. He was full of praise for Pastor Bredberg and the St. Ansgarius congregation. Roos attacked Carlsson for holding reactionary and parochial views. Moreover, *Svenska Amerikanaren* endorsed the speech by the bishop and urged the Swedish people in Chicago to support the Episcopalians.[4]

Although Erl. Carlsson was the principal target of Roos' criticism, he maintained his poise and dignity. The fact that he attended the bishop's lecture showed fraternal respect. Carlsson apparently felt, as events confirmed, that Whitehouse and the Episcopalians were no serious threat to the Swedish Lutherans.

In the year following the bishop's visit to Chicago, Carlsson wrote to Hasselquist identifying the situation in that city: "The St. Ansgarius congregation, as you know from the newspapers, has taken a pretentious name—the Swedish National Church. Last Sunday the *Kyrko-Handbok* (Swedish Service Book) together with *kappan* (Swedish clerical gown) and *krage* (Swedish clerical collar) were introduced. They hope to capture newly-arrived immigrants. . . . But the church remains naturally just as Episcopal as usual. It is altogether a shameful deception designed to bring our countrymen into the Episcopal church." Later in the year he informed Hasselquist that Peter Wieselgren in Göteborg had written to state that Bishop Whitehouse was seeking to persuade the Gustavus Adolphus Foundation to support Bredberg and the St. Ansgarius congregation.[5]

The attempt of the Episcopalians in Chicago to gain a large following among the Swedes did not succeed. Erl. Carlsson was fully aware of the issues but his response showed confidence about the future of his ministry and the congregation.

Erl. Carlsson experienced early in his ministry in Chicago the consequences of general indifference and direct hostility to the church. In a letter to Jonas Swensson in February 1857, he described the situation:

> You regret the spiritual condition among our countrymen and we have reason for the same complaint everywhere. Here in Chicago some have been expelled; others have been refused membership or communion. But most of them become still angrier on that account, throw themselves with fanatical bitterness against us into the arms of other denominations. . . . But with the help of God, truth will win. After we once understand what is right and the Lord points out the road for us, we are determined to advance irrespective of how many people praise or revile, assist, or hinder. It is better to stand on the foundation of truth with both feet even if ten stand at one's side than to stand at the side of the one whom thousands follow.

The letter also discloses the attitude of Pastor Carlsson in the midst of conflict: "We must meet every person with love and humility, but still act sincerely toward him. If the cause is God's, it will not fail. He may indeed try us for a time but when His time comes, His glory will be revealed so much more clearly."[6]

Conflict and criticism of Erl. Carlsson developed with greater intensity in the late 1860s within Immanuel Church. It was related primarily to the new emphasis which some immigrants brought with them from Sweden. The name of C. O. Rosenius was intimately related with the movement in its origin. Later that of P. P. Waldenström dominated in the 1870s. Rosenius, editor of *Pietisten,* had been a source of inspiration to Erl. Carlsson and other *läsare.* Waldenström's teachings about the atonement were rejected within the Lutheran church in Sweden and America. Members of the new movement went beyond the position of Rosenius and embraced the ideas of Waldenström. The early term "Mission Friends" identified them also in the alignment with Waldenström.

Erl. Carlsson had cited two important factors in the views of those who developed the new movement: "1. They were committed to the hyperevangelical course. . . . 2. They wished to build a fellowship of true believers." In describing his understanding of this development he wrote: "They regard the Christian church not as an institution of grace but only as a fellowship of believers. In the typical Reformed view, individuals outside God's kingdom should be born again and become God's children, and they should unite themselves into an association. They could not and would not understand Christ's parable of the great communion in which both the good and the evil participated and the parable of the dragnet, which gathered the good and bad fish." The controversy involved basically the distinction between a *ren församling* (pure congregation) of the *troende* (true believers) which the Mission Friends emphasized in contrast with the *folk kyrka* (people's church) embracing both the "spiritual and worldly" elements, which was the legacy of Swedish Lutheran pastors. Waldenström's doctrine of the atonement later became a paramount issue.[7]

The developments within the Immanuel congregation can readily be traced. Martin Sundin, a recent immigrant, joined the congregation in 1864. The pastor, in consultation with Sundin and upon his urging, organized a mission society within the church. This was not a group of "true believers" in the strict sense. In 1867 and 1868, a sizeable number of Mission Friends, some from Jönköping, joined the congregation. Under the leadership of Sundin and with the consent of Pastor Carlsson, another mission society was organized on December 26, 1868. A room in an old schoolhouse on Wesson Street was rented for a meeting place. The society was called the Swedish Evangelical Lutheran Missionary Association of Chicago. In January of the following year lots were purchased on North Franklin Street for the sizeable sum of $5300, and in October a new mission house was dedicated. Pastor Carlsson participated in the dedication of the structure.[8]

Erl. Carlsson maintained a friendly attitude toward the members of the mission society within his congregation. There were no signs of separation at this time although in Galesburg and elsewhere the movement was becoming increasingly aggressive. The pastor and deacons of Immanuel Church felt it necessary, however, to ask C. J. Lindahl, a city missionary in the employ of the congregation, to resign because he was too energetically promoting evangelistic activities and the sale of *Pietisten* and other literature of this type. He then served for a brief period as a representative of the newly organized mission society. He was succeeded in that position by J. M. Sanngren, who had left the assignment as a traveling missionary for Swedish Lutheran churches.[9]

A letter from Carlsson to T. N. Hasselquist in March 1868, shows that the Chicago pastor was deeply troubled by these developments in his congregation: "The work and anxiety has almost overcome us here. Petitions are circulating in Chicago to form a church to be called *Rena Evangeliska Lutherska Kyrka i Chicago* (Pure Evangelical Lutheran Church in Chicago). Another proposal to form a pure congregation has appeared from another source. At our last deacon's meeting a petition for this purpose was presented by some of our most pious members to form a Lutheran congregation of only true believers." [10]

The situation confronting Carlsson is further described in a letter which he wrote to Hasselquist the following February 1869. This was a confusing time with a mixture of hope and disappointment. In the first part of the letter he wrote optimistically: "The

most important decision at the congregational meeting was the
resolution to build a new church which was adopted unanimously."
Then he described at considerable length some of the problems
already mentioned:

> What shakes our situation here more than anything else is the new
> mission society which attracts many of our members and makes
> them critical of the church and congregation. Our mission's
> committee has had a second meeting with our colporteur, the most
> recent yesterday afternoon, when he and the committee agreed that
> as a result of problems and the mistrust that had arisen between him
> and several of our members, he no longer could carry out his work in
> our congregation with blessing and profit and that he should resign.
> We parted as friends and [C. J.] Lindahl promised not to work
> against our congregation.[11]

Erl. Carlsson then explained to Hasselquist what his response
was to these developments and presented his pessimistic view of the
future: "I am taking a friendly position toward the new society and I
have felt that I should do so since there are many simple and
righteous Christians who have been drawn into it. However, I fear
that they will soon leave the church and go on the separatist road of
error. May the Lord guide it all for the best. Meanwhile it seems very
gloomy."[12]

The first mission meeting of Mission Friends in America was
held in Immanuel Church, July 5-6, 1869. Leaders of the group
included C. A. Björk, J. M. Sanngren, J. Peterson and P. Undeen.
Several Augustana pastors were in attendance including Erl. Carlsson,
G. Peters, and A. Hult. *Hemlandet* had published the following
announcement in June: "A meeting will be held July 5-6 for the
purpose of seeking to achieve a closer bond of union and a more
intimate association for the promotion of missionary endeavor
among our countrymen as well as among the heathen who do not
know God. We like to believe that many share our conviction that
such an association is needed. . . . "[13]

In the course of discussion at the meeting in Immanuel Church
the following question was submitted by an Augustana pastor:
"Since among our Swedish people we have both churches and
pastors, and the gospel is proclaimed in the spoken and written word,
why do you therefore seek to prove the necessity of a distinctive

mission organization?" In response a Mission Friend proposed the following question: "What is the cause of the spiritual decadence which prevails among our Swedish people, in spite of the fact that we have both churches and pastors?" [14]

Although details of the discussion at the meeting are not available it was reported that, "A student from Augustana Seminary stood up and attacked the pastors and their sermons in bitter tones. After such unexpected conduct and shocking mental outburst, he picked up his hat and left the church." At that point Erl. Carlsson took the floor and said: "If the newly organized mission society intends to send such men into the field, it is certain that the church doors will be closed for the society's workers." Calmness soon prevailed as Mission Friends and Augustana pastors spoke in terms of reconciliation and mutual understanding. [15]

The relationship between the mission society and Pastor Carlsson and Immanuel Church continued on a friendly basis for several months. The society held meetings from 8-10 a.m. on Sunday in their property so that members could attend the morning worship service at Immanuel Church. However, wedges of separation began to appear. Augustana pastors became fearful that divisiveness and separation would become a reality. In February 1869, Peter Colseth, an active member of the Immanuel congregation and a close friend of Erl. Carlsson, accused the members of the mission society of undermining the congregation, urged that the new mission building be used as an immigrant shelter, and suggested that "the Mission Friends return to the rock from which they had been hewn." *Hemlandet* and *Augustana*, the latter founded in 1868 to advance the interests of the Swedish Lutherans, wrote critically of the activities of the mission society. [16]

The members of the mission society became increasingly aggressive, critical and independent. Some members felt strongly that arrangements should be made for communion services under the auspices of the society and independent of the congregation. They also urged that other functions, such as weddings and formal services, be held on an independent basis. The fear that Erl. Carlsson expressed in his letter to Hasselquist in February 1869, became a reality within a year. On March 21, 1870, the decision was made to incorporate the Swedish Evangelical Lutheran Mission Church of

Chicago. The separation from Immanuel Church was complete and final. [17]

The new congregation soon celebrated its status with a communion service led by J. M. Sanngren. The Lutheran Synod of Northern Illinois granted ordination to Sanngren although not membership in its ministerium. This action was achieved through the efforts of Charles Anderson, a member of the synod and pastor of the Mission Friends congregation in Galesburg. Sanngren later ordained pastors for Mission Friends. [18]

Erl. Carlsson's response to these developments indicate maturity and an attitude commensurate with Christian imperatives. He obviously was disappointed and at times distressed, but he did not overdramatize the issue or show vindictiveness. Perhaps he thought of his own situation in Sweden long years ago when he had expressed his Christian freedom vis-a-vis Bishop Heurlin. Perhaps the developments were almost inevitable as an expression of certain aspects of the *läsare* movement. It is to be remembered that separatists at this point in time were still Lutheran and continued to use the Lutheran name. In the 1870s a different issue appeared on the horizon with the advent of the ideas of P. P. Waldenström and his view of the atonement. [19]

Moreover, the organization of the new congregation by the separatists made no great impact upon Immanuel Church. The confirmed membership in October 1869 was 1107; in October 1870, following the separation in January of that year, membership was 1260. In the following October it was 1317. The members leaving the congregation for all reasons during each of those three years were 203, 185, and 210. An important factor in assessing the membership statistics must take into account the fact that the late 1860s was a period of very heavy immigration. [20]

Although Immanuel Church moved forward in membership and activities, there were many problems during the five years prior to Erl. Carlsson's resignation in 1875 to become pastor at Andover. In September 1872, P. P. Waldenström presented in *Pietisten* (Sweden) his famous sermon for the twentieth Sunday after Trinity on the doctrine of the atonement. The controversy created by this doctrine fashioned a new situation. Erl. Carlsson has written that the Mission Friends, "Since *Lektor* Waldenström appeared with his new light and learning, namely, that no reconciliation and even no justification occurred in Christ's death, they followed generally that teaching, at least for a while, and so went from one extreme to another."[21]

The newly organized congregation of the Mission Friends served as a rallying point for the dissenters and their friends in Immanuel Church. The impact of the new controversy is reflected somewhat in membership statistics. The communicant membership in 1871-72 was 1362 and two years later, 1873-74, it was 1360. In that period 236 names were stricken from the Immanuel Church records; new confirmands and other new members cancelled out the substantial losses incurred by the atonement controversy. Pastor Carlsson was the object of great criticism by some members. John Enander wrote to Hasselquist in October 1874 about the strife in Immanuel Church where he was a member, and expressed great regret at the prospect that Pastor Carlsson would be leaving the church. O. Fritiof Ander has written: "The old pastor and able leader, Erland Carlsson, was practically compelled to resign over the question of 'saved members.' " He also noted that, "His resignation did not solve the problem and in 1875 a group of 'New Evangelicals' proposed to call a church meeting to determine who was saved." [22]

Pastor Carlsson has written about relationships with another denomination: "The congregation and I had very good relations with the Methodists at the outset. We visited personally and attended each others meetings." Pastor S. B. Newman of the Swedish Methodist Church and Carlsson worked effectively together during the cholera year 1854. But two obstacles developed which detracted from this era of good feeling according to Erl. Carlsson:

> 1. The Methodists began to exert efforts to attract Lutherans to their congregations.
>
> 2. The Lutherans became almost scared over the manner in which the Methodists converted people, whereby as soon as they could get anyone to stand up and go to the 'mourner's bench' or altar to receive prayers in their behalf, that person would then be declared to be converted and won for Christ. They had the custom of praising God and declaring how many people had been converted that evening and had become children of God."

Although he understood the basis for the Methodist belief, which was quite contrary to Lutheran doctrine, nevertheless "it pleased him to have found some among you Methodists who are concerned about sin and evil, and these are the precious jewels of your congregation." [23]

The Methodists and Lutherans lived peaceably side by side until 1861 when the Methodist pastor, A. J. Anderson, presented a lecture in which the differences between the two denominations were clearly emphasized. The critical nature of the presentation caused the deacons of Immanuel Church to request Carlsson to respond to what they viewed as an attack upon Lutheran doctrine. When Lent was over, he presented the Lutheran position. He wrote about this episode: "Everything became quiet thereafter and never again has there been any conflict since that time between the two denominations." Pastor Carlsson's attitude toward the Methodists was expressed earlier in a letter to Jonas Swensson: "The Methodist storm usually passes quickly when left alone. On a suitable occasion one must lay mild but appropriate stress on the one-sided or false among them and afterwards leave them alone." [24]

The Swedish Baptists started work in Chicago about the same time as Lutherans. There were some problems in the early years for a few members of Immanuel Church who had heard the Baptist position presented by L. L. Frisk, but no serious controversies developed. It was not until the middle 1860s that the Baptist work was established on a firm basis. The records do not provide evidence of serious strife between the Swedish Lutherans and the Swedish Baptists in Chicago at any time. [25]

Erl. Carlsson experienced conflict and criticism beyond the area of religion and denominational differences. C. F. Peterson, a keen observer of men and events in the Chicago Swedish community in the early years, has written about "the two embattled camps," which developed. Broadly speaking, one was the church group led by Erl. Carlsson and the other was the more secular, liberal group whose leaders were journalists Herman Roos and Isidore Kjellberg, and officers of the Svea Society. Different philosophies of life and personal ambitions were decisive elements in the conflict. [26]

An interesting description of Erl. Carlsson in this context has been given by George M. Stephenson, distinguished historian of Swedish American culture: "A disciple of pietistic pastors in Sweden whose examples he emulated in word and deed, he became the target for the most bitter attacks of enemies. . . . He minced no words in condemning the sins of the community and of individuals, whose names were even mentioned from the pulpit." In sermons he attacked drinking, card playing, dancing, and membership in secret societies. He was described as "a mighty preacher of the law" (in the context of the "Law and the Gospel"). Moreover, "Carlsson was strong enough to put his seal upon anything with which he was associated. The Swedish Lutheran church [in Chicago] was known quite simply as 'Carlsson' church." [27]

An early leader of the attack on what was called *"den prästvalde"* (preacher's hierarchy) was Herman Roos. He had been a journalist on *Aftonbladet, Nya dagligt allehanda* and other newspapers in Sweden. He became in 1866, the second editor of *Svenska Amerikanaren,* the liberal journal that challenged *Hemlandet,* with its strong Augustana Synod connections. Roos has been described by Alfred Soderström as "the founder of the liberal Swedish American press" and by Ernst Skarstedt as "the honest free-thinker's standard bearer" and "the first who with genius and energy attacked . . . the threatening preacher hierarchy." C. F. Peterson has pointed out that Roos, together with two faithful friends, Charles Eklund and Nils Anderson, "were very zealous in the attempt to lead the Swedes into a new spiritual channel and to form a somewhat modified cult in church and social thinking. The base for their cloverleaf operation was the Ansgarii [Protestant Episcopal] congregation led by Pastor Jacob Bredberg." [28]

Erl. Carlsson and Immanuel Church were close at hand for the attack. The conflict developed primarily in the columns of *Svenska Amerikanaren* and through replies in *Hemlandet.* When Roos retired as editor of the former paper, he was succeeded by A. P. Sundelius, who to the amazement of everyone changed from a defender of Lutheran pastors in his previous position as editor of *Hemlandet* to a bitter attacker in his new assignment. Carlsson did not take pen in hand to answer his critics. Most of the polemics from the church group were written by Hasselquist. The Chicago pastor maintained his position steadfastly and confidently.

In 1869 a new combatant confronted Erl. Carlsson and the alleged "Lutheran hierarchy" in the person of Isidor Kjellberg. His first visit in America lasted from the latter part of 1869 to the spring

of 1872. In January 1870, correspondence from America by
"Isidor K" appeared in *Göteborgs-Posten* and *Arbetaren,* a working-
man's paper in Göteborg. After journalistic experiences in Minneapolis, Kjellberg edited and published *Justitia* in Chicago from
February 1871 to October of that year, when fire destroyed the
paper and printing plant. [29]

Kjellberg was caustic in his attack on Lutheran pastors. He
"could not reconcile himself to the . . . *läsare* pastor, who preached
sermons heavily charged with the 'law', threw away the manuscript,
and stormed and exhorted in orthodox American revivalist fashion,
even to the extent of indulging in personalities." He was critical of
Erl. Carlsson as chairman of the Board of Directors of Augustana
Seminary because he felt that, "The preachers left Augustana
Seminary more narrow and intolerant than when they entered and
graduated with scarcely any trace of learning. In his opinion the
Swedish Lutheran Church was more harmful than salutary. . . . He
advised the immigrants to join pure American congregations in order
to become thoroughly Americanized and assimilated." [30]

The most bitter attack upon Erl. Carlsson appeared over the
signature of "Isidor K" in *Göteborgs-Posten* on April 3, 1870.
Kjellberg described the Chicago pastor as follows: "Pastor Carlsson's
appearance is like guttapercha in that at the behest of the spirit that
controls the inner mechanism, it can momentarily express all kinds
of emotion. Outside the church it always shows a smiling counte-
nance. In the pulpit it is almost on all occasions full of tears; he cries
gladly and well. . . . But he can suddenly change his tone and
appearance. The gracious smile disappears from his lips, and fearful
to behold, he thunders the most horrifying prophecies about God's
approaching wrath and hell's torment." [31]

The attack went beyond personal appearance and responses. He
wrote about Carlsson as a pastor: "The pope in Rome has scarcely
larger or more complete domination over his followers than this
preacher has over the members of his congregation." Moreover,
Kjellberg attributed grandiose schemes to Erl. Carlsson: "There is
even consideration of a plan that when the new church has come into
its full flowering, it will be arranged so that he will be designated the
Swedish bishop in the United States and that he is working hard to
get the 'university' at Paxton [Augustana College and Theological

Seminary] moved to Chicago, which will then become the capitol of the Swedish Lutheran Church in America." [32]

Kjellberg also indicated the reasons for his attack upon Carlsson: "To warn prospective immigrants about one of the biggest and most dangerous 'spiritual runners.' It would be too bad if he should receive support for his 'humbug church' in which charlatanism and hate are continually preached in God's name." [33]

Peter Wieselgren, well-known Göteborg clergyman and Carlsson's close friend, wrote to the Göteborg newspaper a few days after Kjellberg's article stating that several people had urged him to answer the critic's attacks. His refusal to do so was based on his policy not to engage in personal polemics. Moreover, he and others knew that "Pastor Carlsson was an honorable man." [34]

Kjellberg received support from some sources. *Öresund Posten* (Hälsingborg) argued that "Carlsson's sermons are just as full of personalities as 'Isidor K's' articles." *Svenska Amerikanaren* supported Carlsson. Kjellberg was criticized for his attacks on the Chicago pastor in a long article late in April under the rubric, *Skandalskrivaren Isidor K* (Scandal Writer, Isidor K.). The editor of *Svenska Amerikanaren*, after describing the faithful service of Pastor Carlsson as a clergyman, counselor of immigrants, and friend of the poor and ill, wrote as follows: "What you say, *Herr* Isidor, is a lie, an infamous lie, from beginning to end. That *Svenska Amerikanaren* is no friend of clergymen is generally well-known. . . . [However], we know Pastor Carlsson as a noble, honest, friendly person and clergyman and it is for that reason that we read with detestation and horror the scandalous attack on his personal and public character."[35]

C. F. Peterson, an observer of the Chicago scene beginning in 1870, has written about the situation as follows: "One hears much talk about the Swedish pastoral clericalism in Chicago during the first twenty-five years. But it was not as dangerous as it sounded. Seen by the right light as cast into the so-called iron-age, the complaint of clericalism was far from tyrannical, even if at times it seemed high-handed." Peterson emphasized that "the pastors were the only ones to whom the confused immigrants could look with hope of help and guidance, not only in spiritual but also in temporal matters. The pastors held a certain tutelage which was far from being domineering." [36]

There were occasional hecklers who attended the services at Immanuel Church. They were not really interested; some may have come out of curiosity; others were critical of what seemed to be the equivalent of the Church of Sweden, to which they were hostile. A contemporary has written that "occasionally, especially at evening services, the preacher was interrupted with pointed and insidious questions." But the Swedish Lutheran Church had less trouble of this kind than the Swedish Methodist congregation. It is reported that during a revival "windows were broken, doors kicked out, and noise was made by beating on tin pans and other 'cymbals' while the pious people inside sang their *Zionssånger.*"[37]

Erl. Carlsson became involved in criticism related to the visit of Christina Nilsson to Chicago in 1870. Jenny Lind had been an ambassador *par excellence* for Sweden in 1850 when the great singer inspired great audiences with her superb vocal achievement and interesting personality. Two decades later, Christina Nilsson, the great opera singer from Småland, Erl. Carlsson's home area, also scored great triumphs in 1870-71, 1873-74 and a finale in 1883-84.

Erl. Carlsson, who was always interested in promoting Swedish culture as well as the welfare of his congregation, wrote to Peter Wieselgren in October 1870, seeking a letter of introduction to Christina Nilsson. He pointed out that Immanuel Church had recently built a new church and that the congregation had a $20,000 debt. A benefit concert by the famous singer would be a great blessing. He sought Wieselgren's help since he understood that it was difficult to make contact with the famous singer. The Svea Society was also active in trying to capitalize on the visit of Christina Nilsson. In an article with the rubric "An Invitation," appearing in the October 11 issue of *Svenska Amerikanaren,* a committee of twelve, including O. G. Lange, Axel Silversparre, and C. J. Sundell, announced that the public was invited to attend a grand reception for the Swedish singer under the auspices of the Svea Society. This action was rather unusual since its members were clearly separated from the mass of Swedish immigrants by wealth, culture, ideas and social status.[38]

Christina Nilsson presented four concerts in Chicago beginning on December 19, 1870, but no performance was a benefit for Immanuel Church. *The Chicago Tribune,* in full reports, reviewed the performance in glowing terms. The Swedes were proud of their famous compatriot from the homeland and sought to honor her. After considerable controversy between the "church element," represented by Erl. Carlsson and his associates, and the "secular element," identified primarily with the Svea Society, a national festival under the sponsorship of "the Swedes of Chicago and the Svea Society" was arranged through the leadership of John Enander, editor of *Hemlandet* to honor the famous visitor. According to the *Chicago Tribune,* on December 21, shortly after 8 p.m., Christina Nilsson, "wrapped in furs which left but her eyes visible," appeared outside the Sherman House, escorted by Mr. Lange, Chicago's first Swede. A long procession of carriages, illuminated by torchbearers on horseback, drove slowly north on Clark Street, with the final destination, the corner of Wells and Indiana streets, the location of the German Hall.[39]

The *Tribune* reflected on the reception that the great artist received as she entered the hall: "It was a touching scene, this demonstration to the new queen of song. Here in the heart of the American continent, she was surrounded by her countrymen and countrywomen, proud to do her honor, proud to be associated with her even by the slender tie of nationality." Speakers were C. J. Sundell, Mr. Lange, Colonel Eastman, Joseph Medill, editor of the *Tribune,* and others. John Enander read a poem written for the occasion. The gift of a wreath, composed of gold leaves, representing laurel, with two birds between each pair of gold leaves, with pearl letters, "C. N.", formed a beautiful tribute.[40]

A banquet followed in the attractively decorated hall. The *Tribune* reported that, "Eating began, and there was a generous flow of soul and wine, and any amount of sociability and good feeling." Pastor Carlsson and some members of his congregation, and other Swedish pastors, were in attendance at the banquet. They left without sharing in the wine and without attending the ball which followed the banquet. John Enander, who also left before the ball, reported that, "Many people were sad that Christina Nilsson would participate in such sinful recreation." Hasselquist and Erl. Carlsson were criticized for attending one of her concerts a few days later. [41]

Christina Nilsson gave two benefit concerts in Farwell Hall in 1871 for Swedish congregations, institutions and organizations, and for Augustana College and Theological Seminary in Paxton. Isidor Kjellberg used the occasion to mock and ridicule the pastor of Immanuel Church for being so closely associated with the famous singer. He wrote in *Justitia:*

> Erl. Carlsson will now say: "Dear members, take Christina Nilsson, the virtuous and generous actress, as an example, for she is certainly a person according to God's purpose. . . . Go to church today and to the theatre tomorrow."

Kjellberg wrote fancifully that he soon expected to see an announcement for the members of Carlsson's congregation over the pastor's signature, urging them to attend a festive *soiree.* There would be dancing until four o'clock in the morning. Good beer and Swedish punch would be served at a modest cost. Carlsson's critic speculated that the income would be used to build a large concert hall in Chicago. [42]

Erl. Carlsson was often in the midst of conflict. Some aspects may have been based on personal factors; others were related to different philosophies and points of view. Carlsson represented the church and the distinctive witness of the *läsare* and conservative tradition. Some of his critics had embraced a secular and rationalistic view. The antagonists on both sides were capable and articulate advocates of their interests. This was an interesting period, full of activity, and with substantial divergence in life style and thought.

FOOTNOTES

[1] References to relations with Unonius are found *supra*, pp. 30-31. The quotation about the Episcopalians is in *Korsbaneret,* 1881, p. 78. Various issues involving the Episcopalians and the Augustana Synod are discussed in detail by Carl Henrik Lyttkens, *The Growth of Swedish-Anglican Intercommunion, 1833-1922* (Lund: C. W. K. Gleerup, 1970), pp. 16-72; 160-72.

[2] Gunnar Westin, *Lutheraner, Anglikaner, Reformerta. Kyrkohistoriska uppsatser* (Uppsala: J. A. Lundblads förlag, 1935), pp. 216-19; Hugo Söderström, *Confession and Cooperation* (Lund: C. W. K. Gleerup, 1965), pp. 162-63; Carl Henrik Lyttkens, *The Growth of Swedish-Anglican Intercommunion Between 1833 and 1922,* pp. 169-170.

[3] Westin, *Lutheraner, Anglikaner, Reformerta,* pp. 220-21; *Hemlandet* July 16, 1867; *Svenska Amerikanaren,* July 24, 1867; George M. Stephenson, "The Stormy Years of the Swedish Colony in Chicago Before the Great Fire," *Transactions of the Illinois State Historical Society,* 1929 (No. 36), p. 172.

[4]*Svenska Amerikanaren,* July 24, 1867.

[5]Erl. Carlsson to T. N. Hasselquist, Chicago, April 13, 1868, November 23, 1868.

[6]Anders, "Select Letters to Jonas Swensson, 1856-58," pp. 54-55.

[7]Erl. Carlsson, *Korsbaneret,* 1882, pp. 179-80; Arden, *Augustana Heritage,* pp. 160-87.

[8]C. V. Bowman, *Missionsvännerna i Amerika* (Minneapolis: Minneapolis Veckoblad Publ. Co., 1907), pp. 48-56.

[9]*Ibid.,* p. 56.

[10]Erl. Carlsson to T. N. Hasselquist, Chicago, March 11, 1868.

[11]*Ibid.,* February 4, 1869.

[12]*Ibid.*

[13]Bowman, *Missionsvännerna i Amerika,* p. 58; Karl A. Olsson, *By One Spirit,* pp. 214-15; Arden, *Augustana Heritage,* pp. 168-69.

[14]Bowman, *Missionsvännerna i Amerika,* p. 59, translated and cited by Arden, *Augustana Heritage,* p. 169; *Covenant Memories. Golden Jubilee. Swedish Evangelical Mission Covenant, 1885-1933,* pp. 50-51.

[15]Bowman, *Missionsvännerna i Amerika,* p. 61.

[16]Arden, *Augustana Heritage,* pp. 168-69; Karl A. Olsson, *By One Spirit,* 200-201.

[17]Karl A. Olsson, *By One Spirit,* pp. 200-221, 226. Erik Brolund in his book *Missionsvännerna. Jämförelser och studier* (Chicago: Mission Friends Publishing Co., 1938), pp. 68-73 is very generous in his description of Pastor Carlsson and his zeal for evangelical Christianity.

[18]Arden, *Augustana Heritage,* p. 170.

[19]See the following for a discussion of P. P. Waldenström's views of the atonement: Karl A. Olsson, *By One Spirit,* pp. 105-120 and Arden, *Augustana Heritage,* pp. 174-88.

[20]"Statistical Table," *Korsbaneret,* 1881, p. 126.

[21]Erl. Carlsson, *Korsbaneret,* 1882, p. 179.

[22]"Statistical Table," *Korsbaneret,* 1881, p. 126; J. A. Enander to T. N. Hasselquist, October 4 and August 2, 1875, cited in O. F. Ander, *T. N. Hasselquist,* pp. 165-66.

166   THE STORY OF ERLAND CARLSSON

[23]Erl. Carlsson, *Korsbaneret*, 1882, pp. 177-78; Newman, *Sjelfbiografi*, p. 154; N. M. Liljegren, N. O. Westergreen, and C. G. Wallenius, *Svenska Metodism i Amerika* (Chicago: Svenska M. E. bokhandels föreningens förlag, 1895, p. 211.

[24]Erl. Carlsson, *Korsbaneret*, 1882, pp. 178-79; Anders, "Select Letters to Jonas Swensson," p. 53.

[25]Adolph Olson, *A Centenary History. As Related to the Baptist General Conference of America* (Chicago: Baptist Conference Press, 1952), pp. 79-80, 93-97; Erl. Carlsson, *Korsbaneret*, 1882, pp. 176-77.

[26]C. F. Peterson, "Blickar mellan kulisserna i Chicago's Svenska verld för 35 år sedan," *Valkyrian* (New York), V, 34; Ulf Beijbom, "Erland Carlsson och Den Svensk-Amerikanska kyrkan," *Älghults-Krönika*, 1966, p. 35.

[27]Stephenson, "The Stormy Years of the Swedish Colony in Chicago Before the Great Fire," p. 168; C. F. Peterson, "Några svenska Chicagominnen," *Valkyrian* (New York), III, 409.

[28]Alfred Söderström, *Blixtar på tidnings-horisonten* (1910), p. 74; Ernst Skarstedt, *Pennfäktare. Svensk-Amerikanska författare och tidningsmän* (Stockholm: Albert Bonnier, 1930), p. 158; Peterson, *"Blickar mellan kulisserna i Chicagos Svenska verld för 35 år sedan";* Ulf Beijbom, "The Printed Word in a Nineteenth Century Immigrant Colony: The Role of the Ethnic Press in Chicago's Swede Town," *The Swedish Pioneer Historical Quarterly*, XXVIII (April, 1977), 87-89.

[29]George M. Stephenson, "Isidor Kjellberg," *Swedish American Historical Bulletin* (St. Peter, Minn.), II, 31-34.

[30]Stephenson, "Isidor Kjellberg," pp. 35-36.

[31]*Göteborgs-Posten*, April 3, 1870.

[32]*Göteborgs-Posten*, April 3, 1870. Kjellberg continued his attacks on Erl. Carlsson and the Augustana Synod in his lecture in Stockholm in 1883: Isidor Kjellberg, *Föredrag om Amerika hållet i Stockholm den 18 Febr. 1883* (Stockholm, A. W. Björcks förlag, 1883), pp. 36-40.

[33]*Göteborgs-Posten*, April 3, 1870.

[34]*Ibid.*, April 8, 1870.

[35]Stephenson, "Isidor Kjellberg," p. 37; *Svenska Amerikanaren*, April 5, 1870.

[36]Peterson, "Några Chicago minnen," p. 410.

[37]Peterson, "Några Chicago minnen," p. 409; Newman, *Sjelfbiografi*, p. 131.

[38]Erl. Carlsson to Peter Wieselgren, Chicago, October 31, 1870, Westin,

Emigranterna och kyrkan, p. 284; *Svenska Amerikanaren,* October 11, 1870; Beijbom, *Swedes in Chicago,* pp. 267-70, 280-86.

[39] John A. Enander, "Då Christina Nilsson kom till Chicago," *Prärieblomman kalender för 1900* (Rock Island: Augustana Book Concern, 1900), p. 53; *The Chicago Tribune,* December 20, 21, 22, 1870. For description of the Svea Society, see Johnson and Peterson, *Svenskarne i Illinois,* pp. 256-59, E. Gustav Johnson, "Chicago Swedes Organized 'Svea' a Century Ago," *Swedish Pioneer Historical Quarterly,* VIII (1957), 115-29, and Beijbom, *Swedes in Chicago,* pp. 267-74.

[40] *The Chicago Daily Tribune,* December 21, 1870; Enander, "Då Christina Nilsson kom till Chicago," pp. 53-54.

[41] *The Chicago Daily Tribune,* December 22, 1870; Enander, "Då Christina Nilsson kom till Chicago," p. 61.

[42] *Justitia,* June 24, 1871. The members of *Svea* turned down their share of the benefit concerts because they felt that the one-twelfth granted them was not a fair distribution. Kjellberg congratulated *Svea* for this action. *Justitia,* June 10, 1871.

The Carlsson Grandchildren at Rostad

Pastor and Mrs. Carlsson with the Familie
of Son Eben and Daughter Emmy Eva

Pastor Carlsson and Immanuel Church
Confirmation Class, 1867

Pastor Carlsson's Funeral Service in
Immanuel Church, Oct. 25, 1893

12

Family and the Larger Society

Erl. Carlsson's career was supported and enriched immeasurably by a happy family life. That day in May 1855 when Eva Charlotta Anderson and he were married in Chicago was a memorable day. The Carlssons multiplied each others contributions to God and man by merging the sterling qualities which each one possessed.[1]

Eva Carlsson soon established herself as a person with fine personal resources. She was "equipped with great understanding and with the highest degree of friendliness and hospitality. With her piety and zeal for the Lord's work and mankind's welfare, she was such a great help and encouragement in her husband's extensive and exacting work." The Carlsson home was known in a wide circle as a refuge for distressed countrymen. Emmy Evald, the Carlsson's second daughter, remembered as a child her mother carrying out big kettles of meat-ball soup with potatoes and carrots to hungry and penniless immigrants in the backyard of their home. Contemporary records show that the parsonage served at times both as a kind of immigrant home and hospital. Mrs. Carlsson was always there to help and encourage.[2]

When the need for providing aid to ill immigrants became urgent in the early 1860s, Pastor Carlsson rented and equipped a house near Illinois Street for that purpose. Mrs. Carlsson was briefly manager and nurse. A large part of every day was devoted to taking care of ill and discouraged men, women, and children. She, however, never neglected home and family. Mrs. Carlsson had innumerable friends throughout midwestern Swedish America who had remembrances of her loving care and concern. She was always active in church organizations. Her support and spirit was an important factor in making it possible for Pastor Carlsson to carry on his great and varied ministry.[3]

Emmy Evald has described her mother as follows:

> First of all she was a gentle and loving mother in the home. In the second place, she was a kindly and devoted mother for the whole Immanuel congregation, the largest mother church in the synod. Moreover, she was a helpful and sacrificing mother for thousands and thousands of Swedish immigrants. She had time for everyone, she was friendly towards all, and she had a sweet smile for all.[4]

After the death of her husband in 1893, Mrs. Carlsson lived at the home of her daughter Emmy and Pastor Carl Evald, in the parsonage home of Immanuel Church. She was active in the congregation until shortly before her death on July 11, 1911. Her family and a large circle of friends in Chicago and elsewhere mourned the passing of this fine Christian woman.[5]

Eight children were born into the Erland Carlsson family. Four lived beyond the early period of birth—Annie Fredrika, Emmy Christina, Ebenezer, and Samuel. Annie, a young woman of great talent and charm, died in 1880 in Sweden, where she had gone for reasons of health, a few years after her marriage to Pastor Carl Evald of Immanuel Church. Emmy became the second wife of Pastor Evald in 1883. She was the dynamic supporter of this gifted pastor in enriching and expanding the life of the congregation for twenty-six years until his death in 1909.[6]

Emmy Evald was the greatest leader among women in the Augustana Synod and in Swedish America generally. Born in Geneva, Illinois, September 18, 1857, she studied in *Mamsell* Fryxell's school in Kalmar, together with Annie, from 1870 to 1873. Emmy was a student at Rockford Seminary for three years where she was a friend of Jane Addams of Hull House fame. She was also well acquainted with Susan B. Anthony, famous leader of the women's suffrage movement, and she worked fervently with her in behalf of women's rights. Emmy Evald served as president of the Lutheran World's Womens' Congress at the World Columbian Exposition in Chicago in

1883. She led delegations in behalf of woman's suffrage to hearings before committees of the Illinois Legislature and the Congress of the United States.[7]

The dynamic leadership of Emmy Evald resulted in lasting contributions to the building of the Kingdom of God, especially in missions. She was the key person in bringing a group of women together at a meeting of the Augustana Synod at Lindsborg, in June 1892, when the Women's Missionary Society of the Augustana Synod was organized. Her parents had invited the wives of pastors and lay delegates attending the synod meeting to assemble at Rostad, their country home near Lindsborg, on Friday, June 3, to discuss the possibility of organizing a women's missionary society. Plans were adopted and temporary officers were selected on that occasion. The group met at the parsonage home of Dr. and Mrs. Carl Swensson the following Monday to make official the earlier action at Rostad. Fifty women, led by Mrs. Evald, went as a body to the convention and presented their petition for synodical approval. She served as the effective president of the society for more than four decades. She founded *Mission Tidings*, the official publication of the society, in 1906 and served as a departmental editor for almost three decades. She was the vital force in every aspect of the work of this organization.[8]

During Emmy Evald's presidency of the Women's Missionary Society, seventy-four buildings were erected in the United States and throughout the world for Christian service. She was founder of the Lutheran Home for Women in New York, and manager and director at the time of her death. She was the author of nine historical books and smaller studies. Mrs. Evald was awarded the honorary doctor of humanities degree by Upsala College, East Orange, N. J., and the medal of the Vasa Order by the King of Sweden.[9]

Dr. P. O. Bersell, president of the Augustana Lutheran Church, in his report to synod in June 1947, following Emmy Evald's death the previous year, presented this tribute to her:

> Mrs. Emmy Evald, daughter of the third president of our synod, militant leader in the movement for women's rights, world traveler, soul-stirring speaker, missionary crusader, founder of the Women's Missionary Society of the Augustana Synod and for forty-three years its dynamic president, was a maker of history. The Women's Missionary Society in its world-embracing service and its continued growth in strength is the chief monument to her work.[10]

Ebenezer and Samuel Carlsson were good citizens who made worthwhile contributions to society. The former who was known generally as Eben, was a graduate of Augustana College and a Chicago school of pharmacy. He was a pharmacist in Lindsborg, where he brought his bride, Anna, daughter of Pastor and Mrs. Jonas Swensson, in the spring of 1878. He served as register of deeds of McPherson County and as postmaster at Lindsborg and McPherson. He also had business interests and was a community leader. Eben was twelve years old when he witnessed the effects of the great fire in Chicago in 1871 which made the family homeless. Earlier, when he was six years old, he went with his family to City Hall in Chicago, where his father picked him up, and raised him high so that he could see the remains of Abraham Lincoln who was lying in state. Eben died in 1932. [11]

Samuel Carlsson, a talented young man, began his career as a musician while a student at Augustana College. He taught music in that institution until he moved to Chicago. He was director of the Immanuel Church Choir for several years in the 1890s. He organized and was the leader of string trios and quartettes as well as the director of a well-known chamber music ensemble in Chicago. Samuel Carlsson was a fine performer on the violin. He was at one time part owner of *Svenska Tribunen* and manager of *Foster-landet.* [12]

Happy and supporting family life made important contributions to the career of Erl. Carlsson. He was a devoted family man in the midst of a busy career that made many demands upon his time. Dr. Carl Swensson, who knew Erl. Carlsson from the former's teen-age years to the latter's death in 1893, has described this aspect of the life of the pioneer pastor: "He was exemplary and loveable in his home life. The family altar was especially precious to him. He loved song and music and played violin and flute in younger years. Few had such a good memory and could tell a story as well as Dr. Carlsson. One who had the privilege of being in the family circle will never forget it." Pastor Philip Thelander remembered with deep feeling from youthful years the family devotions in the Carlsson home during his three-month stay in Andover. Erl. Carlsson always opened the devotions with two verses of the familiar hymn, *O Gud! all sannings källa! Jag tror ditt löftes ord* (O God! the source of all truth! The promises of Thy word I do believe) in the *Psalmbok,* no. 260. The members of the family dropped to their knees for the prayers. [13]

Erl. Carlsson was away from home often and for long periods of time during his active career. The busy pastor was always thoughtful about his near and dear ones as indicated by his many letters to them. For instance, in May 1872, when he was visiting in New York, he shared his many experiences in a long letter to his wife. But much space was also devoted to family matters. There were instructions as to action to be taken during the construction of the Carlssons' future home, including the suggestion that Consul Hawkinson would be a good adviser. If Mrs. Carlsson needed more money, C. P. Holmberg would gladly advance it from the pastor's salary account. He expressed the hope that Anna and Emmy, who were students in *Mamsell* Fryxell's school in Kalmar, were well and making progress. He recalled that this was Annie's confirmation day in faraway Sweden. He was thinking especially of her. The father inquired about Eben and Samuel, expressing the hope that they were "good boys." His response on being separated from the family was clear: "There are times when I feel horribly lonesome and I feel a deep inner longing for my dear family and my dear congregation." He concluded the letter by sending greetings to the Hawkinsons, Engbergs, Holmbergs, and Colseths who were close friends within the circle of his many friends. [14]

Erl. Carlsson was a good steward of his own business affairs as well as an excellent administrator in church relationships. However, it is rather surprising that according to the census of 1870 he is listed as having financial resources amounting to $26,000. It is undoubtedly true, as has been said, that, "He made judicious investments that in time yielded substantial returns." He received an inheritance in Sweden following the death of his father, but his financial problems as a student indicate that it was not a large legacy. He had no fixed salary during his early years as a pastor in Chicago; he received only collections, which averaged $180.00 during the 1854-1856 period. Later, his first regular annual salary was $350.00 When the congregation grew in membership, his salary increased. He received considerable income from weddings and other pastoral services. One of Isidor Kjellberg's criticisms of Erl. Carlsson was his affluent economic condition. [15]

The record indicates conclusively that Pastor Carlsson used personal funds effectively to promote the work of the church. In the 1850s, when Immanuel Church was in financial difficulties, he took over the obligation on lots owned by the church. These lots became the site of the Carlsson home. When the manuscript for the new *Psalmbok* was completed in 1865, he provided a loan of $1,000 so that this important volume could be printed. His purchase of lots on Lincoln Street, where the new Carlsson home was built, proved ultimately to be an excellent investment. The income from the sale of the house and lots made it possible for Carlsson, at the time of retirement in 1888, to purchase 240 acres of fine farm land in the Smoky Valley near Lindsborg. [16]

Although Erl. Carlsson's mission as a pastor and leader was primarily among Swedish Americans, he was confronted by problems of adaptation to American life. Moreover, he approached life in his new homeland with the intent of being closely identified with the American scene.

The founders of Swedish Lutheran churches in America during the nineteenth century were united in their views about the future. G. Everett Arden has appropriately described their commitment:

> The early leaders of Augustana were not isolationists, hoping to insulate their people against American influence so as to perpetuate a Swedith ethos, or repristinate the Swedish church on American soil. Indeed, L. P. Esbjörn, T. N. Hasselquist, Erland Carlsson, and Eric Norelius were unanimous in their conviction that the Swedish people ought to identify themselves with their new American home, to become good and loyal American citizens, and that Swedish usage, language, and custom must not become ends in themselves, but must be merely the means for effective recruitment and retention of Scandinavians as members of the Lutheran church in America. [17]

The immigrants were confronted at the outset by the problem of language. Erl. Carlsson immediately recognized that fact and made this comment: "I believed that the Swedish language would be dead in America in twenty years and therefore I prepared myself for the change and studied the English language." This observation came out of experience. A description of Carlsson's use of English is given by a contemporary observer, Dr. Adolph Spaeth, when Carlsson was in

Philadelphia seeking funds for the new church following the 1871 fire: "He could not speak German. We could not understand Swedish. He was forced to use English which he spoke very brokenly but the seriousness of his cause gave him eloquence, and his deep emotion, his unrestrained tears, made him intelligible to everyone. . . . " Carlsson made substantial gains in mastering the English language. The letters that are available in that language are characterized by excellent sentence structure and effective vocabulary. [18]

Although Carlsson's prophecy relating to the disappearance of Swedish in twenty years was in error, partially because of the vast increase in immigration in the 1880s, the statement nevertheless indicates his realistic appraisal of the future role of English. More important than his comment was his action. English was used almost exclusively in the Immanuel Sunday School, which was a tradition established by the Norwegians in Chicago and maintained by the Swedes. In May 1863, Esbjörn wrote to Norelius that the *Catechism* should be translated into English. He argued that "English is coming with great steps. Carlsson uses English with the confirmation children." This was only partially the situation, because Swedish was also used by him in this instruction. As has already been noted, Carlsson was chairman later of the committee assigned by the synod to translate the *Catechism* into English. [19]

The commitment of Erl. Carlsson to language as a vital aspect of Americanization was promoted effectively in his official capacity. The constitution of Augustana Seminary, in 1860, which had been drafted primarily by Carlsson as chairman of the committee, providing for instruction in the Scandinavian languages and in English, was written in English. The minutes of the Board of Directors were in that language from the outset. As chairman of the Board of Directors, in 1879, he was instrumental in the decision that provided for the employment of faculty who could communicate effectively in English. In his presidential report to the synod in 1883, while urging his fellow pastors to become proficient in English and to recognize the importance of that language for the future of the church, he reminded them that God's Word can be preached with equal effectiveness in either language. [20]

The leadership of Carlsson as president of the synod in

promoting the language of the land was applauded by Lutherans of other synods. In a letter in December 1882, Pastor G. F. Krotel, a member of the English Home Missions Committee of the General Council, wrote to Carlsson: "We here in the East, at least on the English side of the house, admire the wisdom and fine Christian liberality manifested by the Augustana Synod in comprehending and taking steps to provide for the true interests of the rising generation. . . . Although you do not love your Swedish tongue less, you have experienced the irresistable forces of the new land, and loving your Lutheran church more than your old language, and determined to do all you can to keep your children in that church, you have wisely determined to provide for them." Krotel concluded his praise for the attitude of Carlsson and his associates: "You are wise and courageous and the future will prove it more and more. You are wise in training your young men for this work, for after all they are the men who will prove most useful in this great transition." [21]

Although the road ahead in the transition from Swedish to English was long and difficult, Erl. Carlsson was aware of future needs and acted accordingly. The practical implications were placed in focus during the years when he served as business manager of Augustana College and Theological Seminary. In February 1888, Grace Lutheran Church, Rock Island, was organized as an English language congregation. Erl. Carlsson and his family were charter members. The support of this pastor, who came out of the Swedish tradition and at that time president of the synod, was an important factor in the origin of this congregation. Two sons of pioneer pastors, Carl L. E. Esbjörn and Joshua Hasselquist, were also charter members. Erl. Carlsson was elected one of three deacons. When the congregation applied for membership in the Illinois Conference, he was the principal advocate who "pleaded for admission with tears in his eyes." After lengthy discussion the congregation was accepted. [22]

The available evidence does not indicate that Erl. Carlsson was involved in public and political affairs. A large Scandinavian meeting was held in Metropolitan Hall, Chicago, in August 1856, to consider the position to be taken in the presidential campaign. Action was taken to support Fremont and the Republican party platform. Speeches were given by Gustaf Unonius, pastor, St. Ansgarius Episcopal Church, and by Paul Andersen, Carlsson's close friend and pastor of the Norwegian Lutheran church. Carlsson is not identified as a participant. His arrival in Chicago only three years earlier might have been a factor. Letters to Peter Wieselgren during the Civil War portray Carlsson's support of the Union cause, but there is no great militancy in his description of this tragic conflict. His name does not appear as a speaker at any of the Scandinavian Union rallies. L. P. Esbjörn was the principal speaker in April 1861, at a meeting which was billed by *The Chicago Tribune* as, "The Scandinavians for the War." Later, one of Esbjörn's sons was killed in the war. Erl. Carlsson was not included among the signers of a Scandinavian resolution, April 20, 1861, "In Defense of the Honor of Our Adopted Country." [23]

The many demands of Carlsson's congregation and the work of the church at large were undoubtedly factors in what seemed to be his non-involvement in public affairs. This was not an uncommon situation for Swedish Lutheran pastors then and subsequently. He maintained a fine balance between the culture of his native Sweden, promoting its best qualities, and the new homeland, which he loved and served day by day. His personal Americanization is apparent from his interest in the language of the land and by his support of American institutions.

FOOTNOTES

[1] For background factors about Eva Carlsson, see p. 34.

[2] M. C. Ranseen, "Immanuels-församlingens pastorsfruar," *Minneskrift-Immanuelsförsamlingen,* p. 50; C. E. Hoffsten, "Dr. Erland Carlsson and Our Early Church Work in Chicago," *My Church,* XIX (1933), 80.

[3] M. C. Ranseen, "Fru Eva C. Carlsson," *Korsbaneret,* 1912, pp. 235-36.

[4] *När och fjerran* (Stockholm, N. D.). In the Erl. Carlsson papers at Augustana College.

[5] Ranseen, "Fru Eva C. Carlsson," *Korsbaneret,* 1912, pp. 238-39.

[6] Ranseen, "Immanuels-församlingens pastorsfruar," *Minneskrift-Immanuelsförsamlingen,* p. 50; Ranseen, "Pastor C. A. Evald," *Korsbaneret,* 1910, p. 163; "M", "Emmy Evald," *Korsbaneret,* 1948, p. 194.

[7]"M". "Emmy Evald," *Korsbaneret,* 1948, pp. 193-97; Charlotte Odman, "She Led a Women's Crusade for Christ," *The Lutheran Companion,* June 1, 1960, reprinted in Nystrom, *A Family of God,* pp. 143-44; *Lutheran Companion,* January 1, 1947; *Immanuel Review* (Immanuel Ev. Lutheran Church, Chicago), January, 1947; "Fru Emmy Evald," C. F. Peterson, *"Sverige i Amerika. Kulturhistorisk och biografiska teckningar* (Chicago: The Royal Star Co., 1896), pp. 275-76.

[8]S. Hjalmar Swanson, *Foundation For Tomorrow. A Century of Progress in Augustana World Missions* (Minneapolis. Board of World Missions, 1960), pp. 322-23; *Woman's Missionary Society, 1892-1927. Survey of Thirty-Five Years Activity* (Chicago: Woman's Mission Board, 1927), pp. 53, 84; Emmy Evald, *"Kvinnornas missionförenings fyrtioåriga verksamhet inom Augustana Synoden,"* *Korsbaneret,* 1933, p. 169.

[9]*Lutheran Companion,* January 1, 1947.

[10]*Augustana Synodical Minutes,* 1947, p. 27, reprinted in Nystrom, *A Family of God,* pp. 212-13.

[11]G. A. Andreen, "Eben Carlsson," *Korsbaneret,* 1933, pp. 322-26; *Lindsborg News-Record,* August 4, 1932.

[12]E. W. Olson, *History of the Swedes of Illinois,* pp. 708, 721-22, 755-61, 794; S. E. Carlsson to C. A. Swensson, Feb. 7, March 13, 1899.

[13]*Fosterlandet,* October 25, 1893; Philip Thelander, "Doktor Erland Carlsson," Ms. 7 pp.

[14]Erl. Carlsson to Mrs. Erl. Carlsson, New York, May 9, 1872.

[15]Beijbom, *Swedes in Chicago,* note from Census of 1870, p. 262; E. W. Olson, *The Swedish Element in Illinois* (Chicago: Swedish-American Biographical Association, 1917), p. 150; *Göteborgs-Posten,* April 3, 1870.

[16]Arvastan, *Den Thomander-Wieselgrenska psalmboken,* p. 192; E. W. Olson, *The Swedish Element in Illinois,* p. 150.

[17]Arden, *Augustana Heritage,* p. 233.

[18]I. O. Nothstein, "The Language Transition in the Augustana Synod," *The Augustana Quarterly,* XXIV (July 1945), 210; *Life of Adolph Spaeth Told in His Own Reminiscences, His Letters, and Recollections,* edited by his wife (Philadelphia: General Council Publication House, 1916), pp. 177-78.

[19]Nothstein, "The Language Transition in the Augustana Synod," p. 210; L. P. Esbjörn to Eric Norelius, Chicago, May 22, 1863, *Tidskrift, 1899,* p. 338. See reference to English catechism *supra,* Ch. IX.

[20]Nothstein, "Selected Documents . . . of the Augustana Synod," *Augustana Historical Society Publications,* X, Part I, 189.

[21]G. F. Krotel to Erl. Carlsson, December 20, 1882.

[22]Nothstein, "The Language Transition in the Augustana Synod," pp. 327-28; Stephenson, *Religious Aspects of Swedish Immigration,* pp. 466-67; C. W. Foss, "Historical Sketch of Grace Lutheran Church, Rock Island, Ill., *The Lutheran Companion,* February 18, 1923.

[23]*Wäktaren,* September 30, 1856. Esbjörn's speech is referred to in *The Chicago Daily Tribune,* April 30, 1861. Other references to Scandinavian participation are found in *The Chicago Tribune* January 19, April 20, October 19, 1861. Erl. Carlsson to Peter Wieselgren, Chicago, July 12, 1861.

13

The Last Years

On April 5, 1875, the fourth Sunday after Trinity, Erl. Carlsson preached his last sermon as pastor of Immanuel Church to what has been described as "a packed house." It was a touching occasion as the dedicated pastor brought his twenty-two year ministry to an end. Many people in the audience had grown old with Pastor Carlsson in their many years of Christian fellowship. Others had been baptized, confirmed, and married by him. Still others had heard his words of Christian hope and comfort as they said farewell to near and dear ones. The pastor reflected on the early years—an immigrant in a strange land, a handful of people at the first service in a rented church, the future full of uncertainty. But pastor and people had faith in God and in His grace and power. The years had passed and the work of the Kingdom of God had moved forward. There were many portraits in the temple of memory that April day in Immanuel Church. What had been done in the name of Christ would cast benevolent shadows far into the future.[1]

Erl. Carlsson left Immanuel Church and Chicago after two decades of more than magnificent service. The strenuous years of hard work had made heavy demands on the health of the pastor who was now in his fifties. The invitation to succeed his friend, Pastor Jonas Swensson at Andover, who had been called from this life in the midst of a great career, was accepted by Pastor Carlsson. He hoped that he might be able to regain full physical strength while living in a rural

181

parish, free from the strain of city life. He preached his first sermon at the Andover Swedish Lutheran Church on May 2, 1875.[2]

Erl. Carlsson's decision to become pastor at Andover was based on the second call issued to him in September 1874, following the first invitation in April. His resignation was read to the congregation on October 25, "with deep feeling on the part of the pastor and congregation." Pastor Carlsson has described the meeting following the announcement of his resignation: "I had never seen the voting members assembled in such great numbers previously. In the most alluring terms I was urged to withdraw my resignation and the congregation promised not only to engage assistants for me but also with greater faithfulness commit themselves to the goals of our congregation and carry out their responsibilities if only I would stay." He promised to consider their request, but in the end, the decision to resign was maintained.[3]

The Andover congregation decided shortly after the arrival of the Carlssons to raze the old parsonage and to construct a greatly needed new one. The Carlssons agreed to pay the costs of the heating system as their contribution to the project. They entered into their new field of labor with dedication and enthusiasm. Members of the Andover congregation, although saddened by the loss of dearly-beloved Jonas Swensson, were thankful that Erl. Carlsson had become their pastor. He was well-known as a frequent visitor at the home of the Swenssons. There were mutual feelings of gratitude and respect between pastor and people.[4]

The decisions of the congregation reflect in an interesting manner the attitude of the time on a variety of issues. Action was taken to enforce the constitution relative to membership in secret societies in 1878. The congregation voted that no new members would be admitted if they belonged to the Free Masons or other secret societies of that type, and current members must resign from such organizations if they wished to continue membership in the congregation. The resolution read as follows: "Since the constitution calls Free Masons and members of other secret societies 'unbelievers,' the congregation does not wish to stamp them as 'infidels,' but calls them 'unbelievers' since they in their religion only acknowledge and pray to a higher being, which even Jews, heathen, and Turks do, and therefore are considered 'unbelievers' by all Christians."[5]

Action was affirmed on the subject of church discipline in 1881. The minutes read: "Some severe church discipline has occurred. Drunkenness, however, has declined substantially. Unfortunately, some are found who have not been freed from this bad depravity which has been deep-seated among the Swedish people."[6]

Erl. Carlsson's interest in education is reflected in the reorganization and strengthening of the congregation's parochial school in 1885. The school year was to be nine months, divided into three terms. One term should be held in Andover and the other two at places within the parish to be determined by the deacons. Instruction should be provided in English, Swedish, Christianity, writing, singing, history and geography. Parents of children of ages seven to fourteen should send their children to the school unless excused by the deacons. The financial support of the school was a congregational responsibility although parents were to contribute $1.50 per child for each term. A public examination under direction of the deacons should be conducted at the end of every term.[7]

The interest of the Andover pastor in youth was further manifested by the organization of the Andover Young People's Society in June 1880. This society had the distinction of being the first youth organization of the Augustana Synod which permitted women to have full membership. Emmy, the Carlsson's daughter, was a key person in organizing this group. She has written about this organization:

> Show me a happier crowd of young people, full of innocent glee and mirth. I have never seen anything like them, neither before or after. They proved to be the most punctual, reliable, alert, active workers of any Young People's Society I ever knew.

The society remodeled the old church. In Rock Island and elsewhere they were known as "Den sjungande Andover ungdom" (the singing Andover youth). Emmy described their activities:

> We would ride along on lumber wagons, preferring them to buggies because we could take everyone along with us. As we filled the wagons, so we filled the air with music. . . . These were the happiest and most carefree years of my life.[8]

Pastor Carlsson was chairman of the Board of Directors of the Andover Children's Home during his pastorate there. The home had been moved to its new location from Swedonia in 1871. Three years later a tract of 100 acres of land had been added. Pastor Carlsson soon provided leadership to build a schoolhouse for the home. In order to raise funds for this project, his daughter, Emmy, and he devised a plan whereby Sunday School children in the Augustana Synod raised money through collection cards. This plan was so successful that it was continued well into the next century. Erl. Carlsson participated in the action which at the synod meeting of 1876 transferred the Children's Home from the synod to the Illinois Conference. This arrangement stimulated greater support through direct local interest. Meanwhile the mission of the home required enlarged facilities, resulting in a twelve-room building being added in 1884. Pastor Carlsson had succeeded in effectively identifying this important social mission of the church.[9]

The church work at Andover progressed in a gratifying manner. Erl. Carlsson was a gifted pastor, preacher, and organizer. Worship services were well-attended and organizations carried on active programs. The people appreciated his pastoral services in time of joy and sorrow. The confirmation classes responded gratefully to his effective instruction. The pastor's interest in music brought Joseph E. Osborn, a fine musician and son of the pioneers, Pastor and Mrs. L. P. Esbjörn, to Andover as church organist in 1877. [10]

The Carlssons experienced great joy and deep sadness within the family circle during their early years at Andover. That October day in 1876, when their first born, Annie, was married to Reverend Carl Evald, Erl. Carlsson's successor as pastor of Immanuel Church, was a happy time. Pastor Carlsson performed the wedding ceremony before the altar in Andover's beautiful church surrounded by a large congregation of well-wishers. The choir and band provided appropriate music. Flaming lanterns and numerous flags added color to the reception following the service in the church. Many gifts witnessed to the love of friends in Andover and elsewhere. But within a relatively short time the joy had turned into anxiety. Annie's health was poor. During the summer of 1880 she went to Sweden in the hope of receiving medical aid. Then one day in the latter part of October of that year a telegram brought the sad news that Annie was dead in Stockholm. Later at the memorial service, the Carlsson family, clad in mourning black, sat with Pastor Evald in the

front benches of Immanuel Church, supported by a large congregation of sorrowing friends. When the service was over, Erl. Carlsson
said quietly to a friend: "Now I feel better, now I am calm again." [11]

Although Carlsson was the pastor of a large rural parish, his
devotion to the general work of the church was maintained and even
enlarged. When Olof Olsson returned to the United States in 1880,
following a stay in Europe, he wrote and lectured extensively about
the need for the Augustana Synod to increase its ministry of mercy.
A good response came from pastors and laymen in the Illinois
Conference. Erl. Carlsson was one of the leaders who urged the
founding of a hospital, preferably in Chicago with its large
concentration of Swedish Lutherans. After extensive discussion in
the Illinois Conference, preliminary plans were developed. When the
Board of Directors met for the organizational meeting in February
1884, Carlsson was elected chairman. [12]

The board took steps immediately to carry out their responsibility. After several unsuccessful attempts to find a location and
building, the decision was made in March 1884, to rent the Erl.
Carlsson home on Lincoln Avenue for $50.00 a month. In May
the hospital was dedicated. The fifteen-bed institution was filled to
capacity until a fire in October stopped activities. The board
proceeded to renovate the building and added a story with four
patients' rooms. The name was changed by the end of the first year
from The Deaconess Institution of the Swedish Evangelical Lutheran
Church to Augustana Hospital. [13]

The leaders of the hospital association sought a permanent
location without success. Inquiry was made of Carlsson if he would
be willing to sell this property, which was the temporary location of
the institution, and adjoining lots. In October 1886, he consented to
do so. It was agreed that the price would be $35,000 with a donation
of $1,000 by the seller. The former Carlsson home thus became the
permanent site of the well-known Augustana Hospital. [14]

These were strenuous years for Erl. Carlsson. He was pastor of a
large congregation, and heavily involved in the institutions of the
church. Moreover, as discussed previously, he had been elected
president of the Augustana Synod in 1881. This involved many
meetings, much travel, and extensive correspondence.

In the midst of many responsibilities, Erl. Carlsson's poor health became a problem. In May 1883, he expressed concern in a letter to Eric Norelius about "severe headaches" and "pains in the chest." This condition continued intermittently and finally he suffered a stroke during the next year. Although his condition improved somewhat, his physician, N. H. Lowry, M. D., at Woodhull, Illinois, warned him in a letter on June 16, 1884: "Knowing the important office you hold in the synod and the coming meeting of the same at your place, I deem it a duty I owe to you as your physician, to warn you to abstain from taking an active part in any discussion, to avoid all excitement, and mental work and worry. Your condition is such that any undue mental work will surely prove detrimental to you. Rest and quiet are absolutely necessary for your recovery." [15]

When the synod met at Carlsson's Andover congregation June 19-26, 1884, he was able to preside at the sessions and to carry out his responsibility. That he took his physician's warning seriously is proven by the fact that at the synod meeting he asked to be relieved of his position as president "on the grounds of my worsening health." For reasons that are not fully clear, but based quite likely on the esteem in which he was held, his request to be relieved of the presidency was not granted. He continued to serve until the synod session of 1888. [16]

The stroke which afflicted Erl. Carlsson in 1884 seriously impaired his faculties for a considerable time. Eric Norelius reported that it was impossible for Carlsson to preach and conduct the affairs of the congregation for some time. He was assisted by the faithful and dedicated Pastor August Johnson, who took care of much of the pastoral work. Johnson, a son of the congregation, was ordained at the meeting of the synod at Andover in 1884. He became Carlsson's assistant immediately thereafter. Pastor Carlsson continued to struggle with bad health. In 1885 and 1886 he sought medical assistance in Chicago and reported that he was using medicine that had been so helpful to Professor Olof Olsson and Jonas Engberg. In the autumn of 1886 he was unable to attend the annual meeting of the General Council because of illness. In November he wrote to Norelius: "I love the pastoral calling and wish above all to continue with it. But ever since the stroke I am overcome from time to time with great dizziness, especially during and after preaching. Moreover, my advanced years and lessened strength make it almost impossible for me to continue my pastoral calling." [17]

At the meeting of the Board of Directors of Augustana College and Theological Seminary on December 29, 1886, Erl. Carlsson was called to serve as general manager. He explained to Norelius that he would also "take over the spiritual care of students. This important part of the work and responsibility of our school has been neglected too much." The Andover congregation, realizing their pastor's poor physical condition, reluctantly accepted his resignation. He assumed his new position in July of the following year. He also continued as president of the Augustana Synod until July 1888. [18]

Carlsson exerted his best efforts under great physical handicaps in the new position at Augustana. He also served as treasurer. He had been able to do desk work at Andover and he continued to do so at the college and seminary. However, it soon became apparent that the assignment exceeded his physical resources. At the beginning of 1888, Samuel, his son, became his assistant, an arrangement that was helpful. However, the veteran pastor and leader had critics. Dr. Carl Swensson, his long-time friend and admirer, has written about this situation: "He could not endure as much as formerly, and least of all in matters involving misinterpretation and misunderstanding. That happened to him at Rock Island. The heavy work became heavier than previously, his strength weakened, he thought certainly that they wanted to get rid of him. Many others thought the same as Dr. Carlsson in this matter." [19]

Erl. Carlsson was seriously concerned about his physical condition and other problems. He wrote to Eric Norelius in October 1888: "I cannot endure this demanding work and the accompanying concerns and anxieties. . . . I often feel tired of life's toil and long for home, home with Jesus where the tired pilgrim will find peace and rest. I have, however, nothing to complain of but my bad spirit and I will place myself completely in Jesus' hands." Early in 1889 he resigned as business manager at Augustana. In February, his son Samuel wrote to Carl Swensson: "His resignation as B. M. [business manager] was accepted with a vengeance as you no doubt know or expected, yet he must serve till some one else can take the place." The resignation was effective with the meeting of the synod in June of that year. Later (1890), while sharing experiences with his old friend, Eric Norelius, who was serving briefly as editor of *Augustana*

Carlsson wrote: "When you have a free moment, write to me about the situation and developments. I have been there [Rock Island] and I can understand in a measure what you and others experience on the basis of the way I was treated." [20]

Erl. Carlsson's physician suggested to him that a change in climate would be good for his health. The Carlssons moved to Lindsborg, the well-known Swedish community in the Smoky Valley of central Kansas, in the early summer of 1889. They had visited in the home of Eben and Anna Carlsson in Lindsborg for three weeks during the previous September. Moreover, Lindsborg was the home of Dr. Carl Swensson, pastor of Bethany Church and founder and president of Bethany College. Carl was the son of Carlsson's close friend, Pastor Jonas Swensson, and a great admirer of the venerable pioneer pastor. Carlsson's financial situation was such that he was able to buy a 240-acre farm a short distance northeast of Lindsborg. There he arranged for the construction of a spacious two-story house with modern facilities, on the site of a pioneer log cabin. He called the place Rostad, suggesting a place of peace in memory of Rostad in Kalmar, the school where Anna and Emmy had been students in the 1870s. The change in life style, the quiet of rural living, and the freedom from official responsibilities, were factors in his improved health. He declined public assignments except that Carl Swensson persuaded him to serve as a member of the Board of Directors of Bethany College and to conduct occasional church services in Lindsborg. [21]

Dr. Swensson has written about Erl. Carlsson's years at Lindsborg:

> At Rostad lives an old veteran, an eagle with a broken wing, who with full heart, enthusiasm, and youthful spirit worked hard in his younger years, but now his hair is grey and body stooped. He is one of the Lord's worn-out fighters and instruments in Augustana Synod's large and brave army. . . . If I now go to the window in the corridor [of Old Main on the Bethany Campus], I see over there in a grove of trees the beautiful square building at Rostad, surrounded by maple trees and poplars, and back of it, the wheel of the windmill swings around suddenly, to bring water to the main building, kitchen, cellar, wash house, and the large barn and other buildings. Over there lives the old, beloved veteran and his faithful, hospitable

wife. . . . Gratitude of thousands is part of the reward God gives for
such a life and career as his. . . . Thanks be to God for faithful,
unselfish service. Thanks be to God that we have him among us out
here as counselor and guide for the younger and inexperienced
warriors. Rostad! God's peace be with you dear friends out there. [22]

Erl. Carlsson spent the days in the Smoky Valley observing the
response of nature to the changes of the seasons. He viewed from his
wagon the wave-like wheat fields getting ripe unto harvest and the
flowering of the trees in the orchard with the promise of late summer
fruit. He visited regularly with Eben, his son, and Samuel, the other
son, spent considerable time with his parents. The former took over
the management of the Rostad land in 1892. The Lindsborg
community was pleased to have the Carlssons as residents. There was
time for reading and reflection, for writing and answering letters.
Eric Norelius, who had been requested to write the history of the
Swedish Lutheran churches in America, had asked Carlsson to submit
a copy of his autobiography. In August 1889, he promised to write
the story of his life, expressing the opinion that "it should not take
too long." It was not until the following April that the assignment
was completed. One factor had been poor health. Norelius sent
advance sheets to Carlsson which included the former's revisions. [23]

Erl. Carlsson was soon involved in the life of a farmer. The
column of local items in the *Lindsborg News-Record* described the
activities of the former Chicago pastor and former president of the
Augustana Synod. In the middle of December 1889, the newspaper
reported that Pastor Carlsson had sold twenty tons of broomcorn to
Anderson Bros. at $100.00 a ton. In the next week's issue the readers
learned that he had had his cattle dehorned. In February of the new
year, the Lindsborg newspaper reported that "Rev. Carlsson market-
ed four porkers in this city Monday that weighed 1900 lbs. They
brought 8½ cents per lb. for a total of $61.75. That number of lbs.
of corn in the ear would bring the big sum of $3.52. It pays to feed
your corn to hogs." Erl. Carlsson was not unfamiliar with farm life
since he had grown up on a farm in Småland. In Chicago the
Carlssons kept at least one milk cow regularly. When Pastor and Mrs.
Olof Olsson stayed with them in June 1869, enroute to their new
home at Lindsborg, Mrs. Olsson reported with surprise in a letter to a
friend in Sweden that the Carlssons had a cow that produced ten

gallons of milk daily. [24]

Life on the farm near Lindsborg provided new experiences and some of them were frightening. Shortly before Christmas in 1889, he drove to Lindsborg with a team of young horses. When driving on the Bethany College campus between the Main Building and the Ladies Hall, something scared the horses. The pastor tried his best but he was not able to stop the runaway. He was knocked down in the wagon and when the horses finally stopped, he had suffered a slight concussion which caused him to lose consciousness for a brief time. In March of the following year he and some members of the family were enroute to Lindsborg. The horses were suddenly frightened and ran away at great speed. The wagon-tongue broke so it was not possible to guide or control the horses. The consequences might have been serious as the wagon rolled over, broke up, and threw the passengers to the ground. Carlsson described the situation as follows: "Through God's miraculous protection we escaped so no one was injured in life or limb although we were badly shaken up and received some minor bruises." [25]

There were festive times at Rostad when the genial hospitality of the Carlssons brought enjoyment to their guests. Reunions were held regularly when Erland and Eva welcomed their children—Emmy, Eben, and Samuel—and their families. Several grandchildren enjoyed the many attractions on the farm and each others company. Carl and Alma Swensson were frequent visitors. The president of Bethany College came often to consult with the veteran pastor and church leader. Swensson's sister, Anna, and her husband, Eben Carlsson, were residents of the area. Visitors at Bethany College were often guests of the Carlssons. Some of them were pastors and church leaders who reminisced with Erl. Carlsson about the passing of the years.

Dr. G. H. Trabert, well-known pastor and leader in the Lutheran church in Pennsylvania, recalled his visit at Rostad in May 1893, when the distinguished guest was Bishop Scheele of Visby, the official representative of the Church of Sweden at the great Jubilee of that year. Although Trabert was impressed with the bishop, his thoughts centered more upon his host. He remembered when he first met Pastor Carlsson after the Chicago fire in 1871—"his voice still ringing in my ears as he pled for aid in rebuilding his church." There was "no one in the church for whom I had higher regard." When

Trabert came west to begin English home missionary work, no one welcomed him more heartily than Erl. Carlsson. Carlsson also had remembrances. He recalled his conflict with Bishop Heurlin of Växjö four decades earlier, and the hostility to the immigrant church of some members of the church hierarchy. But a different situation prevailed now. Visiting with him at Rostad was Bishop Scheele, an ambassador of good will from the Church of Sweden, bridging the gap of historic misunderstanding between the church in the old country and the Augustana Synod in the new homeland. [26]

Although Erl. Carlsson was no longer active in the work of the Augustana Synod, he was interested in developments and at times, he had great anxiety. In November 1889, he wrote to Eric Norelius about rumors that Carl Swensson wished to sell *Framåt*, a weekly Swedish newspaper. Carlsson understood that an approach might be made to the Augustana Book Concern, and if this did not result in purchase, some people in Chicago might acquire *Framåt* for publication there. He regretted this prospect, writing to Norelius: "I wish with all my heart to unify our scattered strength within the synod even relative to publications. For your interests as editor of *Augustana*, for that of *Augustana*, and our synod in its entirety, I felt it best to tell you about it." In the following year he was concerned about rumors that the English speaking pastors and congregations who were members of the synod, were thinking of dissolving their bonds with the parent group. He viewed this potential development as "grim for the synod"—being divisive, undermining the older Swedish congregations, and regressive, by delaying the growth in the use of English in the synod. [27]

Moreover, Erl. Carlsson was concerned about the future of church work among Swedish Lutherans in America. In July 1890, he confided to Norelius:

> In regard to our synod I see its future as being very dark and I suffer from bad and depressing pessimism. Not only are all our treasuries empty, but what is worse, internal love and trust disappear more and more. . . . Instead of allowing business to be transacted openly and honestly, it often happens, as Dr. T. N. H. [Dr. T. N. Hasselquist] writes in the last number of *Augustana*, that it is carried on through secret agreements. All this witnesses to an inner rottenness and decay."[28]

The veteran pastor also felt himself out of touch with the main stream of developments. In response to a letter from a discouraged Norelius, who felt that he must resign as editor of *Augustana* for a number of reasons, including poor health, Carlsson wrote: "I readily understand, on the basis of my own experience, how difficult it is for those who have taken such an active and direct part in God's Kingdom, our synod, missions, and school affairs, to find it necessary to withdraw from the work, and in addition, see things take a warped and wrong direction. But what can we do? Only leave our own and our denominations affairs in His hands Who has all power in heaven and on earth." [29]

Erl. Carlsson's last years were made more meaningful because of his close friendship with Eric Norelius. His correspondence includes many letters which clearly show what this friendship meant to him. While at Andover, he urged Norelius again and again to come for a visit, writing in English in otherwise Swedish letters, that, "We may take sweet counsel together" and "improve our time." He told Norelius, "My wife and I count your wife and you not only among our best friends but we feel as if you were our closest relatives." When the Carlssons lived in Rock Island, Erland urged his tired and ill friend and his wife to join them in their household, saying: "We have lots of room for you both in our hearts and in our house." They could live in the rooms which Professor Bartholomew had occupied. Moreover, this would give Norelius an excellent opportunity to work on his historical project. In Lindsborg he wrote to his friend: "I have the great pleasure every Saturday to have a visit with you in *Augustana* which comes regularly and is a very welcome guest. I share fully the point of view which you take and I am glad to say that at least around here *Augustana* is generally liked." Later he urged the Norelius' to visit in Lindsborg. An added attraction was that Leonhard, their son, would find horses to ride on the Carlsson farm. [30]

Dr. L. G. Abrahamson has reported on Carlsson's preoccupation with thoughts of life and death: "He occupied himself especially by digging deeper into the secrets of the word of God, to grasp more intimately the many important questions of the heart, and of time and eternity, and to prepare himself for the departure which he felt was close at hand." When I visited him in the autumn of 1892, I asked him what principally engaged his thoughts. He answered: "I am preparing myself to die." [31]

Although Erl. Carlsson was surrounded by love and affection and should have possessed resources from the knowledge that he had been a true and faithful servant of God and man, he was often restless and discouraged. The stroke and the accompanying paralysis continued to impair his faculties. There were times of spiritual anxiety, too, for this honest man. Professor Nils Forsander writes about this feeling: "Solicitude about his own salvation and that of others followed him all his life, and in Lindsborg, with tears in his eyes, he discussed with his family and friends the fear at last in finding himself like one of the five foolish virgins in the famous parable of Jesus."[32]

As time passed, Pastor Carlsson's physical condition varied. During some periods he seemed to be regaining his former strength. In 1892, he went to the sanatorium in Battle Creek, Michigan, for treatment and baths. In a letter to his Chicago friend, Charles Holmberg, in August 1892, he described his situation in the context of the big questions:

> Through God's great grace my long illness has been useful and helpful to me. It has been for me a quite unexpected lesson in learning how to be satisfied and quiet before God's holy will. I begin to see and understand that God's good and gracious will is best for us and I say and pray from my heart: "I will follow your way, O God, and not that of man. My Lord is faithful and never fails a struggling soul. He says: 'Live fully in my grace for my grace is mighty in him who is weak.' "

Among Pastor Carlsson's visitors at Battle Creek was Pastor John Telleen. He wrote about his contacts with his ill friend: "Those days I cannot forget. They revealed to me how much he lived unto God and how highly he valued our Lutheran confession both in doctrine and practice."[33]

The future began to look bright for the veteran pastor as his health improved substantially after returning to Lindsborg. He looked forward with keen anticipation to the great events scheduled on the campus of Augustana College in June 1893. In the first week of that month, a great jubilee commemorated the historic occasion in Sweden three hundred years earlier when the Council of Uppsala

decisively rejected the Counter Reformation. Erl. Carlsson left
Rostad and Lindsborg for the last time with a group of one hundred
people, including Bishop Scheele of Sweden, enroute to Rock Island
in order to participate in the great celebration. [34]

The day of jubilee dawned clear and bright, splashing the
campus with sunshine. A crowd of people the like of which had
never been seen in Rock Island gathered at the college and seminary.
Special trains brought the throngs from far and near. An observer
pointed out that, "the whole place swarmed with fellow countrymen," numbering perhaps 20,000. A huge tent made it possible for
an audience of 6,000 to listen to great music and to hear a series of
inspiring addresses. The Bishop of Visby, K. G. von Scheele, the
distinguished representative of Sweden, and Dr. Eric Norelius,
pioneer pastor and former president of the Augustana Synod, were
the principal speakers. [35]

In the midst of the great throng were two persons—Erl. Carlsson
and Eric Norelius—who shared in the events with deep feeling and
who, in themselves, represented more than words can adequately
describe. What these veterans talked about that day as they walked
slowly on the campus would be interesting to know. Perhaps they
recalled that August day four decades earlier when twenty-year-old
student Eric Norelius met thirty-year-old Pastor Erl. Carlsson at
Chicago for the first time. They had much upon which to reflect.
They were surrounded by a great crowd of witnesses, literally and
figuratively. They had shared energetically and effectively in building
the Kingdom of God among their countrymen. The proof of it was
around them everywhere.

June 9, 1893, must truly have been a time of joy for Erl.
Carlsson on the Augustana campus. He had been a member of the
Board of Directors uninterruptedly from the founding in 1860 until
1889 when poor health caused him reluctantly to step down. He had
been chairman of the board for nineteen years, chairman of the
finance and support committee, the driving force in planning
buildings, and business manager and treasurer. What he saw—the
great crowd and the beautiful campus—inspired the great man as
shadows began to gather on the path of his life. His eyes fastened
long and joyfully on what our generation affectionately calls Old
Main. Here stood in beauty and dignity the beautifully designed

stone structure which perhaps owed more to him than to anyone else in the world. He smiled approvingly as he pointed to the cupola which he, almost alone, had fought for in the building committee. His gaze encompassed the attractive portico with its broad stairs and marble columns. Business manager Jesperson had succeeded in having a sturdy stone retaining wall built along Seventh Avenue to mark off the campus.

When Erl. Carlsson viewed this attractive scene, he burst out saying: "I thank God that I could live to see all this completed, for which I fought so hard." His prayers had been answered. Other prayers were raised then and later in gratitude for the dedication of the venerable friend of Christian teaching and learning. [36]

Across the street from Old Main and a brief space to the west stands Erland Carlsson Hall, a fitting tribute to the great pastor and champion of education. He has been appropriately described by Conrad Bergendoff, himself a stellar figure in the history and tradition of Augustana, as "its most influential personality between 1860 and 1889."[37]

Eric Norelius described joyfully Erl. Carlsson's presence at this festive occasion in 1893. He seemed to be so much like himself again after an illness of several years. How entirely different now in contrast to the time when his faculties were limited and his strength numbed. However, his youthful vigor was gone and observers noted no traces of his previous impulsiveness which had been part of his temperament. Then Carlsson's long-time associate continued:

> But that which always made him pure gold in his character stood out now, purified and purged. For the one who writes these lines, he seemed a good deal transformed. His mind was clear, his thinking deep, and his piety, sincere and earnest.... His heart was full of Christian love and he hardly knew how he should conduct himself in order to show that love to those associated with him.[38]

On the Sunday following the great day of jubilee, Norelius went with Carlsson to Andover where they were distinguished guests of the congregation. He heard him preach there for an hour on the text for the second Sunday after Trinity, Luke 14:25-35. The visitor observed that he spoke "with clarity and warmth, presenting what the cost is to be a Christian. Judging by outer appearances one would have reason to think and believe that Dr. Carlsson had a good part of his earthly journey ahead of him."[39]

The events at Rock Island, when Erl. Carlsson relived old times, met many friends, and shared with others the memories of the past as well as the promise to the future, were the prelude to the last months of his life. Following a visit with the Evalds in Chicago, he took a lake trip to Sister Bay, Wisconsin, where a relative lived. This was to be a time of rest and recuperation. Although not feeling in full strength, he conducted services in the little Swedish Lutheran church there.

The plans for a longer stay at Sister Bay were interrupted when he suffered another light stroke. He was brought to Chicago where he stayed in the parsonage home of Dr. and Mrs. Evald. His wife and others gave him tender and loving care. Shortly after arrival in Chicago, Pastor Carlsson had another attack. He did not talk much these last days although on one occasion when his resources made it possible, he restated his credo which had been central to his life:

> I believe in the forgiveness of sins. I rest on Jesus the Rock. I die in the faith that I preached. I go home now to be with the Lord forever. I will meet the dear ones who have gone home before me. May my dear ones, who remain, come later and may no one be missing in the Father's house.[40]

The hourglass of Erl. Carlsson's earthly life was running out. Dr. Carl Swensson went to Chicago to see his old and esteemed friend for whom the shadows were gathering. He earnestly recorded his remembrances of that last visit: "He suffered much from inner concern and skepticism towards the end. His soul was full of great anxiety. This was the last chastening, and thereafter, all was quiet and peaceful again. I saw a happy smile a few days before his last farewell. Then the inner voice said to me: 'This is the morning's crimson glow of eternity's beautiful day.' " On October 19, "He slept away quietly and peacefully like a tired child." He had attained the age of 71 years, 1 month, and 20 days. His wife, sons Eben and Samuel, and daughter Emmy, all the children with their families, were there to say farewell. [41]

On Wednesday, October 25, relatives and friends assembled to honor and mourn the memory of Dr. Erland Carlsson. At 12:30 p.m. a brief service was conducted by Pastor John Telleen in the parsonage home of Pastor and Mrs. Carl Evald in Lake View. Seventy-five carriages brought the mourners to Immanuel Church where a crowd estimated at 3,000 had gathered inside and outside the large building. Sermons and tributes were presented by Dr. Olof Olsson, president of Augustana College and Theological Seminary and by Dr. Carl Swensson, president of Bethany College, in Swedish, and by Dr. W. A. Passavant in English. Resolutions of condolence were read from many churches, institutions, and organizations. Congregational singing, choir, quartette, and solo numbers provided appropriate messages in music. A journalist reported that, "The beautiful church was heavily draped in deep black and on every hand was seen the insignia of death." The altar service was conducted by Pastor P. J. Svärd, president of the Augustana Synod, assisted by Pastor Philip Thelander, a close friend and admirer. Emil Larsson was the organist.[42]

Following the impressive and lengthy service in Immanuel Church, the long funeral cortege moved slowly to Graceland Cemetery. Since it was already dark when the cortege arrived there, a lantern was procured to provide light for the committal service. A great quiet prevailed as the burial service of the Augustana liturgy was read in the language of the old country by President Svärd. Then Pastor Evald requested the people to join in singing the familiar hymn, "Nearer My God to Thee." The silence, following the singing, was broken by the firm voice of Dr. Carl Swensson as he uttered these words: "This disciple dieth not." [43]

FOOTNOTES

[1] Erl. Carlsson to Eric Norelius, Andover, Ill., May 5, 1875; J. A. Enander to T. N. Hasselquist, Chicago, April 26, 1875.

[2] Erl. Carlsson to Eric Norelius, Andover, Ill., May 5, 1875.

[3] *Minnes-Album, Svenska Evangelisk Lutherska församlingen i Andover, Illinois. Sextioårs-festen 1910* (Rock Island: Augustana Book Concern, 1910), p. 54.

[4] *Ibid.*, p. 55.

[5] *Ibid.*, p. 61.

[6] *Ibid.*, p. 62.

[7] *Ibid.*, pp. 65-67.

[8]Arden, *Augustana Heritage,* p. 207; Emmy Evald, "Some Memories of Old Andover," *Andover Church Tidings. Eighty-fifth Anniversary Year Book, 1850-1935,* p. 7.

[9]"Gold and Silver. Two Notable Augustana Anniversaries," *My Church,* III (1917), 62-63; G. Everett Arden, *History of the Illinois Conference, Augustana Evangelical Lutheran Church,* p. 29.

[10]*Minnes-Album, Andover, Ill., 1910,* p. 61.

[11]C. A. Swensson, *Förgät-mig-ej. Fosterlandsk och Luthersk ungdomskalender för jubelåret, 1893* (Chicago, 1893), pp. 85-86.

[12]*Illinois-Konferensen, 1853-1903,* pp. 97-102.

[13]*Ibid.,* pp. 103-04.

[14]*Ibid.,* 105.

[15]Erl. Carlsson to Eric Norelius, Andover, Ill., May 26, 1883; N. H. Lowry, M.D., Woodhull, Ill., to Erl. Carlsson, June 16, 1884.

[16]*Augustana synodens protokoll, 1884,* p. 22.

[17]Erl. Carlsson to Eric Norelius, Andover, Ill., March 24, 1885, April 20, 1886, November 24, 1886.

[18]Norelius, *De Svenska Lutherska . . . historia i Amerika, I,* 437; Erl. Carlsson to Eric Norelius, Rock Island, Ill., January 12, 1887.

[19]*Fosterlandet,* October 25, 1893.

[20]Erl. Carlsson to Eric Norelius, Lindsborg, Ks., October 17, 1888, February 19, 1890; Samuel E. Carlsson to C. A. Swensson, Rock Island, February 6, 1889.

[21]Erl. Carlsson to Eric Norelius, Lindsborg, Ks., September 24, 1888; Abrahamson, "Doktor Erland Carlsson," *Minneskrift-Immanuelsförsamlingen,* p. 43; *Lindsborg News-Record,* August 4, 1932.

[22]C. A. Swensson, "Rostad," *Förgät-mig-ej,* pp. 77-79, 89; Hjalmar Nilsson, "Rostad i Kalmar och Rostad i Kansas," *Älghults-Krönika, 1959,* pp. 25-31. Elizabeth Jaderborg [Selma Lind], "Rostad," *Living in Lindsborg and Other Possibilities* (Lindsborg: Lindsborg News-Record, 1967), pp. 14-15.

[23]Erl. Carlsson to Eric Norelius, Lindsborg, Ks., August 6, 1889, February 25, 1890, April 2, 1890.

[24]*Lindsborg News-Record,* December 13, 1889, December 20, 1889, February 7, 1890. Mrs. Olof Olsson to Mrs. C. W. Weinberg, Chicago June 21, 1869.

[25] Erl. Carlsson to Eric Norelius, Lindsborg, Ks., December 28, 1889, March 7, 1890.

[26] G. H. Trabert to Mrs. Emmy Evald, Warren, Pa., October 27, 1893.

[27] Erl. Carlsson to Eric Norelius, Lindsborg, Ks., November 16, 1889, July 26, 1890.

[28] Erl. Carlsson to Eric Norelius, Lindsborg, Ks., July 26, 1890.

[29] *Ibid.*

[30] Erl. Carlsson to Eric Norelius, Andover, May 26, 1883, February 2, 1884, May 15, 1884; Rock Island, September 24, 1888; February 10, February 14, 1890, Lindsborg, Ks.

[31] *Minneskrift-Immanuelsförsamlingen,* p. 43.

[32] Forsander, *Lifsbilder,* I, 126.

[33] Erl. Carlsson to Charles Holmberg, Battle Creek, Michigan, August 1, 1892. J. Telleen, "Rev. Dr. Erland Carlsson," *My Church,* VII (1921), 55-56.

[34] *Fosterlandet,* October 25, 1893.

[35] *Augustana* (Rock Island) June 10, 1893; Bergendoff, *Augustana. A Profession of Faith,* pp. 89-90.

[36] *Augustana,* October 26, 1893.

[37] Bergendoff, *Augustana. A Profession of Faith,* p. 91.

[38] Norelius, "Doktor Erland Carlsson," *Korsbaneret,* 1894, p. 119.

[39] *Ibid.,* p. 121.

[40] John Telleen, "Doktor Erland Carlsson," *Korsbaneret,* 1894, p. 128.

[41] Telleen, "Doktor Erland Carlsson," *Korsbaneret,* 1894, p. 128-29; Carl Swensson, *Fosterlandet,* October 25, 1893.

[42] *Augustana,* November 2, 1893; Telleen, "Doktor Erland Carlsson," *Korsbaneret,* 1894, pp. 129-33; Telleen, "Rev. Dr. Erland Carlsson," *My Church,* VII (1921) 55-56; *Lindsborg News,* October 27, 1893.

[43] Telleen, "Doktor Erland Carlsson," *Korsbaneret,* 1894, p. 133.

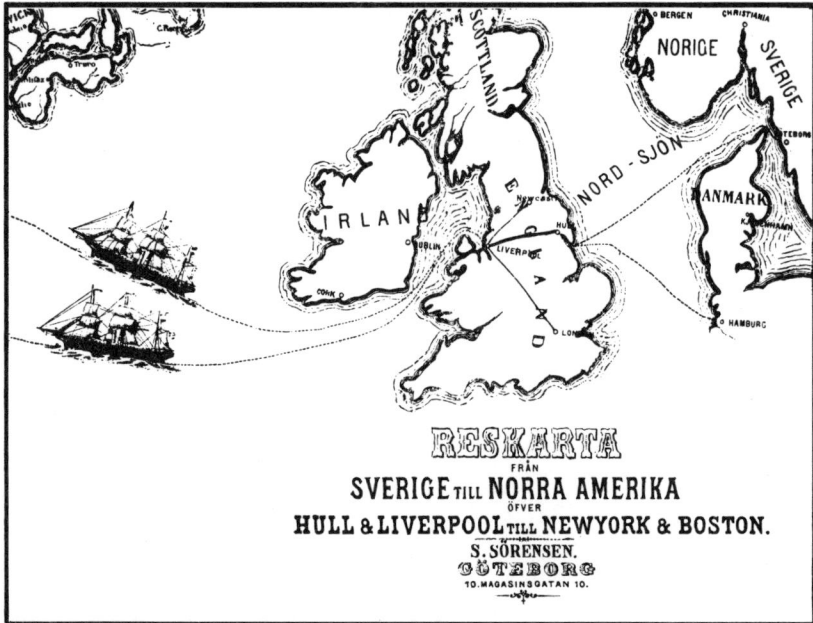

Travel Routes from Sweden across the
  Atlantic

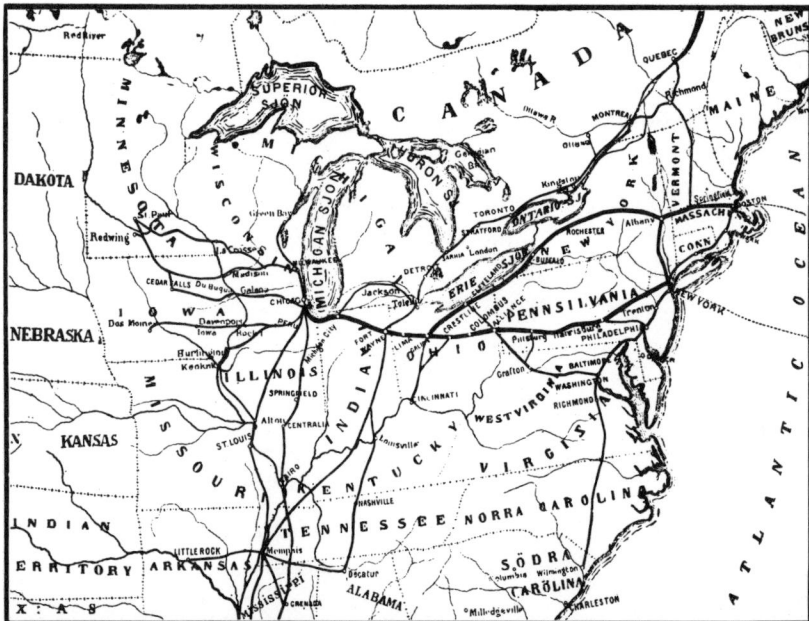

Travel Routes from New York and Boston
  to Chicago and the Midwest

14

An Appraisal

The circumstances of passing years strengthened and refined the sterling qualities of Erl. Carlsson's character. The response to change and development was nourished and fashioned in the framework of abiding principles. The serious-minded boy from Suletorp pursued unfailingly his intense desire to become a Lutheran pastor. Over-coming a late beginning and limited educational opportunity, he boldly and prayerfully went to the university at Lund where his intellect and will enabled him to graduate with distinction in theology, and to be ordained a pastor in the Church of Sweden.

The young pastor was soon confronted by challenges from the ecclesiastical hierarchy, but his firm trust in God and steadfast belief in His grace and power enabled him to survive, and finally to succeed. Then came the call to far-away America with its challenge to Christian service among his countrymen. The future was destined to be heavy, but with the promise of greater things.

Life as an immigrant pastor in the turbulent Chicago world of the 1850s called forth his greatest resources of body and spirit. From lowly and uncertain beginnings, amidst great adversity, the pastor advanced the work of the Kingdom of God within his steadily growing congregation and elsewhere. Immanuel Church was more than a name to thousands of immigrants: it became a central point in their lives, where, for longer or shorter periods of time, they found spiritual comfort, personal encouragement and meaningful guidance from the friendly pastor. Soon he became a leading force in the work of the church at large among Swedish Lutherans—in education, in publications, in the ministry of mercy, and in the organization and development of a free Lutheran church.

The timid lad from Suletorp in Älghult's parish was pastor of the congregation in Chicago which during his life-time became the largest and most influential congregation among Swedish Lutherans in America, and towards the end of his career he was elected president of the Augustana Synod. Small wonder that a later generation in his home parish struck off a large bronze plaque commemorating the distinguished record of this native son. But transcending all of these achievements was Erl. Carlsson, pastor and preacher of the Word of God, which declared unto sinners the grace, mercy, love, and forgiveness of God through Jesus Christ.

What enabled Erl. Carlsson to become the man and pastor known in the annals of history resulted from a combination of many factors. The conflict with Bishop Heurlin at Växjö in early years was a turning point. Personal integrity and commitment to Jesus Christ and the church were at stake. In a situation which seemed to be providential, he received through his good friend, Peter Fjellstedt, a call to serve Swedes in America. It is quite likely, as L. G. Abrahamson has pointed out, that if the future immigrant pastor had stayed in Sweden, he would have become *Kyrkoherde* Erland Carlsson, a worthy calling indeed, but scarcely one of the dimension that was his as pastor and church leader in America. The conflict which brought him to the New World came not by chance. The basic issues were to be decisive all his days until the shadows lengthened and the day was done.[1]

Erl. Carlsson's personality possessed qualities of strength and weakness, and as is quite common, there is often only a thin line separating these factors. Contemporary observers write that, "Carlsson's style was strong and vigorous almost to the end of his life." He has been described as "average in size, quick in his movements, firm in expression." He was his own man, so to speak, in that he held firmly to principle. He had chosen for his motto, as pointed out earlier, the following words which he wrote in English on the first page of the first volume that contains the Immanuel Church records: "Relying upon divine assistance I am determined to declare the truth openly and faithfully, whatever difficulties are thrown in my way."[2]

The decisive nature of Erl. Carlsson's character was portrayed effectively by Dr. Carl Swensson in an article at the time of the former's death:

> He was a man of firm convictions and would not easily change a position he had taken, or change a declared point of view. Endowed with a fiery temperament, rare energy, unusual executive ability, he obviously became a leader. He must personally see his opposition in the white of their eyes, and this he did courageously and as a real man. One could almost add that at times he did so willingly and gladly, exactly like a veteran and victorious officer.[3]

Erl. Carlsson's adherence to principle was occasionally the decisive factor when his temperament displayed strong and almost uncontrollable feeling. It has been pointed out that, "One must not be surprised that his independence was disliked by some people. He was friendly but he maintained without wavering what he knew was right. A person who makes many friends must also have some enemies." He has also been described as "lacking the tact and diplomacy possessed by some others." One observer recalled a "situation when he rose up with indignant wrath against behavior which lacked openness and fairness."[4]

The record includes situations in which Carlsson's volatile temperament caused him problems which he later lamented. When L. G. Abrahamson recorded his remembrances of the Chicago pastor for the fiftieth anniversary historical publication of Immanuel Church in 1903, he praised the long-time distinguished pastor of the congregation, but he realistically described the man whom he so greatly admired:

> He had faults and he could not conceal them. He had an impulsive temperament and we know that it sometimes played ugly tricks upon his otherwise sound judgment. But he suffered from it and he had the courage to ask for forgiveness from the people whom he thought he might have hurt. He could not maintain bitter feelings against anyone.[5]

E. W. Olson, well-known Swedish American author and editor, has presented a balanced view of Pastor Carlsson in words that honor him while at the same time recognizing some of his problems. He wrote: "To know Reverend Carlsson was to love and to esteem him. For the young people in particular he had a peculiar attraction. Socially he was free and natural and a fine conversationalist. That his independence was distasteful to some is not to be wondered at." The Chicago pastor was never known to deviate "a hair's breadth" in matters of principle. In appraising Erl. Carlsson he wrote further:

> But to ascribe to him a perfection which was not his would not be honoring his memory. He had his faults . . . which we cannot here overlook. Among them was a hot and excitable temper which would often get the better of his judgment in the course of public declaration. He was himself fully conscious of his shortcomings which caused him honest regret, and he was not too proud to apologize to anyone whom he felt guilty of having done an injustice or injury.[6]

Erl. Carlsson acknowledged his faults and he knew that he was a sinner who needed grace and forgiveness. In a letter to T. N. Hasselquist in March 1874, in a context that cannot be clearly identified, he shared his problems with this pastor friend: "Thanks for your letters and for your patience with me. I am not surprised that it has been tested. As far as I am concerned, I am both impatient and fed-up with myself. But what shall I do? May God have mercy upon me, forgive me, and help me. Brother, forgive me and help me." Here was an honest man reflecting upon life and its manifold problems.[7]

The ultimate appraisal of Erl. Carlsson's life and work resides in his character and personality and in his mighty contribution to the Kingdom of God. A vital description is found in the testimony of his contemporaries. The immigrant pastor had been in America scarcely a month when young Eric Norelius met him in Chicago. The latter's diary for September 17, 1853, describes the personal qualities of the newly-arrived pastor:

> Carlsson received me with the greatest kindness and showed me so much love and sympathy that I was actually surprised. Here I was met not only with gracious words, but with deeds of love. He insisted that I should make my home with him. I told him how penniless and poverty-stricken I was. Indeed, I said that I had nothing but the rags on my back and my Greek New Testament, which I took out of my pocket and showed him. With tears in his

eyes he said to me: "You are most heartily welcome to stay with me.".... My meeting with Rev. Mr. Carlsson occurred on Saturday, September 17 and I will never forget that hour.[8]

Another future Augustana pastor and leader, John Telleen, also remembered Erl. Carlsson's kindness and understanding in trying times: "And well do I recall a visit to my room at Paxton [Augustana Seminary] as Pastor Carlsson looked around and saw the humble furnishings and a few books and as his eyes filled with tears, he said: 'Poverty is no disgrace my boy. David Livingstone was raised poor. So was Peter Fjellstedt, and many whom God has owned had to go through this schooling. Look to God always and you will never be put to shame.' "[9]

Jonas Swensson, who became president of the Augustana Synod, was grateful to Carlsson for kindness during early and difficult years in America. A few months after arrival at Sugar Grove, Pennsylvania, in October 1856, the pastor and his wife had the thrill of a visit with the Carlssons in Chicago as expressed in a letter: "May I thank you most heartily for the long and pleasant visit which my wife and I enjoyed with you. ... I cannot tell you how happy I became to converse with you because prior to that time everything seemed so strange to me in America, so I almost began to wonder if I ever would find the same Christian spirit as in the old fatherland. Thus our mutual interests strengthened and encouraged me." [10]

The friendly quality of Erl. Carlsson received testimony from people of varied points of views. J. G. Princell, a controversial figure who continued his controversial ways as pastor of Gustavus Adolphus Lutheran Church, New York, had good remembrances of the Chicago pastor. In youthful years he had been superintendent of the Immanuel Sunday School and Pastor Carlsson's assistant. He wrote as follows: "Yes, you old, unforgettable brother, I greet you and thank you still, as you were then—*primus inter pares*—the first among equals. How well you understood how to hold your *primus* behind but your *pares* in front. Whenever you guided or led you always did so with gentle, soft reins. Everything went so well—forward, upward, homeward." In Princell's old Bible was this inscription: "Given by my father-like friend, Erland Carlsson in 1869." Philip Thelander recounted from youthful years that Carlsson suggested he be addressed in letters only as "My fatherly friend." [11]

This deep-seated interest in people, so evident from the first days of his pastorate in America, characterized his entire career. Arthur Bernhard Carlson, in a comprehensive and excellent study of pastoral care among four Swedish clergymen, has summarized his findings about Erl. Carlsson in these words:

> Carlsson's genuine love for people made him responsive to every indication of human need. . . . He regarded himself as the shepherd of all his people. He responded to every request for pastoral services. He sought to minister to each person's present need. Carlsson's faith in God's ability to change human behavior, however unresponsive in the past, made his ministry effective with many who had previously refused counsel.

This scholar further emphasized that, "Carlsson viewed the basic needs of food, housing, work, and health as pastoral concerns. Where they were wanting, he and his congregation sought to meet them. . . . Carlsson gave himself unsparingly in pastoral support of the sorrowing, depressed, and guilt ridden. He enlisted the prayers and personal visits of church members to assist him in this ministry." [12]

The kindly and genial nature of Erl. Carlsson was a mighty resource for his pastoral services. These qualities were accompanied by intense devotion to his responsibility as a preacher of the Word of God. L. G. Abrahamson has recalled this aspect: "To proclaim the Word of God for the purpose of saving sinners, to point the way to heaven for his fellow men, to respond to his listener's deep and tormenting questions of the heart and conscience was his dearest work." Olof Olsson and Carl Swensson, associates and friends, who frequently listened to Carlsson's sermons, gave this interesting appraisal in 1881: "Pastor Carlsson is much liked as a preacher. His sermons are always simple and clear. They are fervent—from the heart and above all, Biblical. We believe that we are not in error if we declare that in the later years, they have become more substantial, probing the depths together with witnessing to rich personal experience of Christian truth." [13]

Erl. Carlsson's patience and spirit of reconciliation in pastoral relationships was also a great asset. His attitude from early years, as reflected in a letter to Jonas Swensson in December 1856, provided a norm for his career: It is important not to take sides too hastily but to remember that one belongs to all and has duties to all. If trifles cause unrest, it is best to keep silent about them, not only publicly but also in personal contacts. But when one is compelled to bring up such matters and reprimand, one must do it with seriousness and love, after first having solicited divine assistance. [14]

Certain aspects of Erl. Carlsson's portrait emerge—sincere friend of man, understanding pastor, inspiring preacher, dedicated churchman. These qualities and others had a positive influence far beyond the boundaries of his own parish. Eric Norelius was in an admirable position to evaluate his long-time friend and occasional adversary. He points out that in forms of worship, church order, and constitutional provisions, Immanuel Church became the model for other congregations. Chicago's central location was a factor since almost all pastors were observers at one time or another of developments there in the early years, but he emphasized that, "The real reason is found in the first pastor." Then he cited the decisive factors: "Firm in doctrine and practice, loving good church order and possessing the ability to initiate and sustain it, he nurtured his congregtation from the beginning, not only as a Christian, but also as a well-ordered congregation, and when those two elements are united, the congregation is strong." Norelius has also appropriately pointed out that, "Erland Carlsson was neither a poet or a philosopher. He was not inclined to be speculative by nature. He has a thoroughly sound and practical type of mind." This quality enabled him to develop exceptional abilities in administration and leadership. [15]

Later observers confirm the appraisal of the veteran Norelius in regard to the range of Erl. Carlsson's contribution to the church at large. L. G. Abrahamson, long-time editor of *Augustana,* has written: "He always had a clear view of what was good for our church and his judgment on important questions within our denomination has always carried much weight. And what has contributed mightily in giving him this recognition has been the circumstance that people were convinced that he always took the position that was best for the general welfare rather than for his own interests." [16]

The achievement of Erl. Carlsson was possible because he lived from a great depth of being. A consensus appraisal summarizes the deep source and abiding power in these appropriate words:

It was especially Pastor Carlsson's consummate Christian charac-

208   THE STORY OF ERLAND CARLSSON

ter which impressed all who came into contact with him. He was a
man of prayer. The Word which he shared with those who heard him
preach, nourished his own soul. His life's and heart's fellowship with
God set a stamp upon his whole personality. [17]

FOOTNOTES

[1] Abrahamson, "Doktor Erland Carlsson," *Minneskrift-Immanuelsförsamlingen,"*
p. 36.

[2] John Telleen, "Rev. Dr. Erland Carlsson," *My Church,* VII (1921), 52; C. A.
Swensson, "Rostad," *Förgät-mig-ej, 1893,* p. 79; Norelius, *De Svenska
Lutherska . . . historia i Amerika,* I, 375.

[3] *Fosterlandet,* October 25, 1893.

[4] Abrahamson, "Doktor Erland Carlsson," *Minneskrift-Immanuelsförsamlingen,*
p. 44; Telleen, "Rev. Dr. Erland Carlsson," *My Church,* VII (1921), 52.

[5] Abrahamson, "Doktor Erland Carlsson," *Minneskrift-Immanuelsförsamlingen,*
p. 44.

[6] E. W. Olson, *History of the Swedes of Illinois,* pp. 478-79.

[7] Erl. Carlsson to T. N. Hasselquist, Chicago, March 9, 1874.

[8] Arden, *Journals of Eric Norelius,* p. 127.

[9] John Telleen, "A Memoir of Erland Carlsson," 5 pp. (n. d.).

[10] Jonas Swensson to Erl. Carlsson, Sugar Grove, Pa., October 27, 1856; Evald B.
Lawson, "Some Jonas Swensson Items," *The Augustana Quarterly,* XIV
(April, 1935), 168.

[11] J. G. Princell, "Hälsning," *Minneskrift-Immanuelsförsamlingen,* p. 106;
Josephine Princell, *J. G. Princells levnadsminnen* (Chicago, 1916), pp.
13-14; Philip Thelander, "Doktor Erland Carlsson," ms. 7 p.

[12] Arthur Bernhard Carlsson, "Pastoral Care in the Faith and Practice of Four
Selected Swedish Churchmen." Unpublished Ph.D. dissertation, Boston
University Graduate School, 1962, pp. 193-94. Examples of Carlsson's
concern for persons are found in "Sjelfbiografi," pp. 38-49 and in
Norelius, *De Svenska Lutherska . . . historia i Amerika,* I, 421-29.

[13] Olof Olsson and C. A. Swensson, "Pastor Erland Carlsson," *Korsbaneret,*
1881, p. 70; Abrahamson, "Doktor Erland Carlsson," *Minneskrift-
Immanuelsförsamlingen,* p. 39.

[14]Erl. Carlsson to Jonas Swensson, Chicago, December 23, 1856; Anders, "Select Letters to Jonas Swensson, 1856-58," p. 53.

[15]Norelius, *De Svenska Lutherska . . . historia i Amerika,* I, 384; Norelius, "Doktor Erland Carlsson," *Korsbaneret,* 1894, pp. 123-24.

[16]Abrahamson, *"Augustana-synoden," Jubel-Album, 1893,* pp. 44-45.

[17]Abrahamson, "Doktor Erland Carlsson," *Minneskrift-Immanuelsförsamlingen,* p. 44.

Några råd och underrättelser

för

Utwandrare

till

Amerikas Förenta Stater

af

Erl. Carlsson,
Evangelist-Lutherst Prest.

———————⋆———————

Werjö, 1854.   H. S. Cederschiöld.

Title-page of Carlsson's Immigrant Guide

APPENDIX

SOME ADVICE AND INFORMATION
FOR IMMIGRANTS
TO THE UNITED STATES OF AMERICA
By Erland Carlsson
Evangelical Lutheran Pastor
Vexiö, 1854. H. G. Cederschiöld
(Translated by O. V. Anderson)

Our Evangelical Lutheran Conference has enjoined me to prepare a guide for immigrants concerning both temporal and spiritual matters. However, since this commission can not be fulfilled in time to benefit this year's immigrants, because of lack of time and incomplete knowledge of conditions in this country, I look upon it as a duty to present in a short article some bits of advice and information which, through the newspapers in the homeland, may possibly be made common knowledge.

Concerning emigration, I believe that one can neither endorse nor advise against it unconditionally. However, it is lamentable that it is undertaken by the great majority so thoughtlessly and without plan. Many succumb to the sufferings and dangers of the trip and the difficulties of the first years. One can not in advance decide who should and who should not emigrate. Nor is it my intention now to enter into any discussion of this question. I only wish to say: No one should be hasty in deciding to emigrate, and all who have decided to do so should prepare themselves for many difficulties, both physical and spiritual. For America, too, is a country where both sin and sorrow dwell. For this reason it is with a certain anxiety that I have received information through letters from the homeland that it is believed that the emigration this coming summer will be large, particularly from certain sections of Sweden. However, may the long, adventuresome journey be accompanied by as few inconveniences as possible, and may even the lines which I pen herewith in some measure contribute to that end.

First and foremost I must in the most decided manner advise against taking the trip via England (Hull and Liverpool). Everyone who came by way of these places last year has bitterly complained about the difficult passage and the treatment received; and especially those who were sent via this route by a certain Mr. J--n in Gothenburg. For Swedish emigrants it is undeniably best to go direct from a Swedish port to America. At least a few opportunities are given each year for such a passage from Gothenburg, Stockholm, Gävle, and Carlshamn. But before one sets out for one of these places with the intention of beginning a voyage, one should, through correspondence or through a representative of some well-known shipping company, sign a contract in which not only the conditions of payment of passage should be decided, but also with which captain and which ship and at what time the trip shall be begun. This contract, for which a downpayment is made when it is received, is exchanged for a new one at the time of the complete payment of the fare. Also, in both of these contracts, the port of disembarkation should be plainly stated. Immigrants to North America's western states have really no choice of port of arrival than New York or Boston. Sea voyages for the lowest possible prices are, to be sure, made to Quebec in

Canada, and the journey inland is made for the same price as from either of the above-named places; but since Quebec is under English rule and its laws for the protection of immigrants are by no means as strict as the American, passengers aboard ships bound for these places are not only horribly crowded together, but in general are poorly treated. To dock at New Orleans is likewise inadvisable unless the trip from Sweden is undertaken in the fall, for example, in the month of September.

If, therefore, passage from a Swedish port to New York or Boston can not be had, I consider it best to go via Hamburg. There a company may be found called *Allgemeine Bureau für Auswanderer,* von Knorr and Holtermann. Those who sign a contract for passage with this company will be transported on Rob. M. Sloman's large and remarkable "Paket-Schiffe" direct from Hamburg to New York. Among all of last year's immigrants I have not met any who experienced a more pleasant and better sea voyage than those who came by this route and who employed this company. Not only did they have ample room on board, but in addition good and more than sufficient food, together with many other benefits; while, on the contrary, those who went by way of England had to endure a pretty severe fasting-cure. Last summer ships with emigrants from the above-named concern departed the first and fifteenth of every month. The price varied. During June and July, space between-decks [steerage] for adults cost 106:23 sk. rgs. and 90:32 sk. s. m. for children from one to eight years old. Prudence, however, should demand that more complete details be procured in advance by writing either Messrs. Knorr and Holtermann or Messrs. Ullberg and Gramer (Hamburg, grosse Bleichen No. 18), or else by addressing Consul Hamfeldt, who because of his good will and helpfulness toward our poor immigrants is deserving of both thanks and praise, and this all the more so since General Consul S––– in H–––– ordinarily dismisses them with the answer, "I don't concern myself at all with immigrants," even if that which is requested is not more than, for example, simply to take a look at a draft and state if it is in legal order.

It is also a matter of very considerable importance to have Swedish money exchanged for American currency. Those who have larger sums do best by taking a draft, when they can obtain a dollar for 3.36 to 3.32 rgs., according to the varying rate of exchange. When this business is transacted, it would be best to procure the advice and the help of a dependable man who is experienced in business affairs. On the other hand, those who do not own much more than what they need for the trip, may, after the ocean passage is paid, exchange what is left over for gold. In Hamburg last year one could get as much American currency as one wished for 3.36 sk. rgs. per dollar. In Gothenburg they have usually, however, had to pay from 3.40 to 3.44 sk., which is altogether too high. Swedish silver coins, in whole and half-species, can be taken along to America. For one of the former and two of the latter, one dollar and six cents is paid in New York. In Boston, last summer, a certain Swede had contrived to prey upon poor immigrants by tricking them into paying a specie and some shillings for each dollar.

Concerning the time for the voyage, it is impossible to decide when it can be most suitably undertaken. Each time of year has both its disadvantages and its advantages. No one, however, should start out later than the last part of August or the beginning of September unless one is thinking of going via New Orleans, but in this case the trip can be taken somewhat later. Implements and other things ought not to be taken along at all; or at least only the fewest possible. Good dress clothes and work clothes, two and at the most three outfits, together with good bedclothes as well as a quantity of linen—this is all, except that each emigrant ought to be equipped with flannel or wool to wear nearest his body. This is of the greatest importance, not only for the sea voyage, but also for residence here, if one is not to be stricken soon after arrival by the severe intermittent fever, called "fever ague." Likewise, emigrants ought not to forget to provide themselves with a quantity of good Swedish books, because such can not be bought here without ordering them from Sweden. In addition to the *Bible,* Luther's *Postils,* and some other good devotional book, for example, Arndt's *True Christianity,* they may take along psalmbooks, catechisms, Barth's *Bible History,* and A.B.C. books. When buying Psalmbooks, Thomander and Wieselgren's edition should be preferred, especially since here in this country it is beginning to be used with predilection by our countrymen and it is very likely that it will displace the one generally used in the homeland. To be sure, our countrymen, when they have come over here, will soon hear other advice concerning these devotional writings and Christian books than this which I have given; for, instead of being advised to procure such and to use them, they will be admonished, if not to burn them up entirely, then certainly to throw them away. "Away with Luther, away with the *Catechism,* away with every word of man!" so it goes. "We have the *Bible,* and that is enough." But one should not allow oneself to be confused by this. It is the sectarian—the spirit of error—who shouts so, and it is not the love of truth which drives him on; he wishes simply in this way to make room for his own "word of man," for his own human devices. One will often also hear the same condemnation concerning our church's customs and practices. In place of these, others are brought in, by which men are soon confused, with injury to their souls, inasmuch as upon these very things much greater weight is laid than our Lutheran Church ever placed upon the external form. But enough concerning this.

As to provisions, sufficient information may be had in the seaports, and if one goes via Hamburg, one does not need to supply provisions. It would perhaps be well, however, to provide oneself with a few pounds of prunes, etc., for fruit soup, a few bouillon cubes ("buillon de Poche"), together with a few bottles of good red wine and Madeira. Particularly those who have small children I would advise to buy from an apothecary a few pounds of arrowroot (Maranta arundinacea), which can be prepared into a pleasant-tasting, healthful, and nourishing drink, by first making a dough of this flour and then pouring on as many quarts of boiling water as one uses tablespoons of flour. This is stirred together well and boiled for a few minutes over a fire. Afterward a little sugar and wine may be added to suit the taste. This drink is not only the most suitable for suckling babies during the ocean voyage, but is particularly useful for older persons in case of sickness.

During the voyage, under no circumstances must one allow oneself to be overcome by indifference concerning oneself and others, which always accompanies sea sickness. One must stay out of bed and in motion, promenade the deck, work the pump, be busy with sewing, crocheting, and whatever else one can do. This contributes to health and comfort.

Having arrived at an American port, immigrants must with great care protect themselves against the many swindlers who, by means of false words and fine representations, offer their guidance and service. In Boston our countrymen have had much help from a Swede named Willeston, and in general those who have come by way of this port have enjoyed good treatment. In New York greater difficulties are met. From there, several roads go west, and the choice between them becomes so much more difficult, since crowds of runners try to solicit business for the various companies; however, there are only two between which there can be any question of choice, namely, Hudson River Railroad and New York and Erie Railroad. Both of these are well known, although on the latter many extortions were committed last year. However, conditions improved in the fall. In New York, Pastor Hedström (for several years pastor of a Swedish Methodist congregation there) has with great willingness and solicitude undertaken to help his countrymen. Pastor Hedström has always recommended the New York and Erie Railroad, but since Hudson River Railroad enjoys fully as great confidence and since a Swede named Aspelin, through whom immigrants have received honest and dependable travel aid, is to be found at the office of the latter, I do not know which road I shall recommend. That which may be the choice of route consequently depends on which road quotes the lower price. Certainly there should, in this connection, be room for no difference, since the state by law, in the most careful manner, has decided not only the price of passage between the various cities, but also how much baggage may be taken along free, and what must be paid for overweight (see *Caution to Passengers,* published in New York, July 1853, by the Commissioners of Immigration). But most immigrants will find that these careful regulations by the state are often scorned.

Thus, although the city mayor decided, for last year, upon 100 pounds free baggage for every adult passenger, and, for example, a $2.50 charge for every hundred pounds overweight from New York to Chicago, nevertheless all Swedish immigrants who traveled on the Erie road were tricked and forced to pay $3.00 for every hundred pounds which they had in excess of 50 pounds.

When the ticket for the journey inland is received, it must be inspected carefully to see if it is good, and good for the whole journey. Normally, on top of all tickets reads, "By canal," "By steamboat," or "On the Lake," which words must be stricken out, and in their place "By railroad" must be written in, or still more correctly, the name of the railroad stated. If this is not done, immigrants will be compelled either to make a long and troublesome journey via canals and over the great lakes or else, if this is to be avoided, pay an additional fare or at least two dollars for each person on the way.

Those who travel on the Erie road are taken a short distance (about thirty English miles) from New York by steamer, then via railroad to Dunkirk and from there by steamer over Lake Erie to Detroit. If one travels via the Hudson River Railroad, one entrains in New York. The road starts in the city near the harbor (the station is at the foot of Canal Street) and runs through Albany and Troy and other cities to Buffalo; from there one travels by steamer across the above-named lake to Detroit. Then the journey continues via Michigan Central Railroad to Chicago. Occasionally immigrants are taken from Dunkirk and Buffalo by steamer to Toledo and from there via Michigan Southern Railroad to Chicago. This way is considered somewhat better than via Detroit, although I can not see any real difference between these two lines. From Chicago, railroads and canals stretch out in every possible direction. Those who want to go to

Southern and Central Iowa, ought to go by the Rock Island Railroad, but to Northern Iowa and Minnesota it is best to go via the Galena Railroad.

All chests, trunks, and bags should be carefully marked with the owner's name and destination. One is not allowed to take along large provision boxes on the railroad. At transfer points everyone will have to see to it that he gets his own things. If one follows belongings as they are moved by company employees, one will avoid taking the wrong road or train. A common swindle to which immigrants are subjected is simply this, that they are hospitably invited to get what they need and wish, for money of course, by that miserable class of men, the innkeepers, with the assurance that the train will not leave for some hours yet. In this manner they are often detained until the train is gone, must remain at least another day, pay high prices for room and board, and may consider themselves lucky if they are not also more or less robbed. But it is impossible to enumerate and warn against the scores of dangers and frauds to which poor immigrants are exposed. I will, however, before I close, call their attention to another item or two.

Perhaps it will be enough simply to warn people not to accept paper money before they have learned to know which banks are good, not to lend their money carelessly, and to exercise great caution during the journey by railroad. All newcomers must, to begin with, submit themselves to the strictest diet, entirely refraining from all kinds of fruit as well as whiskey. If this is not observed, they may not live very many days here.

It is known that slavery exists in America; for with all its freedom and all its Christianity this fair land has nevertheless not as yet progressed so far that it has been able to do away with or blot out this dark spot. To be sure, it is only the Negroes over whom this darkness of thralldom rests, but even white people may well be on guard. No newcomer who is seeking a place of service or work ought to hire out for longer than a month. The majority of those who have indentured themselves for one or several years have bitterly regretted it; and when one considers more carefully how newcomers, unfamiliar with the language and other conditions, often are treated, one sees therein something akin to slavery. But that which bears a closer relationship to slavery, and has awakened in me grief and indignation, is that children often have been beguiled away from their parents. Promises are given to clothe and rear children, keep them in school, in a word, "to take care of them." Parents are urged to sign a paper, written in a language that they do not understand, containing a waiver of all rights to the children until they have reached legal age (a girl at 18 and a boy at 21 years). Many parents have been foolish, heartless, conscienceless enough to give away their children thus, oftentimes the only, but always the dearest, possession they brought along when they stepped upon American soil. Even if one child or another may be well enough provided for, even better than with his parents, I nevertheless do not believe that parents have the right to give away their children in this manner. If they knew the persons with whom the children are left, or remained in their vicinity, one could not say so much about it; but now the children are entrusted to total strangers, whose religion—if they have any at all—one does not know. Parents go to one place, the children are brought to another, most often several hundred miles apart; and I have met parents who never after got information about their children or even had any hope of ever seeing them again in this life, and who would have considered themselves vastly more fortunate if they had followed their children to the grave instead of throwing them out into the world in this manner.

Shortsightedness has often presented this willingness to "take up children," as it is called, as a visible evidence of self-sacrificing love. I thought so, too, to begin with, but soon I thought otherwise. In our company two mothers died who left several children, among them some very tiny ones. In New York we hoped to find such much praised love, but in vain. And, alas, we were no more fortunate in Chicago. Generally people inquired of us concerning the age of the children, if they were pretty and healthy, and when we answered that they were very small, sickly, and feeble, no one wished to take them. I went away distressed and thought: That which frightened them was just that which ought to induce a friend of Jesus to "receive these little ones." Certainly there are many praiseworthy exceptions here, but I have wanted to present this as evidence that all is not gold that glitters in America, even if this is a land of gold, and that the renowned willingness to "take up children" is not always a love of children, nor love for Him who said, "He who receives one such in my name receives me." More often it is that self-love which seeks its own, wherefore only children of ten or twelve years of age or older are wanted.

Perhaps I ought also to say something concerning the spiritual frauds and seductions to which our countrymen have been exposed in this country but this would make my article all too long. Instead I urge each and every immigrant to procure and make himself thoroughly acquainted with a little book called *Skiljelärorna hos åtskilliga Christna bekännelser belysta af Guds Ord* (The Distinctive Doctrines in the Several Christian Confessions Enlightened by God's Word) by R. Graul, printed in Stockholm by Norstedt and Sons, 1849. (It would be very desirable if the book dealers in the seaports from which emigrants depart would furnish their book stores with an adequate number of copies of this little book, in order that they might be available for those who want to procure the same.) He who makes himself conversant with the contents of this book will derive great benefit from it, when he comes under the influence of the many intellectual winds which blow in the spiritual atmosphere of America. If he has, in addition, come to a living experience of that truth, spirit, and power which is found in our church and its glorious doctrines, then he will certainly not do as many of our countrymen who have arrived here have done, thoughtlessly or frivolously sell his birthright as a Lutheran, "pure Word and pure Sacraments," for a mess of pottage, cooked together out of empty promises of some earthly benefits and a self-chosen spirituality spiced with bitter rantings about the church back home and a few Bible passages, twisted and torn from their context. Concerning this, much could be said, but I close with the apostolic exhortation: "Beloved, believe not every spirit, but prove the spirits whether they are of God, because many false prophets are gone out into the world" (I John 4.1).

Finally, a few words to the many unknown correspondents in the homeland who have taken it upon themselves to send letters to their relatives and friends who have come over here, enclosing them in envelopes sent to me with the request that I would see to it that they are forwarded to the right persons. This trouble I am certainly willing to take upon myself, and I shall do what I can to forward the letters promptly. But it is impossible for me to pay the postage in addition. I have received several letters for persons who are either dead or who have moved to another place without leaving their address. I have been obliged to pay postage due to get their letters at the post office, for some, 42 cents and for others 84 cents, and of late my expense for such letters has amounted to several dollars. I always pay postage when my own letters are sent, and my friends in the homeland do the same thing; and I must herewith give notice that after the first of next July, I will not redeem a single letter sent with postage unpaid. It is erroneously imagined by many that letters arrive more safely when postage is not paid in advance. I do not believe that. The reason why so many letters go astray is that they have an indistinct or incorrect address. Nor do letters on which postage has not been paid arrive any sooner than the stamped ones. This is much more dependent upon the route by which they are sent. The fastest and most regular is undeniably "via Liverpool" since from there English and American government mail-steamers depart each Wednesday, making the trip over the Atlantic in ten to twelve days. Many fear that even if postage is paid when a letter is mailed, it must nevertheless be redeemed when it arrives; but this is not so. If full postage is paid (i.e. the franti mark (so de Porto)) at one place, it does not need to be paid at the other. To be sure, a number of complaints have been made about some postmasters. I would rather believe that these are ungrounded, at least there has never arisen the slightest reason for complaints against the post office (Vexiö, Carlshamn, Sölwesborg, etc.) from which I have received my letters. However, should it be that fraudulent methods are employed in post offices here or there back home, this matter is easily taken care of. One simply returns the envelope to the writer of the letter, who then certified under oath before a qualified person, that the full postage was paid at the time the letter was mailed, whereupon the matter will be taken up for legal action and will be accompanied by serious consequences for the guilty party.

I now close these lines with the warmest, sincerest well-wishes for my old, beloved fatherland. May God's Spirit, grace, and blessing always rest over her and her people! May especially the many and important matters which are now in the making there be given a solution and development which will be rich in blessings for both church and state! We love our fatherland and remember her in our prayers. We hope also that praying hearts in the homeland will not forget to intercede in faithful prayer for us and our striving for God's kingdom and for the welfare of souls. May the Lord also keep and guide by His protecting hand those who undertake the long voyage in order to find here a new homeland, a home, and then a grave; and may we all some day receive an inheritance in the abode of light.

Chicago, Illinois, North America, April 24, 1854.

BIBLIOGRAPHY

KEY

ACL – Augustana College Library, Rock Island, IL
BCL – Bethany College Library, Lindsborg, KS
GUB – Göteborg University Library, Sweden
LCAA – Lutheran Church in America Archives, Chicago
LUB – Lund University Library, Sweden
LV – Landsarkivet in Vadstena, Sweden
NA – United States National Archives and Records Service,
Washington, D.C.

MANUSCRIPTS

"Elghults födelse och döpbok, 1800-1831." Birth and baptismal record (LV).

"Elghults husförhörslängd, 1825-1830." Household examination roll (LV).

"Testimonium vitae för Erland Carlsson: Rector och Consistorium Academicum i Lund, den 9 December 1848" (ACL).

"Utdrag af Protocollet hållet uti Theologiska Faculteten i Lund d. 6 April 1848 and d. 6 December 1848" (ACL).

"Antavla för Erland Carlsson," by Catharina Svensson (ACL).

"Sjelfbiografi, 1853-54 af Erland Carlsson" (LCAA).

"The Ship's Manifest of the *St. Patrick,* New York, August 25, 1853" (NA).

"Records of the Evangelical Lutheran Immanuel Church, Chicago, Illinois, 1853-75" (LCAA).

"Minutes of the Board of Directors of Augustana College and Theological Seminary, 1860-93" (ACL).

"Minutes of the Faculty of Augustana College and Theological Seminary, 1860-93." (ACL)

"The Erland Carlsson Papers" (ACL). Four file books of letters received and seventeen copy books. The majority of items deal with the later years of his life.

"The L. P. Esbjörn Papers" (ACL).

"The T. N. Hasselquist Papers" (ACL).

"The Eric Norelius Papers" (ACL).

"The Olof Olsson Papers" (ACL and LCAA).

"The Carl Aaron Swensson Papers" (BCL).

"The Jonas Swensson Papers" (ACL and BCL).

"The Peter Wieselgren Papers" (GUB).

Miscellaneous: *Letters,* P. A. Ahlberg (ACL), A. Andreen (ACL), Samuel Carlsson (BCL), Erland Danielsson (ACL), J. V. Dahlstedt (LUB), John Enander (ACL), G. Hammar (LUB), G. F. Krotel (ACL), George Trabert (LCAA), C. W. Weinberg (LCAA), General: G. A. Andreen (ACL), C. A. Lund (ACL), Peter Peterson (LCAA), John Telleen (ACL), Philip Thelander (LCAA).

NEWSPAPERS

Augustana. Månatlig tidskrift för Lutherska kyrkan i Amerika, 1869-73 (Chicago). (Merged with *Rätta Hemlandet* in 1869. Known after 1873 as *Augustana, Luthersk kyrkotidning).*

Augustana. Luthersk kyrkotidning, 1874-89 (Rock Island and Moline). (Continued as *Augustana och missionären vecko-tidning för kyrka och mission,* 1879-89).

Augustana Tidning för den Svenska Lutherska kyrkan i Amerika. 1889-93 (Rock Island).

Hemlandet, det gamla och det nya, 1855-75 (Galesburg and Chicago).

Justitia, Mar.-Oct., 1871 (Chicago).

Nya Svenska Amerikanaren, 1873-77 (Chicago).

Nya Wexjö-Bladet, 1853-58.

Det Rätta Hemlandet, 1856-73 (Galesburg and Chicago).

Svenska Amerikanaren, 1866-73 (Chicago). (Continued as *Nya Svenska Amerikanaren).*

Svenska Amerikanaren, 1877-93 (Chicago). (A continuation of *Svenska Posten).*

Wexjö Stifts-Tidningar, 1852-53.

Miscellaneous issues of *Barometern* (Kalmar), *The Chicago Daily Tribune, Fosterlandet* (Lindsborg and Chicago), *Göteborg-Posten, Kansas Conference Lutheran* (Lindsborg, KS), *Lindsborg News, Lindsborgs-Posten, Lindsborg Record, Lunds Missions-Tidning, Lutheran Companion,* (Rock Island), *När och fjärran* (Stockholm), *Wäktaren, tidning för stat och kyrka* (Stockholm).

PERIODICALS

Almqvist, Sten. "An Immigrant Letter Concerning the Chicago Fire," *The Swedish Pioneer Historical Quarterly,* XXII (Oct. 1971), 212-20.

Ander, O. Fritiof (translator and editor). "Some Letters Pertaining to the Proposed Minnesota Synod," *The Augustana Quarterly,* XII (Oct. 1933), 358-70.

_____. "Some factors in the Americanization of the Swedish Immigrant, 1850-1890," *Journal of the Illinois Historical Society,* XXVI (Apr.-July 1933), 136-50.

_____. "Augustana-kyrkan vid sitt sekelskifte," *Kyrkohistorisk årsskrift.* Stockholm. LXI (1960), 146-84.

Anders, J. Olson. "Select Letters to Jonas Swensson, 1856-58," *Swedish-American Historical Bulletin.* St. Peter, Minn. V (June 1932), 50-60.

Beijbom, Ulf. "The Oldest Swedish Parish Records of Chicago," *The Swedish Pioneer Historical Quarterly,* XX (Apr. 1969), 57-75.

_____. "The Printed Word in a Nineteenth-Century Immigrant Colony: The Role of the Ethnic Press in Chicago's Swede Town," *The Swedish Pioneer Historical Quarterly,* XXVIII (Apr. 1977), 82-105.

Bergendoff, Conrad. "The Sources of the Original Constitution of the Augustana Synod," *Augustana Historical Society Publications* V (1935), 85-106.

_____. "National Aspects of the Lutheran Church in America," *The Augustana Quarterly,* III (1924), 154-69.

_____. "The Cultural Heritage of the Augustana Synod," *The Augustana Quarterly,* XIV (Oct. 1935), 347-52.

"The Chicago Fire," *Chicago History. Magazine of the Chicago Historical Society,* 1971 (Fall), pp. 196-244.

Enander, J. A. "Chicago-branden," *Valkyrian,* V (1901), 632-40.

Forsander, Nils. "Några blad ur Augustana Synodens historia, åren 1848-1870," *Kyrkohistorisk årsskrift,* IV (1903), 203-209.

Foss, C. W. "Historical Sketch of Grace Lutheran Church, Rock Island, Ill.," *The Lutheran Companion,* Feb. 18, 1923, pp. 157-58 and an editorial, p. 156.

Johnson, E. Gustav. "Chicago Swedes Organized 'Svea' a Century Ago," *The Swedish Pioneer Historical Quarterly,* VIII (Oct. 1957), 115-28.

Lawson, Evald B. "Are Changes in Our Liturgy Desirable? A Symposium," *The Augustana Quarterly,* XIII (Oct. 1934), 307-20.

_____. "Some Jonas Swensson Items," *The Augustana Quarterly,* XIV (Apr. 1935), 157-79.

_____. "Some Footnotes to the Study of Our History," *The Augustana Quarterly,* XX (Apr. 1941), 109-23.

_____. "The New York Conference of the Augustana Lutheran Church and Its Place of Founding," *The Swedish Pioneer Historical Quarterly,* V (Apr. 1954), 35-55.

Lindberg, Conrad Emil. "The Influence of the Pioneer Pastors from Sweden on Theological Education in the Augustana Synod," *The Augustana Quarterly,* VII (June 1928), 118-27.

Nelson, Clifford Ansgar. "A Pertinent Historical Letter—with Comments," *The Augustana Quarterly,* XXIII (Jan. 1944), 22-30.

Nothstein, I. O. "The Language Transition in the Augustana Synod," *The Augustana Quarterly,* XXIV (July 1945), 209-23; (Oct. 1945), 327-46.

Odman, Charlotte. "A Great Leader Gone. Mrs. Emmy Evald, Lover of Missions Dies," *The Lutheran Companion,* Jan. 1, 1947.

_____. "She [Emmy Evald] Led a Women's Crusade for Christ," *The Lutheran Companion,* June 1, 1960.

Olson, Oscar N. "William Alfred Passavant and the Augustana Synod," *The Augustana Quarterly,* XXIV (July 1945), 224-41.

Olsson, Augustus G. "Three Pioneer Pastors," *The Augustana Quarterly,* XV (Jan. 1936), 45-54.

Olsson, Nils William. "Documents. The First Constitution of the St. Ansgarius Church of Chicago," *The Swedish Pioneer Historical Quarterly,* I (Oct. 1950), 18-22.

Peterson, C. F. "Några svenska Chicagominnen. Efter branden," *Valkyrian,* III (1899), 407-11.

_____. "Isidor Kjellberg, Agitatorn," *Valkyrian,* I (1897), 33-35.

_____. "Blickar mellan kulisserna i Chicagos Svenska verld för 35 år sedan," *Valkyrian,* V (1901), 34-36.

Pleijel, Hilding. "The Church from which Came the Founders of the Augustana Synod," *The Augustana Quarterly,* XXVII (July 1948), 205-18.

Reinertsen, P. J. "The Division of the Scandinavian Evangelical Lutheran Augustana Synod," *The Augustana Quarterly,* XII (July 1933), 248-65.

Stephenson, George M. "Background of the Beginning of Swedish Immigration, 1850-75," *The American Historical Review,* XXXI (July 1926), 708-23.

_____. "The Founding of the Augustana Synod: Illustrative Documents," *Swedish-American Historical Bulletin,* XII (Mar. 1928), 1-52.

_____. "The Stormy Years of the Swedish Colony in Chicago Before the Great Fire," *Transactions of the Illinois Historical Society,* XXVI (1929), 166-84.

BOOKS

Ander, O. Fritiof. *T. N. Hasselquist. The Career and Influence of a Swedish-American Clergyman, Journalist, and Educator.* Rock Island, 1931. (Augustana Historical Society Publication, I)

_____. *The Cultural Heritage of the Swedish Immigrant. Selected References.* Rock Island, 1956. (Augustana Library Publication, no. 27)

Ander, O. Fritiof and Nordstrom, Oscar L., eds. *The American Origin of the Augustana Synod from Contemporary Lutheran Periodicals, 1851-1860.* Rock Island, 1942. (Augustana Historical Society Publication, no. 9)

Anders, John Olson. *The Origin and History of Swedish Religious Organizations in Minnesota, 1853-1885.* Rock Island: Augustana Book Concern, 1932.

Andreas, A. T. *History of Chicago.* Chicago: The author, 1884. 3 vols.

Andreen, Gustav. "The Early Missionary Work of the Augustana Synod in New York City in 1865-66," *Augustana Historical Society Publication,* II (1932), 1-26.

Angle, Paul M. *The Great Chicago Fire.* Chicago: The Chicago Historical Society, 1946.

Arden, G. Everett. *Augustana Heritage. A History of the Augustana Lutheran Church.* Rock Island: Augustana Press, 1963.

──────. *History of the Illinois Conference, Augustana Evangelical Lutheran Church.* Rock Island, 1953.

──────. *The School of the Prophets. The Background and History of Augustana Theological Seminary.* Rock Island: Augustana Theological Seminary, 1960.

Arvastan, Allan. *Den Thomander-Wieselgrenska Psalmboken.* Stockholm: Svenska kyrkans diakonisstyrelsens bokförlag, 1949.

Backlund, J. Oscar. *A Century of the Swedish American Press.* Chicago: Swedish American Newspaper Company, 1952.

Baeckström, Brita (ed.). *Karta över Sveriges kyrkliga indelning.* Stockholm: Svenska prästförbundet, 1977.

Barton, H. Arnold. *Letters from the Promised Land. Swedes in America, 1840-1914.* Minneapolis: Published by the University of Minnesota Press for the Swedish Pioneer Historical Society, Chicago, 1975.

Beijbom, Ulf. *Swedes in Chicago. A Demographic and Social Study of the 1846-1880 Immigration.* Chicago: Chicago Historical Society and Uppsala: Studia Historica Upsaliensia, 1971.

──────. *Amerika, Amerika! En bok om utvandringen.* Stockholm: Natur och Kultur, 1977.

──────. "Från slum till förort. Chicago Swede Town." *Utvandring. Den Svenska emigrationen till Amerika i historiskt perspektiv.* Edited by Ann-Sofie Kälvemark. Stockholm: Wahlström och Widstrand, 1973. pp. 179-211.

Bergendoff, Conrad. "The Sources of the Original Constitution of the Augustana Synod," *Augustana Historical Society Publication,* V (1935), 85-106.

──────. "Augustana. A People in Transition," *The Swedish Immigrant Community in Transition,* ed. by J. I. Dowie and E. M. Espelie. *Augustana Historical Society Publication,* no. 20, pp. 197-208. Rock Island, 1963.

──────. "The Role of Augustana in the Transplantation of a Culture Across the Atlantic," *The Immigration of Ideas,* ed. by J. I. Dowie and J. T.

Tredway, *Augustana Historical Society Publication* no. 21, pp. 67-83. Rock Island, 1968.

_____. *Augustana. A Profession of Faith.* Rock Island, 1969. (Augustana Library Publication no. 33).

Blomén, Sven. *Älghult. Vår hemsoken.* Nybro: Johansson och Svenson boktryckeri, 1955.

Boethius, Axel and Olauson, Åke (editors). *Vår Svenska stam på utländsk mark.* Stockholm: Riksföreningen för svenskhetens bevarande i utlandet, 1952.

Boethius, Bertil. "Erland Carlsson," *Svenskt biografiskt lexikon.* VII, 569-75. Stockholm: Albert Bonniers förlag, 1927.

Bowman, C. V. *Missionsvännerna i Amerika.* Minneapolis: Veckoblad Publ. Co., 1907.

Brolund, Erik. *Missionsvännerna. Jämförelser och studier.* Chicago: Mission Friends Publishing Company, 1938.

Carlson, Arthur Bernard. "Pastoral Care in the Faith and Practice of Four Selected Swedish Churchmen" [Henrik Schartau, Carl Olof Rosenius, Erland Carlsson, Jonas Swensson]. Ph.D. dissertation, Boston University Graduate School, 1962.

Carlsson, Erl. "Annandag Pingst," *Korsets predikan af pastorer inom Augustana-Synoden.* II, 387-401. Rock Island: Augustana Book Concern, 1885.

Centennial Essays. Augustana Lutheran Church, 1860-1960. Rock Island: Augustana Press, 1960.

Church, William Conant. *The Life of John Ericsson.* New York: Charles Scribner's Sons, 1907. 2 vols.

Clemenson, Gustaf. *Lessebo 1658-1856.* 1954.

Covenant Memories. Golden Jubilee. Swedish Evangelical Mission Covenant, 1885-1935. Chicago: Covenant Book Concern, 1935.

Dahllöf, Tell G. *I utvandrarnas spår. En bok om Sverige och Amerika.* Stockholm: Verbum, 1975.

Dahlsten, A. W. "Några ord om Augustana College och Seminarii första början," *Minnen från jubelfesten Augustana College och Augustana-synodens femtio års-jubileum, den 5-15 juni 1910.* pp. 41-43. Rock Island: Augustana Book Concern, 1910.

Forsander, Nils. "Erland Carlsson," *Lifsbilder ur Augustana-Synodens historia.* I, 101-27. Rock Island: Augustana Book Concern, 1915.

Gerberding, G. H. *The Life and Letters of W. A. Passavant, D. D.* Greenville, Pa.: The Young Lutheran Co., 1906.

Hawkinson, Eric G. *Images in Covenant Beginnings.* Chicago: Covenant Press, 1968.

Hildebrand, Karl and Fredenholm, Axel. *Svenskarna i Amerika.* Stockholm: Historiska förlaget, 1925. II.

Historic City. The Settlement of Chicago. Chicago: City of Chicago, Department of Development and Planning, 1976.

Holmgrain, O. V. "Augustana-Synodens förlagsverksamhet," *Minneskrift med anledning af Augustana-Synodens femtioåriga tillvaro, 1860-1910.* pp. 293-318. Rock Island: Augustana Book Concern, 1910.

_____. *Augustana Book Concern, 1889-1914. Festskrift.* Rock Island: Augustana Book Concern, 1914.

Illinois-Konferensen, 1853-1903. Rock Island: Augustana Book Concern, 1903.

Janson, Florence Edith. *The Background of Swedish Immigration, 1840-1930.* Chicago: The University of Chicago Press, 1931.

Johnson, Emeroy. *Eric Norelius. Pioneer Midwest Pastor and Churchman.* Rock Island: Augustana Book Concern, 1954.

Johnson, Eric and Peterson, C. F. *Svenskarne i Illinois. Historiska anteckningar.* Chicago: 1880.

Kälvemark, Ann-Sofie. *Utvandring. Den Svenska emigrationen till Amerika i historiskt perspektiv.* Stockholm: Wahlström och Widstrand, 1973.

Larson, Esther Elizabeth. *Swedish Commentators on America, 1638-1865. An Annotated List of Selected Manuscript and Printed Materials.* New York: The New York Public Library and Chicago: The Swedish Pioneer Historical Society, 1963.

Lawson, Evald B. "Music, Art, and Architecture in Our Church," *After Seventy-five Years, 1860-1935.* pp. 119-35. Rock Island: Augustana Book Concern, 1935.

_____. *Two Primary Sources for a Study of the Life of Jonas Swensson.* Rock Island, 1957. (Augustana Historical Society Publication, no. 17).

Liljegren, N. M., Westergreen, N. O., and Wallenius, C. G. *Svenska Metodism i Amerika.* Chicago: Svenska M. E. bokhandels föreningens förlag, 1895.

Ljungmark, Lars. *Den stora utvandringen.* Stockholm: Sveriges Radio, 1965.

Lund, Emil. *Minnesota-Konferensens av Augustana-Synoden och dess församlingars historia.* Rock Island: Augustana Book Concern, 1923. 2 vols.

Lundeen, Joel W. *Preserving Yesterday for Tomorrow. A Guide to the Archives of the Lutheran Church In America.* Chicago: 1977.

Lundstedt, Bernhard. *Svenska tidningar och tidskrifter utgifna inom Nord-Amerikas Förenta Stater. Bibliografiska öfversigt.* Stockholm: Kungl. boktryckeriet. P. A. Norstedt söner, 1886.

Lyttkens, Carl Henrik. *The Growth of Swedish-Anglican Intercommunion between 1833 and 1922.* Lund: C. W. K. Gleerup förlag, 1970.

Mattson, A. D. *Polity of the Augustana Synod.* Rock Island: Augustana Book Concern, 1941.

Minneskrift 1858-1908 tillegnad Minnesota-Konferensens af Ev. Luterska Augus-tana-Synoden 50-års jubileum, den 7-11 Oktober 1908. Minneapolis: 1908.

Minnesskrift med anledning af Augustana-Synodens femtioåriga tillvaro 1860-1910. Rock Island: Augustana Book Concern, 1910.

Naeseth, Henriette C. K. *The Swedish Theatre of Chicago.* Rock Island, 1951. (Augustana Library Publication, no. 22, and Augustana Historical Society Publication, no. 12).

Nelson, Helge. *The Swedes and the Swedish Settlements in North America.* Lund: C. W. K. Gleerup, 1943. I.

Newman, S. B. *Sjelfbiografi.* Chicago: Svenska Metodist bokladens förlag, 1890.

Norelius, Eric. *De Svenska Luterska församlingarnas och Svenskarnes historia i Amerika.* Rock Island: Lutheran Augustana Book Concern, 1890-1916. 2 vols.

——————. *T. N. Hasselquist. Lefnadsteckning.* Rock Island: Lutheran Augustana Book Concern [1900].

——————. *Early Life of Eric Norelius, 1833-1862. A Lutheran Pioneer.* Translated by Emeroy Johnson. Rock Island: Augustana Book Concern, 1934.

——————. *The Journals of Eric Norelius. A Swedish Missionary on the American Frontier.* Translated and edited by G. Everett Arden. Philadelphia: Fortress Press, 1967.

Nothstein, I. O. (ed.). *Selected Documents Dealing with the Organization of the First Congregations and the First Conferences of the Augustana Synod and Their Growth until 1860,* Rock Island, 1944-46. (Augustana Historical Society Publications, nos. 10-11). 2 vols.

Nystrom, Daniel. *A Ministry of Printing. History of the Publication House of Augustana Lutheran Church, 1889-1962.* Rock Island: Augustana Press, 1962.

——————. (ed.). *A Family of God.* Rock Island: Augustana Press, 1962.

Ochsenford, S. E. *Documentary History of the General Council of the Evangelical Lutheran Church in North America.* Philadelphia: General Council Publication House, 1912.

Olson, Adolf. *A Centenary History as Related to the Baptist General Conference of America.* Chicago: Baptist Conference Press, 1952.

Olson, Ernst W. "Augustana Book Concern: Publishers to the Augustana Synod. History of Its Activities Since 1889, with Introductory Account of Earlier Publishing Enterprises," *Augustana Historical Society Publication.* III (1933), 3-80.

——————. *Augustana Book Concern. Publishers to the Augustana Synod Since 1889.* Rock Island: Augustana Book Concern, 1934. (Identical in contents with volume listed above).

——————. "Early Letters to Erland Carlsson," *Augustana Historical Society Publication,* V (1935), 107-133.

_____. *En bokhandels-historia*. Chicago: The Engberg-Holmberg Pub. Co., 1910.

_____. *History of the Swedes of Illinois*. Chicago: The Engberg-Holmberg Publishing Co., 1908. I.

_____. *The Swedish Element in Illinois. Survey of the Past Seven Decades*. Chicago: Swedish-American Biographical Association, 1917.

_____. *Olof Olsson. The Man, His Work, and His Thought*. Rock Island, 1941. (Augustana Historical Society Publictation, no. 8).

Olson, Oscar N. *Olof Christian Telemak Andrén. Ambassador of Goodwill*. Rock Island, 1954. (Augustana Historical Society Publication, no. 14).

_____. *The Augustana Lutheran Church in America. Pioneer Period, 1846-1860*. Rock Island: Augustana Book Concern, 1950.

_____. *The Augustana Lutheran Church in America, 1860-1910*. Rock Island: Executive Council of the Augustana Lutheran Church, 1956.

_____. *A Century of Life and Growth. Augustana [Synod] 1848-1948*. Rock Island: Augustana Book Concern, 1948.

Olsson, Karl A. *By One Spirit*. (History of the Evangelical Covenant Church in America). Chicago: Covenant Press, 1962.

_____. "Peter Paul Waldenström and Augustana," *The Swedish Immigrant Community in Transition*, ed. by J. I. Dowie and E. M. Espelie. *Augustana Historical Society Publication* no. 20, pp. 107-20.

Olsson, Olof. "Vid Doktor Erland Carlssons begrafning." His *Samlade Skrifter*. Rock Island, 1912. III, 467-69.

Peterson, C. F. *Sverige i Amerika. Kulturhistoriska och biografiska teckningar*. Chicago: The Royal Star Co., 1898.

Pierce, Bessie Louise. *A History of Chicago*. Vol. II: *From Town to City*. New York: Alfred A. Knopf, 1940.

Princell, Josephine. *J. G. Princells levnadsminnen*. Chicago: 1916.

Runblom, Harald and Norman, Hans (editors). *From Sweden to America. A History of the Migration*. Minneapolis: University of Minnesota Press and Acta Universitatis Upsaliensis, University of Uppsala, 1976.

Runeby, Nils. *Den nya världen och den gamla. Amerikabild och emigrations-uppfattning i Sverige, 1820-1860*. Uppsala: Studia Historica Upsaliensia, 1969.

Ryden, E. E. "Early Publication Ventures," Nystrom, Daniel, *A Family of God*, pp. 88-89.

Rönnegard, Sam. *Lars Paul Esbjörn och Augustana-Synodens uppkomst*. Stockholm: Svenska kyrkans diakonistyrelses bokförlag, 1949.

_____. *Prairie Shepherd. Lars Paul Esbjörn and the Beginnings of the Augustana Lutheran Church*. Translated by G. Everett Arden. Rock

Island: Augustana Book Concern, 1952.

_____. *Utvandrarnas kyrka. En bok om Augustana.* Stockholm: Diakonistyrelsens bokförlag, 1961.

Scott, Franklin D. *Sweden. The Nation's History.* Minneapolis: University of Minnesota Press, 1977.

Sjöström, Carl. *Smålands nation i Lund, 1668-1921. Biografiska och genealogiska anteckningar.* Lund: 1922.

Skarstedt, Ernst. *Svensk-Amerikanska folket i helg och söcken.* Stockholm: Björck och Börjesson, 1917.

_____. *Pennfäktare. Svensk-Amerikanska författare och tidningsmän.* Stockholm: Albert Bonnier, 1930.

Spaeth, Adolph. *Life of Adolph Spaeth Told in His Own Reminiscences, His Letters, and Recollections of Friends.* Edited by his wife. Philadelphia: General Council Publication House, 1916.

Stephenson, George M. *The Founding of the Augustana Synod, 1850-1860.* Rock Island: Augustana Book Concern, 1927.

_____. *The Religious Aspects of Swedish Immigration.* Minneapolis: The University of Minnesota Press, 1932.

Sundbärg, Gustav. *Betänkande i utvandringsfrågan och därmed sammanhängande spörsmål.* Stockholm: Kungl. boktryckeriet. P. A. Norstedt och söner, 1913.

Swan, G. N. *Swedish-American Literary Periodicals.* Rock Island, 1936. (Augustana Historical Society Publication, no. 6).

Swanson, S. Hjalmar. *Foundation For Tomorrow. A Century of Progress in Augustana World Missions.* Minneapolis: Board of World Missions, Augustana Lutheran Church, 1960.

Söderström, Alfred. *Blixtar på tidnings-horisonten."* 1910.

Söderström, Hugo. *Confession and Cooperation.* Lund: C. W. K. Gleerup bokförlag, 1965.

Unonius, Gustaf. *A Pioneer in Northwest America, 1841-1858. The Memoirs of Gustaf Unonius.* Edited by Nils William Olsson and translated by Jonas Oscar Backlund. Minneapolis: Published for the Swedish Pioneer Historical Society by the University of Minnesota Press, 1950-60. 2 vols.

Walan, Bror. *Invandrarna och kyrkan.* Stockholm: Gummessons bokförlag, 1963.

Wentz, Abdel Ross. *The Lutheran Church in American History.* Philadelphia: The United Lutheran Publication House, 1923.

Westin, Gunnar. *Emigranterna och kyrkan. Brev från och till Svenskar i Amerika 1849-1892.* Stockholm: Svenska kyrkans diakonistyrelses bokförlag, 1932.

_____. *Lutheraner, Anglikaner, Reformerta. Kyrkohistoriska uppsatser.*

Uppsala: J. A. Lundblads förlag, 1935.

Westman, Erik G. and Johnson, E. Gustav. *The Swedish Element in America.* Chicago: Swedish-American Biographical Society, 1934. IV.

Witting, Victor. *Minnen från mitt lif som sjöman, immigrant och predikant.* Worcester, Mass., 1904.

ANNUALS

"A". "Svenska evangeliska Lutherska församlingen i Andover och dess historia," *Korsbaneret. Kristlig kalender för 1880,* pp. 60-119.

Abrahamson, L. G. "Illinois-konferensens 75-års jubileum," *Korsbaneret,* 1925. pp. 34-55.

Almqvist, Sten. "Erland Carlsson, 1822-1972." *Älghults-Krönika, 1972,* pp. 29-39.

Andreen, G. A. "Eben Carlsson," *Korsbaneret,* 1933. pp. 322-26.

Augustana Synodens Protokoll, 1860-1893. This is the citation in footnotes for: *Protokoll hållet vid Skandinaviska Evangeliska Lutherska Augustana Synodens årsmote,* 1860-1883, and *Officielt referat öfver förhandlingarna vid Skandinaviska Evangeliska Lutherska Augustana Synodens årsmote,* 1884-93. Also appropriate years of *Minutes of Annual Convention of Augustana Synod.*

Beck, Victor E. "Augustana and the Printed Word," *Augustana Swedish Institute Yearbook,* 1962-1963, pp. 15-30.

Beijbom, Ulf. "Erland Carlsson och den Svensk-Amerikanska kyrkan," *Älghults-Krönika,* 1966, pp. 27-38.

Bengtson, C. O. "Änkefru Emmy Evald," *Korsbaneret,* 1936, pp. 139-53.

Bergendoff, Conrad. "How the Augustana Church Came to Be," *Augustana Annual. Yearbook of the Augustana Evangelical Lutheran Church,* 1960. pp. 41-47. Rock Island: Augustana Book Concern, 1960.

Bjerking, Arvid. "En Hällebergas Amerikaresa 1853" *Älghults-Krönika,* 1959, pp. 69-73.

Blomén, Sven. "Ut-och inflyttning från och till Älghult åren 1854-1945," *Älghults-Krönika,* 1947, pp. 88-90.

Carlsson, Erl. "Svenska evang. Lutherska Immanuels-församlingen i Chicago, Ill.," *Korsbaneret,* 1881. pp. 73-126; 1882, pp. 132-180 (Erl. Carlsson's history of Immanuel Church, Chicago).

Dahlén, Esther. "Bondpojken från Suletorp, som blev president för Augustana-synoden i Amerika," *Älghults-Krönika,* 1947, pp. 55-67.

Enander, J. A. "Då Christina Nilsson kom till Chicago," *Prärieblomman kalender för 1900.* pp. 50-61. Rock Island: Augustana Book Concern, 1900.

BIBLIOGRAPHY   229

Esbjörn, L. P. "De Svenska Lutherska församlingarnas i N. Amerika uppkomst,"
  Korsbaneret, 1885. pp. 33-51. (Address at Uppsala pastor's meeting, June
  14, 1865).

Evald, Emmy. "Kvinnernas missionsförenings fyrtioåriga verksamhet inom
  Augustana synoden," *Korsbaneret,* 1933. pp. 167-73.

"Emmy Evald," *Korsbaneret,* 1948. pp. 193-97.

"Gold and Silver. Two Notable Anniversaries," *My Church. An Illustrated
  Lutheran Manual.* Rock Island. III (1917), 62-65.

Hoffsten, C. E. "Dr. Erland Carlsson and Our Early Church Work in Chicago," *My
  Church.* XIX (1933), 74-84.

Illinois konferensens protokoll, 1878-88; *Illinois konferensens referat,* 1889-93.

Malm, Alba. "Mera om Rostad," "Rostad i Kalmar och Rostad i Kansas,"
  Älghults-Krönika, 1959, pp. 31-32.

Mattson, Carl E. "Register över uppsatser om Svensk-Amerika och Svenska-
  Amerikaner," *Year-Book of the Swedish Historical Society of America,* VI
  (1916-17), 89-120.

Minutes of the Mississippi and Chicago Conferences, 1853-60. See also
  Augustana Historical Society Publications, X.

Minutes of the Synod of Northern Illinois, 1851-60. See also *Augustana
  Historical Society Publications,* X.

"The Mississippi Conference," *My Church.* IX (1923), 28-34.

Nilson, Hjalmar. "Rostad i Kalmar och Rostad i Kansas" *Älghults-Krönika,*
  1959, pp. 25-32.

Norelius, Eric. "Återblick på Augustana-synodens historia under dess första
  tjugufem år," *Korsbaneret,* 1885. pp. 4-31.

_____. "Guds ledande hand i vår Svenska Lutherska kyrkas historia i
  Amerika," *Korsbaneret,* 1886. pp. 13-45.

_____. "Några hågkomster från året 1854," *Korsbaneret,* 1888. pp.
  107-52.

_____. "Hågkomster från 1855," *Korsbaneret,* 1889. pp. 107-155.

_____. "Hågkomster från 1856," *Korsbaneret,* 1890. pp. 107-135.

_____ (redaktör). "Historiska dokument rörande de Svenska Ev. Luth.
  forsamlingarna i N. Amerika före Augustana-synodens organization 1860,"
  *Tidskrift för Svensk Ev. Luth. Kyrkohistoria i N. Amerika och teologiska
  och kyrkliga frågor.* Rock Island: Lutheran Augustana Book Concern,
  1899, pp. 1-14.

_____ (redaktör). "Bref och utdrag ur bref från L. P. Esbjörn till E.
  Norelius, T. N. Hasselquist och Erl. Carlsson, i kronologisk ordning,"
  *Tidskrift för Svensk Ev. Luth. kyrkohistoria i N. Amerika och för telogiska
  och kyrkliga frågor.* Rock Island: Lutheran Augustana Book Concern,
  1899, pp. 244-354.

230   THE STORY OF ERLAND CARLSSON

_____(redaktör). *Tidskrift för Svensk Ev. Luth. Kyrkohistoria i N. Amerika och för teologiska och kyrkliga frågor.* Rock Island: Lutheran Augustana Book Concern, 1899.

Olsson, Olof and Swensson, C. A. "Pastor Erland Carlsson," *Korsbaneret*, 1881. pp. 67-72.

Peterson, Conrad. "The Beginning of Swedish American Education Prior to 1860," *Year-Book of the Swedish Historical Society of America*, VIII (1922-23), pp. 26-55.

Ranseen, M. C. "Pastor C. A. Evald," *Korsbaneret*, 1910. pp. 155-63.

_____. "Fru Eva C. Carlsson," *Korsbaneret*, 1912. pp. 235-39.

Stephenson, George M. "Some Footnotes to the History of Swedish Immigration from about 1855 to about 1865," *Year-Book of the Swedish Historical Society of America*, VII (1921-22), 33-52.

_____(editor and translator). "Hemlandet Letters," *Year-Book of the Swedish Historical Society of America*, VIII (1922-23), 56-98.

_____. "Isidor Kjellberg: Crusader," *Swedish-American Historical Society Bulletin*, St. Peter, Minn. II (Aug. 1929), 31-51.

Telleen, John. "Rev. Dr. Erland Carlsson," *My Church*. VII (1921), 43-57.

ALBUMS AND MISCELLANEOUS

Abrahamson, L. G. "Doktor Erland Carlsson," *Minneskrift. Illustreradt album utgifvet af Immanuelsförsamlingen i Chicago.* Chicago: Augustana Book Concern, 1903. pp. 33-47.

_____. "Augustana-Synoden," *Jubel-Album, 1893.* Chicago: National Publishing Company, 1893, pp. 23-120.

After Seventy-five Years, 1860-1935. A Jubilee Publication. Seventy-fifth Anniversary of the Augustana Synod and Augustana College and Theological Seminary. Rock Island: Augustana Book Concern, 1935.

Andover Church Tidings. Eighty-fifth Anniversary Year, 1850-1935.

Andover Minnes-Album. Sv. Ev. Lutherska församlingen i Andover, Illinois. Sextioårs-festen, 1910. Rock Island: Augustana Book Concern, 1910.

Bartholomew, E. F. "Erland Carlsson. Memorial Address," *The Alumnus* [Augustana College], I (Nov. 1893), 6-9.

Beijbom, Ulf. "The Swedish Experience of Chicago's 'Melting Pot' ", *Migration and Social Mobility*. A Report of the Second Scandinavian Research Symposium at the Emigrant Institute in Växjö, Sweden, Aug. 28-29, 1972. pp. 6-19.

Bengtson, C. O. *The Story of the Immanuel Lutheran Church, Chicago, Illinois. Seventy-Fifth Anniversary, January 8-16, 1928.*

_____. "Doctor Erland Carlsson," *Immanuel Review* (Chicago), Aug. 1922.

Carlson, Arthur Bernhard. "Pastoral Care in the Faith and Practice of Four Selected Swedish Churchmen" [Henrik Schartau, Carl Olof Rosenius, Erland Carlsson, Jonas Swensson]. Ph.D. dissertation, Boston University Graduate School, 1962.

Carlsson, Erl. Några råd och underrättelser för utwandrare till Amerikas Förenta Stater. Wexjö: H. S. Cederschiöld, 1854.

_____. *Tillförlitliga råd och underrättelser för utwandrare till Amerika, nemligen.* I. Råd och underrättelser. II. Upplysningar om mynt, mat, wigt, prowiantering och kostnader för resan m. m. III. Utdrag af bref från i Amerika wistande svenskar. IV. Ordregister. Carlshamn: Ludwig Lindgrens bokhandel, 1854.

_____. "The Beginnings of Our Benevolent Work," *The Alumnus* [Augustana College], I (Apr. 1893), 172-75.

"Eva Charlotta Carlsson," *Augustana*, July 20, July 27, 1911.

Geneva Lutheran Church, Geneva, Illinois, 1853-1963.

Illustrerad minneskrift af Sv. Ev. Luth. församlingens i Geneva, Ill. 50-års jubileum. Rock Island: Augustana Book Concern, 1903.

The Illinois Conference, 1853-1928. Jubilee Album. Rock Island: Augustana Book Concern, 1928.

Jaderborg, Elizabeth (Selma Lind). "Rostad," *Living in Lindsborg and Other Possibilities.* Lindsborg: Lindsborg News-Record, 1967, pp. 14-15.

Johnson, E. "The Swedes of Chicago," Ph.D. dissertation, the University of Chicago, 1940.

Kjellberg, Isidor. *Föredrag om Amerika hållet i Stockholm den 18 Febr. 1883.* Stockholm: A. W. Björcks förlag, 1883.

Kyrko-Handbok för Augustana-Synoden. Antagen 1895. Rock Island: Augustana Book Concern, 1895.

Lund, Gene Jessie. "The Americanization of the Augustana Lutheran Church." Th.D. dissertation, Department of Church History, Princeton Theological Seminary, 1954.

Lundeen, Joel W. and Weber, Erwin. *Lutheranism in Illinois, 1816-1976. The Story of the Illinois Synod, Lutheran Church in America.* Rock Island: 1976.

Minneskrift. Svenska Ev. Lutherska Immanuelsförsamlingen i Chicago, 1853-1903. Chicago: Lutheran Augustana Book Concern, 1903.

Norelius, Eric. "Hälsningar," *Minneskrift. Svenska Ev. Lutherska Immanuelsförsamlingen i Chicago, 1853-1903.* pp. 77-79.

Olson, Ernest W. "Augustana Loses a Venerable Father," *The Young Observer,* II, (Oct. 1893), 6.

Ranseen, M. C. "Immanuels-församlingens pastorsfruar," *Minneskrift. Svenska Ev. Lutherska Immanuelsförsamlingen i Chicago,* 1853-1903, pp. 52-54.

Rodell, A. "Reverend Erland Carlsson, D. D." *The Alumnus,* Augustana College, I (Jan. 1893), 97.

Rockford, Ill. Centennial. The First Evan. Lutheran Church, Rockford, Illinois, 1854-1954. Rockford: 1954.

Swensson, C. A. "Rostad," *Förgät-mig-ej. Ungdoms kalender för jubel året 1893.* Chicago: 1893. pp. 77-89.

Swensson, C. A. and Abrahamson, L. G. *Jubel-Album, 1893.* Chicago: National Publishing Co., 1893.

Swensson, C. A. "Erland Carlsson, D. D." *Fosterlandet,* Oct. 25, 1893.

Telleen, John. "Indianmissionen," *Jubel-Album, 1893,* pp. 195-201.

Ullen, Marian. *Älghults kyrkor.* Aseda: Älghults kyrkoråd, 1974.

U. S. Census. The Eighth Census. Population of the United States in 1860. Washington: Government Printing Office, 1864.

U. S. Census. The Ninth Census (June 1, 1870) *of the United States. A Compendium.* Washington: Government Printing Office, 1872.

Woman's Missionary Society, 1892-1927. Survey of Thirty-five Years Activity. Chicago: Woman's Mission Board, 1927.

INDEX

Abrahamson, L. G., quoted 97, 98, 192, 203, 206, 207
Ahlberg, P. A., 18
Ahlstrand, *Domprost,* 10
Ander, O. Fritiof, quoted 157
Andersen, Rev. Paul, 19, 30, 31, 56-57, 82, 134, 176
Anderson, C. J., 34, 46, 60, 62
Anderson, O. V., 126. See Immigrant Guide, appendix
Anderson, Petrus, 6
Andersson, Johan, 22
Andover Children's Home, 183-84
Andover Lutheran Church, 181-87
Andreen, A., quoted 48; 76-78; founder, Gustavus Adolphus Lutheran Church, New York City, 79-80; 104
Andrén, O. C. T., 8, 108-09
Arden, G. Everett, quoted 174
Arvastan, Arvid, quoted 121-22
Aschan, *Bergsrådet* Johan Lorentz, 9, 10, 12
Augustana College and Theological Seminary, 106-14, 187
Augustana Hospital, 185
Augustana Synod (Ev. Augustana Lutheran Synod), 37, 131-45

Barometern, quoted 21-22
Battle Creek, Mich., 193
Bergendoff, Conrad, quoted 95-96, 101, 113
Bethel Ship, 24
Bersell, P. O., quoted 171-72
Bohman, J. A., 124
Borås Tidning, quoted 23
Bredberg, Jacob, 150, 159
Bring, E. G., 68
Bring, S. L., 110

Carlshamns Allehanda, quoted 45
Carlson, Arthur Bernhard, quoted 206
Carlson, Peter, 43
Carlsson, Anna Lovisa, 1
Carlsson, Ebenezer, 170, 172
Carlsson Erland, America, departure for, 20-22; Andover Lutheran Church, pastor of, 181-87; Andover Children's Home, chairman, board of directors, 183-84; Augustana College and Theological Seminary. Faculty, interest in, 110-11; founding, role in, 106-07; general manager and treasurer, 187; Jubilee of 1893, 193-95; leadership in, 107-114; relationship with Swedish Lutheran Publication Society, 124-25; reports on, 1862, 108; 1879, 112. Augustana Hospital, identification with, 185. Augustana Synod, 131-45; catechism revision,

136-37; constitution, 135; higher education, 141-42; offices in, 132; organization of, 132-33; president (1881-88), 137-45; resignation, 144-45; reports to, 1870, 134; 1882, 137; 1884, 138-39; 1885, 139-41; 1886, 141-42; 1887, 142; 1888, 144; separation from Norwegians, 133-34; view of, 134, 143-44. Birth and baptism of, 1; brothers and sisters, 1-2; business affairs, 173-74; children, Annie Fredrika, see Mrs. C. A. Evald; Ebenezer, 170, 172; Emmy Christina, see Emmy Evald; Samuel, 170, 172, 187; churches founded by, see Immanuel Church, Chicago and Geneva-St. Charles; missionary work in Minnesota Territory, Illinois, Indiana; clerical garb, 56-57; confirmation, 2, 3. Conflict and criticism. Religious issues, 30-32, 56, 149-51, 151-52, 152-57, 157-58; secular issues, 159-62, 164; general, 10-14. Death of, 196-97; description of, 144, 152, 154, 158-59, 160-62, 202-07; early life in Chicago, 41-48; early years in Sweden, 1-16; education of, 1-8; family and family life, 169-73; General Council of Ev. Lutheran Church (president), 98-99; Grace Lutheran Church, Rock Island, 176; hospitals, interest in, 84, 185; Illinois Conference (president), 97-98; Immanuel Lutheran Church, Chicago. See special entry. *Immigrant Guide,* 125-26, and Appendix; illness, 7, 48, 185, 187-88, 193, 196; Indian Missions (American), 80-82; Lindsborg, resident at, 188-93; marriage of, 37; Minnesota Synod, 90-92; Missionary work. Minnesota Territory, 77-78; Grand Rapids, 79; New York City, 79-80; Indiana, 78-79; De Kalb, 79; Rockford, 76-77; Chisago Lake, 77-78. Mississippi Conference, 96-97; motto of, 202-03; Norelius, Eric, close friendship, 192; ordination of, 9; parents of, see Carl and Stina Carlsdotter Jonsson and Erland Danielson, stepfather; parochial school, 103-05; preacher, 53-55; public affairs, 176-77; residences, 33-34, 76, 182, 187, 188; salary, 44; Scandinavian Emigrant Aid Society, 82-84; sermons, 55; Sweden, visit in, 68-69; Synod of Northern Illinois, 89-90, 94-96; Swedish Lutheran Publication Society, 119-24; Swedish newspaper, 117-19; travel route to America, 22-29; theological examinations, 7-8; tutor, 10

233